lture   Demand

For Agnes Silva Lull

Culture-on-Demand

Communication in a
Crisis World

James Lull

Blackwell Publishing

88299

BLACKWELL PUBLISHING
350 Main Street, Malden, MA 02148-5020, USA
9600 Garsington Road, Oxford OX4 2DQ, UK
550 Swanston Street, Carlton, Victoria 3053, Australia

First published 2007 by Blackwell Publishing Ltd

1   2007

Library of Congress Cataloging-in-Publication Data

Lull, James.
    Culture-on-demand : communication in a crisis world / James Lull.
        p. cm.
    Includes bibliographical references and index.
    ISBN-13: 978-1-4051-6064-3 (hardcover : alk. paper)
    ISBN-10: 1-4051-6064-0 (hardcover : alk. paper)
    ISBN-13: 978-1-4051-6065-0 (pbk. : alk. paper)
    ISBN-10: 1-4051-6065-9 (pbk. : alk. paper)
1. Communication and culture.   2. Communication, international.
3. Globalization.   I. Title.

    P94.6.L848 2007
    302.2–dc22

                                        2006027959

A catalogue record for this title is available from the British Library.

Set in 11.5 on 13.5 pt Bembo
by SNP Best-set Typesetter Ltd, Hong Kong
Printed and bound in Singapore
by C.O.S. Printers Pte Ltd

For further information on
Blackwell Publishing, visit our website:
www.blackwellpublishing.com

Contents

Figures

Acknowledgments

I want to thank Eduardo Neiva for his intellectual contributions, editorial suggestions, and personal support for this project. Jonathan Gray provided superb critical readings of early drafts of the manuscript. Joe Verbalis, Roseanne Anderson, Laura Stovel, Michael Marx, and Andy Wood gave me valuable feedback on various chapters. A Leverhulme Trust Fellowship spent at Goldsmiths College, University of London, provided time and context for development of several chapters. My Mexican colleagues Aimée Vega and Gabriela Pedroza made suggestions that improved the book, as has Jorge Larraín in Chile. Another *Chileno*, David Mateo, has been a great source of inspiration for years with regard to many of the ideas presented here. Jen "GenJen" Stein provided valuable assistance in London. Natalie Jomini, Anya Iyengar, and Phoebe Kitanidis helped me develop the material on human expression. Special thanks to Elizabeth Swayze, my editor at Blackwell Publishing, for her enthusiastic support and excellent editorial guidance, and to Caroline Richards for careful editing of the text.

Introduction

You'll have to forgive my optimism. I was born and raised in a small Minnesota farm town named after Owatonna, a young, Native American "princess" who, legend has it, was restored to good health from her deathbed by drinking the clear, cold water that gushes to Earth from the area's natural mineral springs. That often-frozen but fertile land is also the place where many Scandinavian and northern European immigrants, including my own ancestors, later homesteaded in North America.

Growing up with the triumphant legend of Princess Owatonna may help explain why the perspective I advance in this book doesn't consider human beings to be hopelessly inscribed into determining statuses and roles, imprisoned by the ideological and cultural structures and institutions that surround and guide them.

But let's be realistic. No rational or responsible account of the global scene today can underestimate the destructive intentions, activities, and consequences that are brought to bear by the world's major political, economic, and religious power brokers. We all have personal experiences that testify to the widespread presence of that kind of hegemonic influence. I myself left that idyllic little farm town in southern Minnesota to enlist in the US Army at age 18, only to endure a lengthy tour of duty in Vietnam as a military journalist and broadcaster with the same combat outfit that, as of this writing, was patrolling the mean streets of downtown Baghdad. It was there, in the central highlands of what was then South Vietnam, that many of my friends were killed, and where I personally witnessed with horror some of the same kinds of torture applied to Viet Cong suspects that were meted out by the American military police at Iraq's Abu Ghurayb prison. While in Vietnam I kept trying to determine the purpose for our being there, for the massive violence, the mayhem, the deep sorrow. I found no satisfying explanation. By the time I turned 21 my way of looking at the world, and especially at the United States, had changed radically. Since then, American political and economic hegemony, buttressed by unparalleled military power and cultural influence, has become the predominant ideological force in the world – certainly not always with positive, uplifting consequences. Never before has the power of America been so great as it is today, in fact, and never before has its standing in world opinion been so low.

So, if I'm an optimist, then I'm an informed optimist.

No doubt ideology and culture impact human populations in powerful ways, frequently to their detriment. But that fact alone does not tell the whole story. Whether speeding along in the fast lanes of the information superhighway, or meandering slowly along the winding paths of the cultural countryside, people never function simply as passive subjects, mere victims of their increasingly diverse and interconnected social and cultural worlds. They actively engage those worlds as subjective agents who struggle on their own behalf, and on behalf of their various partnerships, communities, and causes to bring meaning, dignity, influence, and pleasure into their lives.

Because of the United States' massive impact on the world, it's never easy for an American to write credibly about the positive potential of mass media, information technology, and the global flows of culture – among the main themes taken up in the pages that follow. That challenge has never been greater. American hegemony – which could, and should, serve the world as an altruistic, productive, unifying force – has in many ways devolved into just the opposite. Promises of global peace and prosperity that were forthcoming in the West as the Soviet Union disintegrated have yet to be fulfilled. Instead, national and ethnic differences have sharpened: "Since 1989, the world has seen the proliferation of ethnic conflict, the rise of militant Islam, the intensification of group hatred and nationalism, expulsion, massacres, confiscations, calls for re-nationalization, and two genocides of magnitudes unprecedented since the Nazi holocaust" (Chau 2003: 123).

Thankfully, there has been no shortage of critical analyses of American foreign policy and the neoconservative doctrine behind it in the early twenty-first century, especially as the violent intervention in Iraq turned into a shambles. But blaming America or the West ("Occidentalism") for the world's problems today – however tempting and in some ways understandable as that may be – is far too easy, reductionist, and misleading. As recent history makes clear, other potent forces are at work. Fundamentalism in all its primary forms has become the most intractable obstacle to greater inter-civilizational tolerance and understanding. By fundamentalism, I refer to a way of thinking held by groups of individuals who subscribe to an unassailable system of beliefs, desire certainty above all else, and aim to amass the power needed to impose their worldview over others (Sim 2005: 21, 28). We normally think of fundamentalism in religious terms, but nationalist and economic fundamentalisms also exist. They often interact. Alarming evidence of these interfused fundamentalisms can be found in the dictates of American foreign policy, for example, especially as they materialized during the presidential tenure of born-again patriot-businessman George W. Bush.

The United States is distinctly religious among the more developed nations of the world, and the intensifying presence of Christian fundamentalism in American politics and culture is extremely worrisome, especially considering the military and economic might wielded by the world's only superpower. But fundamentalist Islam – whose core cultural values are least compatible with the modern world, and whose ideological force has been least held in check by democratic secular authority – must also be given special critical attention by scholars and citizens. Under the relentless, penetrating gaze of the media, sharp differences between the core principles of Islamic fundamentalism and the basic values of global modernity are becoming increasingly visible, discussed, and debated. The religious cartoon controversy of 2005, the death penalty case of the Afghan man, Abdul Rahman, who was tried for converting to Christianity in 2006, and the killing by religious extremists of three male Iraqi tennis players later the same year for wearing short pants – not to mention all the horrific acts and failed plots of

Islamic terrorists – epitomize the cultural contrasts and demonstrate the international media's ability to bring such differences to light. Because of its extraordinary importance, a straightforward inquiry into the ideological and cultural underpinnings of Islamic fundamentalism, and an exploration of how media, the culture industries, and information and communications technology expose those realities – certainly *not* an assault on Muslim people – serves as the primary analytical theme that runs throughout this book.

Understandably, media coverage of Muslim fundamentalism so far has focused on the acts and plans of deadly terrorism perpetrated by fanatical Islamists. But the problem is much larger than that. As Sam Harris asserts in *The End of Faith*, "the evil that has finally reached our shores is not merely the evil of terrorism. It is the evil of religious faith at the moment of its political ascendancy" (Harris 2005: 130). Harris and others blame all religious fundamentalisms – including Christian fundamentalism and orthodox Judaism – for fueling the global cultural crisis, but also argue that Islam poses special difficulties that must be addressed in a way that is unencumbered by the sometimes unreflective and overly apologetic sentiment of cultural relativism. While the harsh political, social, and economic histories and current conditions of much of the Middle East, as well as the interventionist policies of Western powers, contribute much to the rise of Islamic terrorism, these circumstances do not sufficiently explain the root cause of the problem. Dogmatic religious ideology – which cumulatively permeates and influences the totality of social, cultural, and political practice – has greatly precipitated the downward spiral of the Middle East over many centuries.

Islam has not been "hijacked by terrorists," a catchy claim put forward by politicians and repeated uncritically by the media. Terrorists, as human beings, have themselves been hijacked by a religious ideology and political vision that threatens to brutally eliminate all who oppose it. The terrorists have company. As Syrian-born Islamic scholar Bassam Tibi soberly points out, "the terrorists of New York and Washington were not a crazed gang, inasmuch as they represent an existing significant stream with numerous followers within Islamic civilization. We need to be honest, acknowledge this, and face the corresponding facts" (Tibi 2002: xvi). After researching the lives of the 19 terrorists of 9/11,

Los Angeles Times reporter Terry McDermott (2005) concluded that they were "regular guys" simply unable to say "no" to God. We got the same kinds of reports about the middle-class Pakistani-British men who blew up the underground trains and bus in London four years later. Moreover, the Islamist terrorists weren't "cowards, as they were repeatedly described in the Western media, nor were they lunatics in any ordinary sense. They were men of faith — perfect faith, as it turns out — and this, it must finally be acknowledged, is a terrible thing to be" (Harris 2005: 67). So while various particular groups threaten the world with religious and political terrorism, it is the far broader set of values, practices, and discourses of fundamentalist thought — especially the profound link between religion and culture — that must be critically addressed.

Although religion provides considerable spiritual comfort and guidance for individuals and helps to promote altruism and public service in societies, in the larger sense it also functions as dominant ideology and must ultimately be understood as such. This means that Islam has not simply been converted into political ideology for sinister purposes; the religion itself is deeply ideological and, because of its untestable claims of infallibility, is subject to extreme interpretations and uses. These debilitating tendencies are not peculiar to Islam, of course. Christians, Jews, and Hindus have plenty to account for in the past and the present. Fundamentalist Islam looms as a distinct and compelling case, however, because most of the Islamic world — especially the symbolic center of the Islamic universe, the Middle East — has yet to undergo a transition that even vaguely resembles what Europe and North America underwent during the Enlightenment 300 years ago. Consequently, many Muslim societies have not benefited sufficiently from science and reason to be able to confidently relegate religion to a less conspicuous, more personal, and generally peaceful role. Instead, theocratic authority, repressive and undemocratic political rule, and contiguous cultures of ignorance and poverty interact to stymie social, cultural, and economic development. Muslim societies have had to confront a rapidly modernizing and globalizing world which they are not well prepared to engage. The resulting culture shock has created a crisis of identity that contributes mightily to the rise of religious radicalism.

Lamenting how the rigid and restrictive Islam of the Middle East and South Asia compares with religious and civic life in the West, Irshad Manji, a Canadian Muslim, argues that only the exercise of fundamental civil liberties, especially free expression, can diminish the cultural tendencies that hold back progress in the Arab and Islamic world. Manji implores non-Muslims to challenge Islamic believers to "leverage their freedom" and modernize. "Non-Muslims do the world no favors by pushing the moral mute button as soon as Muslims start speaking," she says. "Dare to ruin the romance of the moment" (Manji 2003: 186, 192).

Doing so has been difficult because religion and religious culture – even the explicitly ideological aspects – have traditionally been considered off-limits to interrogation and criticism, especially in the academic world. This has been particularly true when the Arab-Muslim region is scrutinized. Scholarly attacks on capitalism, communism, fascism, Marxism, nationalism, racism, Orientalism, even feminism, can all be condoned, but the slightest questioning of religious ideology and practice – arguably the most influential social and cultural force in the world today – is steadfastly avoided. Except for religious studies departments on college campuses, where most professors have vested theological interests and dutiful personal biases, religion has been given a pass as an object of critical scientific inquiry. As the philosopher Daniel Dennett observes, all believers of the major religions "have been taught that any . . . questioning is somehow insulting or demeaning to their faith," a way of thinking which conveniently wards off any threat of skepticism (Dennett 2006: 207).

Against all odds, but also in a way that makes perfect sense, Muslim women like Irshad Manji have been at the forefront of the post-9/11 critique of Islamic ideology. In Pakistan, Mukhtar Mai, a victim of a gang rape that had been imposed on her to punish her family, became a global symbol of human rights and women's resistance to tribal Islam. Women authors such as Seyran Ates, Necla Kelek, and Serap Celili have described the practice of selling young women in Turkey to Turkish men in Germany and the pervasive physical and mental brutality many women suffer in the Turkish diasporas there. The film *Chaos* by Coline Serreau in France documents the plight of young Arab women trying to escape homes ruthlessly dominated by men. Ayaan Hirsi Ali, a

Somali Muslim immigrant who was living in Holland at the time, wrote the script for *Submission*, a short film about domestic violence against Muslim women in the Netherlands – a political act that led to the killing of the film's director, Theo Van Gogh, by a Dutch Islamist, and police protection for her.

The struggle over women's rights, more than any other issue, reveals the moral double standard that characterizes much of the mainstream Muslim world. For that reason, the most impassioned and revolutionary voices now being heard are those of women. Most of the women described in the previous paragraphs live in nations where Islam is a minority religion – Canada, Germany, France, Holland – and where the individual rights of all citizens are protected. The women are telling their stories in the West, and are being heard mainly by sympathetic, non-Islamic Westerners. In 2006, however, another outspoken (former) Muslim woman reached a different audience with an even more sweeping and polemical message. Wafa Sultan, a political refugee from Syria living in the United States where she works as a psychologist, appeared on Al-Jazeera, the Arabic-speaking satellite television network based in Qatar, to sternly criticize the very basis of Islamic religion, history, and culture. We are witnessing "a clash between two opposites, between two eras," she said. "It is a clash between a mentality that belongs to the Middle Ages and another mentality that belongs to the 21st Century. It is a clash between civilization and backwardness, between the civilized and the primitive, between rationality and barbarity" (Middle East Media Research Institute 2006).

What all these women have in common, besides unconscionable suffering, a personal awakening, and the courage to stand up to sources of oppression, is the opportunity for the first time in history to air their grievances through channels that are capable of reaching a large audience, giving great exposure and credibility to their subversive messages. Part of Muslim women's relative powerlessness in the past stemmed from a systemic denial to education for many and a near complete lack of access to technologies of expression. Modern mass media, the internet, the culture industries, and immigration to Western nations have changed the landscape immeasurably. New voices have been empowered as a result. Irshad Manji, for example, parlayed a cable television program in

Toronto into a best-selling book, *The Trouble with Islam Today*, which has been translated into dozens of languages and sold around the world. She also hosts a website to inform and recruit other "Muslim refuseniks" to the movement (www.muslim-refusenik. com), and has become a global media personality. International television news reports broke the story of Mukhtar Mai in Pakistan, whose vital cause was picked up by human rights organizations and diffused globally online, creating a high-profile, celebrated role model for women along the way. The writers in Germany published their cultural exposés in European languages, which then attracted considerable attention from electronic, print, and digital media worldwide. The film industries of France, Holland, and elsewhere financed the critical work of Coline Serreau, Ayaan Hirsi Ali, and others. Wafa Sultan's uncompromising assault on Islam originally took the form of essays she wrote for a reformist website hosted by American Muslims. Her comments were repeated, praised, and attacked on Middle Eastern media and websites and, as her fame grew, Sultan was invited to appear on Al-Jazeera. The remarks she made during an interview there (only a small portion of which was cited in the previous paragraph) were immediately translated by the Middle East Media Research Institute (MEMRI), which also made a video clip of her appearance available. It has been accessed more than a million times.

Compare these media developments with what happened in the famous case of the small Danish newspaper that in late 2005 published cartoons depicting Muhammad, the historical figure considered by Muslims to be the main prophet of the faith. Frustrated by an inability to find artists who would render images of Muhammad for a book about his life (for fear of reprisal from extremists), the newspaper solicited and published images of Muhammad "as you imagine him." The images insulted many Muslims. We all know what happened next. Anti-Western rioting continued for weeks throughout much of the Muslim world. Embassies were burned, symbols of Western culture were destroyed, boycotts of Danish imports were imposed, and some 50 people lost their lives – especially in Nigeria, where Muslims attacked Christians and Christians counterattacked to avenge their deaths.

Two discursive themes emerged from the worldwide attention given to the cartoon controversy. First was the question of whether the Danish newspaper – and other media who later supported the principle of free speech and expression by reprinting or transmitting the images – should have published the cartoons in the first place. Islamic religious ideology prohibits *any* graphic depiction of Muhammad. For many Muslims, and not just the extremists, publishing any such representations, especially by non-Muslims, signifies blasphemy perpetrated by infidels against the beloved prophet. Respect for the sanctity of religion, the conservative argument goes, should cause anyone to refrain from making such potential "insults." The second discursive theme concerns the highly visible and immoderate reaction much of the Muslim world gave to publication of the cartoons. International news agencies not only presented images of outraged Muslims demonstrating in various parts of the world, but also investigated how their rage was further provoked by leaders within Islam, including a troupe of mullahs who traveled to the Middle East from Denmark with the expressed purpose of using the cartoons to stir resentment.

The violent reaction to the cartoons spurred *New York Times* columnist David Brooks to argue insightfully that the controversy was not just about different ideas, but about a "different relationship to ideas." He pointed out that in the West, "images, statistics, and arguments swarm around from all directions. There are movies and blogs, books and sermons. There's the profound and the vulgar, the high and the low . . . By swimming in this flurry of perspectives, by facing unpleasant facts, we come closer and closer to understanding" (Brooks 2006: A27). There is little room for absolutes or ultimate truths – the metaphysical certainties that underpin all fundamentalisms – in any civil society. In the case of the cartoon controversy, there was a distinct refusal of dialogue in most of the Muslim world. At minimum, according to Sam Harris, a civil society

> is a place where ideas of all kinds can be criticized without the risk of physical violence. If you live in a land where certain things cannot be said about the king, or an imaginary being, or about certain books, because such utterances carry the penalty of death, torture, or imprisonment, you do not live in a civil society. (Harris 2005: 150)

Any political-cultural force that speaks and acts with a fundamentalist mindset must be subjected to the same powerful criticism and response that was given to oppressive autocracies of the past, including last century's nemeses from the right and left – state fascism and communism. That was the key argument advanced in the seminal work of the twentieth-century philosopher Karl Popper (1945). For Popper, an open mind and the free exchange of ideas are essential for questioning and reducing the power of institutional authority of any kind, and for finding provisional peace among diverse peoples, a principle that applies particularly well in today's globalized environment. In the midst of the cartoon dispute, for instance, Robert Menard, Secretary General of the French-based NGO (non-governmental organization) Reporters Without Borders, said: "I understand that [the cartoons] may shock Muslims, but being shocked is part of being informed" (Menard 2006). And Slovenian cultural critic Slavoj Zizek argues that Islam – as is the case with all religions – must be subjected to a "respectful, but for that reason no less ruthless, critical analysis. This, and only this, is the way to show a true respect for Muslims: to treat them as serious adults responsible for their beliefs" (Zizek 2006: 12).

Social progress always exacts a price. Living in a vibrant democracy means feeling slightly offended all the time because differing opinions must be, and will be, expressed. But criticism of ideology or culture, no matter how necessary or truthful, is not the point at which any good analysis or plan of action stops. Hurt feelings ultimately should help move a society forward. How can this happen?

Karl Popper also believed strongly that sincere and informed optimism, even in the face of formidable structural barriers, is a moral duty. Today's geopolitical realities and sensitivities are daunting indeed, "yet there is terrific promise," according to modernist King Abdullah II of Jordan, a key Middle Eastern Muslim voice in current discussions. Abdullah's sources of inspiration and hope correspond with the central themes promoted in this book. Breakthroughs in the generation of human knowledge, innovation, communication, and education will be crucial. Introspection and self-criticism will be essential. In the landmark Amman Message delivered in November 2004, Abdullah (2004b) asked Muslims to find the courage to adapt to modern complexities and demands by interpreting the Koran and the life of Muhammad in ways that promote a nuanced and relativized sense of global citizenship. This means "honoring all human beings," he said, and recognizes what he calls the Koranic "deep principles" of unity, peace, moderation, and security. King Abdullah imagines "open, modern, civil societies rooted in true Arab-Islamic values" that embrace "tolerance and respect for others, belief in the rule of law, the equal dignity of all people, and the pursuit of excellence" (Abdullah 2004c).

The King of Jordan called for visionaries to come forward – "people with the courage to visualize positive change and the commitment to achieve it" (Abdullah 2004a). One of those visionaries who has gone public with a particularly good idea is Abdullah's royal partner herself. Jordan's Queen Rania argues that real potential exists now for a global moral consciousness to emerge from the widely shared political and cultural discourses that have been instigated and maintained by the expanding reach and impact of contemporary global communication. The near universal ability of people to leverage an unprecedented range and quantity of information and cultural resources, and to help create those resources themselves, have become defining characteristics of the current era. These key developments offer real hope for increasing tolerance and decreasing violence in our ever more connected and populous world.

This book focuses on *how* and *why* today's communications technologies and cultural resources offer that hope. Because of the unprecedented challenges it poses today, the case of Islamic fundamentalism is presented in these pages as the primary illustration of both the problem and the potential long-term solution. But the principles and processes discussed here extend well beyond the contours of current realities. To borrow an expression from sociologist Robert Putnam, who was proposing remedies for the deteriorating American civil society, it is essential today to create "bridging social capital" on a global scale and "to connect with people unlike ourselves" (Putnam 2000: 411). In order to develop this social capital and create greater moral consensus we must first be able to see and hear those "others." That's where the quartet of communication resources featured in this book – mass media, the culture industries, information technology, and personal communications technology – offers such great long-term promise.

Communicating shared values and reaching a meaningful level of moral agreement appeal intuitively because of the humanitarian benefits these ideas seem to promise; such developments might eventually help reduce human suffering. Theoretically, the ideas are attractive because they offer an alternative to the lack of structure and perceived uncertainty of the postmodern world. But as the philosopher Kwame Appiah (2006) has written, any real hopes for developing reasoned, cross-cultural agreement about values may be quite difficult to realize. Basic cultural principles, especially those inscribed in and reinforced by religious myths and rituals, are particularly difficult to dislodge even in the face of incontrovertible empirical evidence to the contrary. Appiah suggests that a better way to overcome the well-guarded boundaries of cultural identity may require "imaginative engagement" and transcultural "conversations" that lead to the gradual acceptance of unfamiliar ideas. He writes, "when it comes to change, what moves people is often not an argument from principle, not a long discussion about values, but just a gradually acquired new way of seeing things" (Appiah 2006: 73).

His intriguing main argument posits that constructive cultural change will occur as we simply "get used to one another" (Appiah 2006: 78). Appiah claims that Western societies, for example, have become accustomed to the category of "gay person" now to the point that social progress concerning homosexuality – acknowledging gay rights and the existence of gay relationships, for instance – can move forward. "I am urging that we should learn about people in other places," he says, ". . . not because that will bring us to agreement, but because it will help us get used to one another" (Appiah 2006: 78).

If the disparate peoples of the world are ever going to fundamentally concur on basic moral principles, as Jordan's Queen Rania suggests, or if they will ever be able to get used to each other, as Kwame Appiah maintains, media and communications technology will be the channels that provide the necessary cultural exposure that can promote the change. In the example Appiah gives, for instance, television and film have played major roles in creating the categories that made gayness familiar, tolerated, even appreciated by large sectors of European and American societies and increasingly in other parts of the world now, too.

The liberating developments discussed here are not the only ones at play, of course. Dominant ideologies and the traditional systems of social practice that make up national, ethnic, and religious cultures continue to exert enormous influence over their populations. Media and cultural institutions routinely serve these entrenched interests. Reactionary crosscurrents of religious, nationalist, and market fundamentalism further inhibit human development. All these enduring influences accumulate to reflect the considerable "demands of culture."

But, most importantly, the nature of much cultural activity is changing swiftly today with enormous effect. Media, information and communications technology, and popular culture permeate everyday life. Individuals everywhere exercise more autonomy than ever before as cultural decision makers. Obviously, the extent of these developments varies according to the structured circumstances in which people find themselves. But widespread global trends toward personal accessing of film, video, music, and TV "on demand" dramatically symbolize how people everywhere are expanding the range and increasing the control of their cultural experiences to accord with their particular needs, wants, and interests.

This side of the social power equation is what I mean by "culture-on-demand," the central theme of this book. The idea of culture-on-demand strongly emphasizes the role of the individual person in cultural activity and the consequences that are brought about by increased cultural fragmentation and autonomy. Individual persons benefit tremendously from recent improvements in the modes of information transmission and cultural exchange. But the potential significance and power of culture-on-demand transcends the limits of self-centered cultural conduct. Individuals and groups can also exploit communication and cultural resources in order to encourage and cultivate much broader kinds of human development.

I'll explain in the following chapters what drives this cultural potential and show how it materializes in everyday life. I begin by discussing how the various globalizations, including religious and media globalization, influence contemporary world affairs. I'll show why the power of human expression resides at the core of the book's cautiously positive outlook. I'll introduce cultural programming, the personal superculture, and the "push and pull of culture" as fresh ways of thinking about the crucial role of the individual person in cultural matters. The theme of globalized Islam recurs throughout the book as we analyze what happens when relatively closed societies confront the openness of today's global communication. We'll explore how intensified media visibility and transparency impact culture and politics throughout the world. And, from an evolutionary perspective that develops throughout the volume, I'll explain why convergent trends in communication and culture ultimately offer the best opportunity for improving inter-civilizational understanding. We will also carefully contemplate the forces that stand in the way of further progress, especially the daunting challenges posed by religious, nationalist, and market fundamentalisms.

The paradigmatic concept to be highlighted as we go forward with the analysis presented here is human communication. Developing cooperative modes of social interaction through human expression and robust communicative exchange has been fundamental to the evolution of *Homo sapiens* as a species so far and holds the key to future progress. How we construct and navigate the multiple frames of reference we use to survive and thrive are the cultural histories now being written.

Those histories have not been, and will not be, bloodless. But they will be more transparent, scrutinized, and hopeful – even when world events are utterly deplorable and discouraging. Stunning examples have become iconic media events of recent history – the falling World Trade Center towers and subsequent terrorist actions, the torturing of prisoners by American military forces and the carnage of sectarian violence in Iraq, the beheading of foreigners by religious fanatics on the internet, the humiliating practices carried out by authorities at Guantanamo Prison, the rioting over religious cartoons, and the destruction of civilian life in the Israeli–Hezbollah conflict, among other visually spectacular incidents. These interconnected, highly symbolic events have been brought to the world's attention *only* because technologically mediated, global communications can no longer be controlled effectively by political leaders and institutions, no matter how powerful, and because people the world over today expect to know what's going on.

The production of images and accounts such as those described in the previous paragraph, the globalized discussions they provoke, and the cultural adjustments that eventually will be made require new ways of thinking about how people invent their ways of being in the world. We may never become a global community of respectful cosmopolites, nor will any variety of fundamentalist thinking ever be fully extinguished. In the short term, reactionary radicalism and violence will increase on all fronts. Hopes for creating sustainable human development in the long term, however, are reasonable and necessary. To be fulfilled, those hopes will depend on the active cultivation of new communication skills and cultural experiences by people everywhere – at minimum by participating in the positive "getting used to each other" process that Kwame Appiah describes. Fortunately, that essential undertaking is already well under way.

Chapter 1

All Eyes on the Global Stage

Before the terrorist attack of 2001 on the USA sharpened critical debates about globalization, British historian Eric Hobsbawm identified a key dynamic that contributed much to the shocking events that would follow. "As the world is integrated in one way by globalization," Hobsbawm wrote,

> it is increasingly divided in another way into a permanently inferior majority of states and a privileged and self-satisfied minority of states. This minority enjoys a self-reinforcing superiority of wealth, technology, and power, and such superiority and complacency are just as likely to be resented now as they were in the old days of imperial supremacies – perhaps more likely, since today's greater availability of information can more easily reveal the discrepancies. (Hobsbawm 2000: 165)

Globalization inherently promises "egalitarian access to products in a world that is naturally unequal and varied" (ibid.: 65). The contrasts have never been clearer to more people.

Global awareness of extreme disparities in living standards and lifestyles provokes much more than terrorist assaults by religious fanatics. Discomfort with current developments – the "march of modernity" attributed to economic and cultural globalization – is felt in many parts of the world. But negative reactions to the material realities associated with global capitalism stand in remarkable contrast with what has taken place throughout the history of Western civilization. The unleashing of entrepreneurial talent, establishment of a merchant class, growth of markets, and the expanding role of consumers all helped bring down oppressive "millennia-old patterns of economic, social, and political life" inflicted on disenfranchised social classes suffering from the punishing structures of "feudalism and monarchism with their emphasis on bloodlines and birth" (Zakaria 2003: 45). The social and industrial revolutions of the United Kingdom and Europe in the eighteenth and nineteenth centuries, as well as the establishment of liberal economic principles in America, were all inspired by the advent of capitalism – itself a radically progressive idea in its time.[1] Similar transformations in the late twentieth century have led to spectacular economic success for China, India, and Israel, among other nations. The economic payoff has been particularly robust for countries that have been willing and able to compete in the fast-moving world economic system since the 1980s, "when globalization truly took shape" (Soros 2002: 117). The economic challenges have heightened tremendously in recent years because today "global capitalism has a speed, inevitability, and force that it has not had before" (Hutton and Giddens 2000: vii).

Throughout modern history capitalism has liberated societies, led to impressive national economic growth, enhanced the quality of life, and enriched cultural experience. But, as David Landes explains in *The Wealth and Poverty of Nations*, what has made this progress possible is the development and dissemination of the knowledge, techniques, and political and social ideologies of Western civilization during the past thousand years (Landes 1999: 513). The cross-cultural consequences of these historical developments have never been uniformly favorable. While some parts of the world and some groups benefit tremendously from the passing of free trade agreements and the presence of expanded consumer options, others continue to confront the extraordinarily harsh realities of social and economic underdevelopment. A United Nations commission rightly concludes that "globalization is forging greater interdependence, yet the world seems more fragmented – between rich and poor, between the powerful and the powerless, and between those who welcome the new economy and those who demand a different course" (United Nations Development Programme 2002a: 1).[2]

The fault lines of those divisions do not develop solely according to geographical region or social class. Ethnic differences and patterns of human migration that bring diverse groups into contact also increase tensions. As Amy Chau (2003) observes, for instance, much resentment and turbulence around the world stems from the uprising of a poor ethnic majority in their own land against a small but rich ethnic minority of "foreigners" – Chinese in Southeast Asia, for example, or whites in Zimbabwe and South Africa, Indians in East Africa, Jews in Russia, Spanish in Bolivia. The same principle applies to the world economic and cultural order. The United States makes up but a small percentage of the world's population (about 4 percent), but dominates the global economy and controls vast industrial, technological, and cultural resources. Because of this discrepancy America is widely resented as the world's "market dominant minority" (Chau 2003: 230).

Distrust, dislike, even hatred of the relatively rich and powerful have intensified despite the fact that in nearly every objective category – hunger, health, literacy, education, income, nutrition, women's rights, life expectancy, infant mortality, transportation, and greater access to a variety of goods and services – there is absolutely no question that the world's poorest people in general are relatively better off now than ever before (see, for example, Giddens 2002b; Hobsbawm 2000; Norberg 2003; UNDP 2002a, 2003a, 2004, 2005; World Bank 2003).

These vital improvements in the human condition have been made possible in great measure by the circulation of ideas, materials, and expertise for which global capitalism is primarily responsible. In many respects, as the data show, the trends are encouraging. But they don't tell the whole story, and they don't reflect what's going on from the point of view of the majority of the world's inhabitants. As United Nations' statistics reveal, three-fourths of the world's population – some four billion people – live in developing countries that lack a stable middle class committed to national economic and political development (UNDP 2002a). Nearly half the world population survives on less than the equivalent of two dollars a day, and 1.3 billion people must get along on one dollar per day (NetAid 2006). While world poverty is decreasing in absolute terms, it remains an enormous problem and the gaps in economic equality are widening. The average income of persons living in the world's richest 20 countries is 37 times greater than that in the poorest 20 (World Bank 2003: 2). Many countries in

Africa and the Middle East have become "terminal world nations," according to one observer, because they are "falling off the planet" (Barber 1995: 55). Interethnic warfare, environmental destruction, gender discrimination, and AIDS continue to disproportionately plague the poorest regions of the world. To make matters worse, virtually all of the increase in the world population in the next 20 years – some two billion people – will take place in developing countries with average incomes of less than two dollars per day (World Bank 2003: 1).

So despite free-flowing, upbeat rhetoric emanating from the West that promises improved living standards eventually for all the world's people, the realities of modernization, development, and globalization speak to other truths. The bottom line is that nations and corporations that benefit most from the global flow of money, goods, information, and technology today are those who were the dominant players in international business *before* the radical intensification of global marketization and exchange took place from the 1980s forward. Any political state or economic corporation that wants to play the game must be well prepared to compete effectively in the world capitalist system. That system was established and refined primarily to benefit the original participants – countries that had a relatively well-educated and trained work force and a political system that encouraged innovation and enterprise. Under these conditions, superpower nations occupy extraordinarily privileged positions in today's economic globalization. Perceptions of that power only increase when commercial products and logos, tourists, and business travelers arrive in less developed parts of the world or when the superpowers exercise their vastly superior political and military might to reinforce and sustain their economic dominance – the Iraq War is but the most recent example.

Globalization, therefore, is understood or "imagined" variously. Mainstream politicians and financial experts tend to see globalization as "circular and integrated," a fundamentally fair and open free-market system that serves the interests of anyone with the skills and motivations to enter the fray. Much of the rest of the world, however, imagines an asymmetrical or "tangential globalization," an inherently unbalanced and unfair economic scheme imposed by – and favorable to – the English-speaking First World

(García Canclini 1999). Especially in the wake of an intensive backlash against the major institutions that regulate world trade and investment – the World Bank, World Trade Organization (WTO), and International Monetary Fund – the fairness of economic globalization as it presently functions is being seriously questioned even by authorities within the system. Former Chief Economist of the World Bank and Nobel Prize winner Joseph Stiglitz is a leading voice for reform. "Globalization," he says, "can be a force for good and it has the *potential* to enrich everyone in the world, particularly the poor . . . The problem is not with globalization, but with how it has been managed" (Stiglitz 2002: ix, 214).

Most economists agree that among the great challenges facing the world in the early twenty-first century is finding ways to regulate global economic activity so that more equitable participation in the conduct of international commerce and finance can be achieved. More even-handed and effectively enforced rules for global economic activity, however, will not be enough in and of themselves to remedy the massive problems of the developing world. Significant improvements in basic education, gender equality, technological infusion, and greater control of crime and corruption, among other issues, must also materialize in developing nations and economies before they can benefit from the economic opportunities that globalization offers. For societies to prosper they must be able to produce capital. As Hernando DeSoto argues, "only capital provides the means to support specialization and the production and exchange of assets in the expanded market" (DeSoto 2000: 209). For him, only the right of every individual to own property alone or with others – "one of the fundamental rights of humankind" (as stated in the United Nations Universal Declaration of Human Rights) – can organize reality into a "conceptual universe" ultimately capable of raising the economic productivity of developing societies (DeSoto 2000: 217, 221).

To say the least, none of this will happen overnight and that's a big part of the problem. The world's economically excluded majority will continue to suffer from the growing disparities of asymmetrical economic globalization and, for many, domestic economic, political, religious, and cultural oppression. Meanwhile, access to information and images – loaded up with cultural values and styles that represent the imagined "easy life" and power of the modern world – increases tremendously.

Globalization is not just a measurable extension of modernity; it is a reflexive portrait of comparative economic, political, and cultural development. What matters most to populations in the developing world are not the gains they have made in the last 50 years against their own long histories of suffering, but the ready comparisons facilitated by media and cultural globalization. The global village has some very poor neighborhoods. Ironically, worldwide diffusion of mass media, information technology, personal communications technology, and many products of the transnational culture industries – all primary pillars of globalization – provide the relatively poor and powerless with the very tools and resources that facilitate unprecedented access to images and accounts that fuel resentment and rage. In this sense, the spread of global culture acts as a mediating, discomforting, influence that prompts "people around the world to constantly reorganize their individual and collective identities" (Notoji 2000: 225). The developing world experiences simultaneous economic scarcity and cultural overload.

The term "globalization" glosses over many big ideas that too often have become conveniently and misleadingly rolled up into one catchy concept. To better understand the complexity of today's globalization, it is necessary first to break the term down into principal subcategories. I've used the expression economic globalization so far to emphasize relative standards of living and earning potential around the world. Political globalization calls attention to transnational developments having to do with international relations, policies, and histories. And cultural globalization usually refers to the symbolic aspects and impacts of the flow of ideas and goods around the world.

The dissemination of religious ideology often is considered to be part of cultural globalization (e.g. Held et al. 1999: 333). Religious globalization is a term that is rarely used, although attempts to spread religious beliefs over vast territories – often enacted or imposed by military force and coercion – dates back at least as far as economic and cultural expansion and exchange. Global emissaries of the world's major monotheistic religions – especially those promoting various strains of Christianity and Islam – have tried throughout history to unify the world in the name of the gods they claim to represent. Contact between persons of different metaphysical philosophies and religious faiths has led to many recruitments and conversions. It has also led to endless disagreements, disputes, wars, and conquests.

Because of its unique and powerful emotional significance to many individuals and groups, religion remains the chief criterion for cultural inclusion and exclusion – particularly in the developing world where people who suffer economic deprivation and despair look for signs of hope and justice. In general, globalization expands awareness of new and competing systems of thought while simultaneously helping galvanize resistance to outsiders. Non-Islamic religious proselytizing on much of the Arabian Peninsula is outlawed, for example, and violators can be put to death. Sectarian violence in Iraq, Lebanon, Pakistan, India, Indonesia, and other countries rages between rival groups within the same religious faith. Catholics and Protestants have been killing each other for years in the United Kingdom. And while President George W. Bush repeatedly praised mainstream Islam and acted to protect Israel's Jewish population, many observers have interpreted the missionary overtones of his Middle Eastern foreign policy as a run-up to Armageddon – the final battle between "good and evil" prophesied in the Bible (Revelation 16:16) that is taken literally by millions of evangelical Christians.

Media Globalization

We add media globalization to the mix in order to stress the enormous importance of mass media, the culture industries, information technology, and personal communications technology in contemporary world affairs, and to analyze their complex relationship to economic, political, cultural, and religious life (Rantanen 2005). Without question, the worldwide communications revolution (especially the merging of satellite-based communication with computerization), the consequent growth of the global information society, and the breathless development of the knowledge economy have been globalization's distinguishing features over the past 30 years (see Giddens 2002a, 2002b; Hutton and Giddens 2000).

The global reach of mass media, popular culture, and the internet can easily be observed everywhere – the Britney Spears tee shirt worn by a young girl in the Venezuelan Andes, a McDonalds restaurant churning out burgers in downtown Moscow, David Beckham's face appearing on billboards in Istanbul, Spanish-language radio stations pulsating through immigrant neighborhoods in Los Angeles. Examples like these of media and cultural globalization disturb many observers – particularly when the cultural forms emanate from the West. The typical objection is that the aggressive, profit-driven practices of mass media and the culture industries routinely expose most of the world's inhabitants to common, often debasing, cultural forms – a process that homogenizes thought and experience, destroys local cultures, exploits their populations, and makes way too much money for the anonymous, often foreign corporate producers who distribute the product globally. These processes have been criticized under the rubric of media imperialism, cultural imperialism, neocolonialism, or even just globalization.

Commentators who describe global developments this way make an obvious yet important point about media influence. Some of their conclusions misrepresent and mislead, however. That's because the homogenizing tendencies that are so plain to see and criticize reflect only part of what's happening in contemporary cultural experience. Even the most fundamental idea that widespread *representation* of cultural forms leads to undifferentiated *reception* of those forms – an unstated assumption that underlies the usual critical argument – simply does not hold true. Active engagement by people everywhere with the ever-increasing abundance of technological and cultural resources has become just as decisive, if not more decisive, than the homogenizing tendencies.

But let's take a step back for the moment from any encouraging prospects for the future. The same developments that inspire hope have also helped fuel the tensions and armed conflicts that characterize world history. Communications media and the symbolic forms they produce and circulate have contributed greatly to impassioned ideological competition and conflict over many centuries.

Very early evidence of what has led to today's global cultural discord was born of the perilous mix of religious difference and media development in the form of book publishing. As former long-time CBS Middle East Bureau Chief Ed Hotaling points out, "the modern Arab envy of the West's good fortune, which still runs deep, was perhaps prefigured at the beginning of Islam, when the prophet lacked a book and saw how well the Christians and Jews were doing with theirs" (Hotaling 2003: 123). Legend has it that God dictated the content of the Koran to Muhammad in Arabic and that the prophet's successors, the Caliphs of Medina, assembled the material into a text by about 650 (Cook 2000: 5–6). Eight centuries later the hegemonic influence of the Catholic Church in Europe began to erode when the printing press was invented and publishers began to distribute religious and secular materials to growing numbers of educated readers – a turn of events that helped bring about the Protestant Reformation and, later, the Enlightenment.

Today, one needs only to see and hear the globalized images and sound-bite rhetoric of Muslim, Christian, and Jewish leaders to realize how vital communications media and cultural forms continue to be to their political and cultural causes. Even the logos of the three major monotheistic religions – the Star of David, the Cross, and the Crescent Moon – have become universally familiar symbols that clearly identify and brand particular belief systems.

Modern Media Development

The modern array of mass media and information technology developed primarily in the West during the nineteenth and twentieth centuries. The penny press newspapers of New York and other eastern seaboard cities of the United States became the first public communications medium to reach a mass (large, popular) audience. Magazines, still photography, and motion pictures emerged as popular media toward the end of the nineteenth century. Radio first appeared in the West in the early twentieth century, followed by terrestrial television in the 1950s, and cable television 20 years later. The final decades of last century brought satellite TV, the internet, mobile telephones, and a wide variety of other digital communications media that continue to proliferate today. The most recent era is so dominated by spectacular advances in communications technology that it has become widely known as the Information Age and, because it is proving to be as historically significant as the advent of manufacturing and modern transportation, this period is also sometimes referred to as the Third Industrial Revolution.

The extraordinary growth of diverse media and communication around the world in recent decades occurred at the same time as global economic markets were expanding at breakneck speed. As the media and information technology industries developed, they began to uniquely shape and strengthen the very global economy that had grown to depend on them. The year 1997 was particularly important for molding policy concerning global telecommunications and the rise of the internet as a political, economic, and cultural force. In that year the World Trade Organization passed a Basic Telecommunications Agreement that liberalized global electronic media activity overall and made generous provisions for foreign ownership of media properties among member states. That same year the office of American President Bill Clinton issued a crucial document – "The Framework for Global Electronic Commerce" – that praised the private sector for driving economic growth in the digital era, recommended a "free trade zone" on the internet, and prescribed an extremely limited regulative role for government over electronic commerce.

Many media critics and political activists were skeptical of these measures, and some were outraged. The White House document on global electronic commerce was "intended to organize the digital age according to rules most helpful to its formulator, the United States," according to Herbert Schiller, a long-time critic of media institutions. The neoliberal bent of American policy, he said, was clearly revealed by "the language of freedom" used to describe the opportunities (for some) that electronic commerce promises (Schiller 2000: 78–9). Specific criticism directed toward the global telecommunications and information technology industries, and toward international economic policy in general, often corresponds with more general charges of cultural imperialism, or even more vividly of "McDonaldization" (Ritzer 1993). Critics from these camps continue to claim that distinctive world cultures are being destroyed by the onslaught of globalized Western, especially American, ideas and products. Proponents of this position fear that the highly visible icons of global commerce are crunching global cultures into a "sterile American monoculture" (Barber 1995).

This perspective is important discursively and it contains more than a kernel of empirical truth. Ownership of the world's largest media, information, and entertainment enterprises is concentrated in the hands of relatively few multinational corporations (Bagdikian 2004). Recognizable global cultural flows do exist and their consequences can be damaging. But media globalization and the rise of the internet certainly don't just serve the narrow interests of the world's most powerful nations and institutions. Nor do they simply corrupt the integrity of pristine cultural groups. To the contrary, trends in global media influence today often decentralize, challenge, and realign traditional vectors of institutional authority in the spheres of politics and culture, just as early printing technology did centuries ago. The impact of the new, non-state-controlled satellite television networks in the Middle East today reveals how the fast-moving terrain of media globalization can upset political and cultural norms in a progressive way. The best example is Qatar-based Al-Jazeera, the pioneering satellite television network in the Middle East, which is feared and criticized by Arab and American elites alike.

Economic globalization, technological development, and the growing infrastructure that supports the information revolution converge to radically expand cultural options by providing access to a seemingly infinite universe of material and symbolic resources. This combination brings about a wide range of consequences that calls into question any claim that transnational media and culture simply overwhelm or undermine their global audiences. The main reasons to reject such an easy and misleading claim include the following:

- The number of media outlets, internet service providers, and culture producers is expanding tremendously throughout the world, inevitably opening up an unprecedented quantity and variety of political and cultural spaces and discourses.
- Global flows of everything – including especially media and cultural products – have changed course, becoming far more

diverse and complex, in some cases reversing the patterns of past imperialist exploits.

- The dominant cultures of relatively developed nations are being challenged by an unprecedented volume of transnational human migrations, which bring with them exogenous cultural materials.
- Piracy of media transmissions, information technology, and cultural goods is rampant worldwide with theft of CDs, DVDs, and software in some countries (China, Vietnam, Russia, Ukraine) hovering around 90 percent or more of all sales.
- "Local" cultures in developing countries stubbornly persist and are often reinforced and strengthened in the face of "outside influence."
- Outside influence typically becomes integrated or "indigenized" into local culture (this can occur in a market-driven way, such as MTV customizing its product for regional and national appeal, or as a receiver-driven process, such as the appropriation of American rap music by indigenous peoples around the world as a medium for expressing political demands and asserting contemporary cultural identities).

The speed and force of media and information technology influence world events at every level and for every purpose – including the conduct of global terrorism. Their effects have been spurred by the precipitous reduction in cost and the widespread availability of professional and consumer communications resources and tools – servers, microchips, fiber optics, mobile phones and calling plans, digital video and still cameras, computer hardware and software, and wide internet access chief among them. All these developments interact with enhanced functionality made possible by the reduced cost and increased speed and efficiency of modern transportation – a factor that contributed tremendously to earlier stages of industrialization and globalization as well.

The "true architectures" of today's "informational capitalism" driving all this political, economic, and cultural activity are institutional and personal networks that can only be facilitated by the blend of high-speed connectivity, interactivity, and flexibility that digital information and communication technologies provide (Castells 1996, 2000). These networks expedite lightning-fast movement of information around the world and efficiently connect global partners in business, industry, and finance. The same resources and concepts have been mobilized to serve a wide range of alternative, non-economic related purposes, too. A global reality check is in order, however, because the dynamic technological, economic, and cultural scenario described here does not much resemble what is happening in many parts of the world.

The Global Divides

Expressions like "digital divide" and "global technology gaps" regularly enter discussions about global human development, and for good reason. While the world's most developed countries enjoy the countless benefits that modern information and communication technologies offer, people who inhabit the least developed countries remain essentially out of the loop. The global gaps are not just digital. Very few people in the world's least developed nations (about six out of every 1,000 persons) even have access to a landline telephone (UNDP 2003a). The same percentage, less than 1 percent, have mobile (cellular) phone service. At the turn of the last century half the world's population had yet to ever make a single telephone call (*National Geographic* 1999). By comparison, there exist more landline telephones and mobile phones than people in the world's most developed countries where mobile communication has become a way of life.

Internet connections in poor countries are even less common than telephone services. United Nations' data indicate that less than two persons per 1,000 in the least developed countries use the internet, compared to more than half the population (and still rising) in the most developed countries. Research and development in the creation and diffusion of communications technology in poor countries is virtually non-existent, and very few scientists and engineers there are being trained in these vital areas (UNDP 2003a).

No quick fix can narrow the global communications technology gap. Despite the long-term importance of communications in national development, other more immediate needs must be met.

The principal Millennium Development Goals pursued by the United Nations concern much more basic issues – ending hunger and poverty, combating AIDS, discouraging armed conflict and genocide, eliminating gender discrimination, promoting basic education, and improving overall economic performance in the poorest countries of the world (UNDP 2003a). Developments in communications that have become central features of everyday life in the world's more advanced countries still don't even show up on the primary list of United Nations' priorities for human development in the poor sectors, although a Digital Opportunity Task Force was established by G8 countries in 2000 to explore ways that poor countries may be able to eventually use information technology to escape poverty.

Globalization extends social divisions that have been apparent throughout modern history. Media and information technology – together with many other influences not all attributable to globalization – accelerate those tendencies, amplify the effects of inequality, and widen the gaps even more. Technological growth cannot simply be injected into situations where poverty, disease, corrupt governments, lack of education, gender discrimination, and religious intolerance define and limit human potential. In contrast to the incredible speed with which advances in information and communications technology take place, economic and cultural conditions greatly slow and limit their diffusion in less developed countries. Quickly bringing about significant improvement in living conditions for an impoverished majority is impossible to achieve.

Lack of economic performance continues to be the primary obstacle to growth in all aspects of human development, including the potential positive utilization of information and communications technology, but it isn't the only factor. Cultural values, histories, and practices also greatly influence the degree to which nations modernize, develop their human capital, and participate successfully in the world system. That's always been true, but today the stakes are higher. Although he simplifies and overstates the case, Thomas Friedman correctly points out that "the most open-minded, tolerant, creative, and diverse societies will have the easiest time with globalization, while the most rigid, uptight, self-absorbed companies and countries, which are just not comfortable with openness, will struggle" (Friedman 2000: 227). Friedman argues that it makes more sense to talk today about differences between the "Fast World" (open, ambitious, innovative, and networked nations) versus the "Slow World" (nations that fear or cannot achieve the speed, demands, and consequences of globalization) than to categorize countries as First, Second, or Third World (Friedman 2000: 46).

Global inequalities eventually provoke strong reactions, especially now that the differences between nations, ethnic groups, and cultures have become clear to many people through the power of international media and the internet. Some of the global "losers" in these comparisons feel humiliated and lash out at the "winners." Terrorism may be the most obvious, blatant, and visible case in point. The humiliation hypothesis is one of Thomas Friedman's main conclusions in his "search for the roots of 9/11" (Friedman 2003). He points not only to mass media and the internet, but to all forms of transcivilizational experience where cultural comparisons are inevitably made – including foreign travel – as triggers of violent reaction. And, as Amy Chau observes, "the spread of the internet and television, even improvements in education – are two-edged swords, often producing growing discontent with growing awareness. Globalization generates not only new opportunities and hopes, but also new social desires, stresses, insecurities, and frustrations" (Chau 2003: 245). Under these circumstances, some of the most rewarding benefits that globalization can bring to the poor are symbolic victories resulting from attention that derives from media events. These can be national team victories in televised sports competitions such as the Olympics or World Cup soccer, for instance, or feats by individual persons from home who are celebrated by international media (sports heroes, politicians, beauty pageant contestants, scientists, writers, human rights activists, and many others), and the most recent category – terrorist leader.

Extreme differences in living standards have also spurred unprecedented levels of transnational migration in recent decades by workers and professionals – usually from South to North and East to West. Modern forms of communication and transportation make human movement around the world faster than ever before and more responsive to opportunity. While these migrations may benefit individuals, they simultaneously drain developing countries of key human resources – particularly bright students and skilled technical talent – which further limits the potential of those nations to grow economically and culturally. No country can compete successfully in global trade without a sufficiently educated and stable workforce, an urbane and enterprising middle class, and an institutional infrastructure that facilitates effective movement of financial and material resources.

For reasons not always entirely of their own choosing, immigrants tend to group together in their new locations and attempt to maintain the cultural traditions they brought with them from their homelands. Cultural maintenance within ethnic diasporas has become much easier to achieve in recent years because a general relaxation of restrictions on international trade and access to modern transportation forms, especially jet air travel, have greatly increased access to material resources such as traditional food, domestic items, clothing, and religious artifacts. Even more crucial is the ready availability of symbolic cultural resources such as popular music, video cassettes, DVDs, and satellite television channels from abroad, and the low cost and convenience of international telephone calls.

The sheer scale and inter-civilizational nature of immigration over the past 50 years have created more entangled and challenging cultural realities for everyone. It isn't just the immigrants and their cultural belongings that are moving around with ease and impact. As David Held and his associates describe it,

> the stratification of cultural globalization is changing rapidly . . . flows have begun to be reversed, primarily through migrations but also through other cultural forms . . . Music, food, ideas, beliefs, and literature from the South and East have percolated into the cultures of the West, creating new lines of cultural interconnectedness and fracture. (Held et al. 1999: 369)

American popular culture (especially movies, music, video games, computer software, and fast food restaurants) travels throughout the world where it finds eager consumers and relentless critics. At the same time, global cultural influence streams into America and the West from everywhere, adding distinctive new elements to current cultural mixtures and interacting with those existing forms to create cultural hybrids. Media and cultural globalization have supplanted traditional routes of transnational influence with a far more intricate web of interactions and impacts. Japanese export of pop music, Pokémon, anime, and television drama, for example, command extraordinary cultural recognition and influence throughout Asia (Iwabuchi 2002). Spanish-language cultural forms permeate Latin America, the Iberian Peninsula, and beyond. Many other examples of intra-civilizational cultural flows could be summoned. Cultural forms travel best among nations whose common languages, religions, cultural values, and habits facilitate easy accommodation and appreciation.

China and the Middle East: Responses to Modernity and Globalization

Globalization in all its forms has always been more multidirectional than commonly imagined, but cultural decentralization has become particularly evident in recent years. China merits special consideration in this regard. Whether under the rule of emperors, nationalists, or communists, China has almost always faced inward for inspiration throughout its political and cultural history. But when the country opened to the West in the 1970s and initiated sweeping economic reform and technology-based modernization under Deng Xiaoping, China guardedly cultivated extensive economic and cultural relations with the most successful capitalist societies of the outside world – especially Japan, the United States, and the nations of Western Europe. Since then, China has become the world's fastest-growing domestic economy, developed enormous international trade balances in its favor, joined the World Trade Organization, and seems destined to become the world's next economic and military superpower. Mandarin Chinese will be the most popular web language by the end of this decade and Chinese political and cultural influence in general is rapidly increasing. China has indeed changed course, albeit cautiously, to look outward – importing ideas, materials, and expertise from the West, particularly in the fields of hard science and technology.

Much of China's economic success can be attributed to the vast opportunities afforded by globalization, yet despite strong measures taken to control potential problems, the government has not been unable to avoid the dangers of a closely connected world. And it isn't just the government that should get credit or bear the blame for what's happening. Economic and political corruption – long a pervasive problem in Chinese society – permeates the over-bureaucratized official channels but also infects the private business sector. International intellectual property theft and patent violations, especially in the technological and cultural areas, run rampant. Trade in erotic literature and pornography is booming. HIV and AIDS have made serious inroads into China. The SARS and bird flu outbreaks have become global health problems.

Fundamental to the Chinese modernization was development of a national, satellite-based telecommunications system. The consequences of this monumental step into the future, however, were not controllable. Instead of simply fulfilling the government's plan for disseminating information and propaganda, television became a powerful force for cultural change, offering alternatives to official ideologies, expectations, and lifestyles (Lull 1991). Professional workers at all levels in the government television industry found ways to express their unofficial opinions about China's political-economic-cultural system; messages produced by television stations were never understood solely as intended by government policy makers; and, most important, Chinese audience members creatively interpreted the official discourses represented on the small screen and passed their often non-conformist opinions around to family, friends, and co-workers. Television stoked the imagination of Chinese viewers, especially the young, and incited a student–worker uprising for freedom and democracy culminating in a standoff at Tiananmen Square in 1989. That media event was covered by a cadre of international journalists and television networks, giving the entire world more than just a shadowy peek into the political and cultural realities of the People's Republic of China – until the government pulled the plug on satellite links and asked the journalists to leave.

Turmoil caused by China's revolutionary movement in the late 1980s continues to influence the East Asian powerhouse now. The country's current economic success stems from ruptures in state policy that were caused directly by the student–worker uprising, which relegated the political apparatus to a subordinate role. China's efforts to contain the impact of outside influence today have become even more difficult with the unstoppable and interacting effects of global popular culture, international mass media, and the agent of national modernization that has succeeded television in the era of globalization – the internet.

Because no economy can succeed today without effective use of information technology and the internet, the challenge for authoritarian governments like China is to find a balance between flexibility and control. That's no easy task. More than 100 million Chinese are connected to the web today, making China the world's second-largest internet user with less than 10 percent of the population involved (Internet World Stats 2006). Advanced information and communications technology is rapidly being imported from Japan and the West and developed domestically. Venture capital for high technology projects flows into the country and many new dot-com companies appear every day. At the same time, the Chinese government arrests people who use the web to criticize the government, promote alternatives to communist-style socialism (including religion and new-age philosophies like Falun Gong), or connect to prohibited political or pornographic sites. The most popular form of access to the web – internet cafés and bars – are strictly regulated and routinely shut down.

Arab and Islamic nations of the Middle East have also tried for centuries to avoid precisely what the Chinese government has had to negotiate in its transformation from a traditional to modern society – the unwanted influence of certain Western cultural values and lifestyles. That's difficult to do when importing technology, machinery, and expertise, of course, because, among other problems, cultural values are embedded deeply in the logic, appearance, and content of the equipment itself, including computer operating systems, software, and domains of connectivity. The content of mass media and popular culture is even more explicit, pervasive, and influential. In the face of these challenges to cultural authority and political ideology, communist and Islamic cultures stridently attempt to prohibit or limit exposure to the forces of modernity and globalization. They do so for the same basic reason: outside influences threaten to discredit the authority of the political and religious elite and call into question the ideological and cultural platforms that legitimize and extend their power.

Diversity, tolerance of competing systems of thought, and dissent are necessary for cultural progress because they contribute to another vital characteristic of success in the era of globalization: innovation. Closed societies don't innovate. And history makes clear that societies that fail to adopt and retain innovations "will be eliminated by competing societies" (Diamond 1999: 407). Structures of political and cultural authority often determine their fate.[3] Historian Kenneth Boulding observed that, "We can be pretty sure that innovation will not be carried on unless it is rewarded, and in traditional societies, where the innovator is looked upon with suspicion and even horror as one who violates ancient dignities and destroys the sacred patterns of society, innovation is not likely to be successful" (Boulding 1969: 340).

According to Boulding, China's technological development in many areas was vastly superior to the West until Europe began to jump way ahead, beginning in the seventeenth century. China's inward vision limited its development. Europe, meanwhile, was diversifying and looking outward. So while China remained stuck with

> folk technology . . . the very disjointed and disintegrated structure of Europe, with its many centers of power, religious and national divisions, its separation of ecclesiastical from political power, and at the same time its active network of trade and communication . . . made that fraction of difference which carried Europe over the watershed into science. China . . . did not make this transition . . . a fact that dominated history for the last 300 years. (Boulding 1969: 347)

In many respects developments in the Arab and Muslim world mirror China's history until the communist revolution and subsequent political opening and economic liberalization began to change the East Asian country's fortunes toward the end of the last century. Islamic nations of the Middle East, however, did not follow the same path and remain mired in severe economic and cultural underdevelopment – "going nowhere," in historian David Landes' frank terms (Landes 1999: 518). This turn of events was not predictable or predetermined. It's commonly known that the

Middle East was once the most advanced civilization in the world. The reflection made by *Newsweek International* editor Fareed Zakaria is typical: "The Arabs belong to a great civilization with a long history of science, philosophy, and military success. They invented algebra, preserved Aristotle when he had been forgotten in the West, and won wars against the greatest power of the day. Islamic art and culture were sophisticated when Europe was in the Dark Ages" (Zakaria 2003:124).

Not only did the Middle East region develop greatly within its geographical territory long before Europe began to cultivate its own civilization, its influence had spread great distances to the West and East. For centuries, much of the robust diversity of plants and animals that originally inhabited the Fertile Crescent – extending from the eastern shores of the Mediterranean Sea to the western plains of the Arab Peninsula – was introduced to Europe and Asia. During the early Middle Ages the Middle East "was technologically advanced and open to innovation" and "the flow of technology was overwhelmingly from Islam to Europe, rather than from Europe to Islam as it is today" (Diamond 1999: 253).

The religion of Islam permeated and began to deeply affect diverse Arab cultures toward the latter stages of the Middle Ages, particularly during the twelfth century. Gradually, for reasons also having to do with changes in climate and culture, Middle Eastern civilizations became more and more isolated. Progress stalled in virtually all areas of intellectual inquiry and cultural life. The consequences have become obvious today. By as early as the seventeenth century, "no one who looked around could be blind to the shifting balance of world power . . . [by then] the loss of might [by Muslim societies] relative to infidel societies became a source of profound despair or active anguish" (Landes 1999: 394).

Now, four centuries later, conditions in the Arab Muslim world relative to the West and to other developing nations have deteriorated greatly. Can the miserable situation ever be reversed or dramatically improved? How do today's global realities affect the chances for recovery? There is no magic bullet, that's for sure, and fantasizing about the glorious past won't help either. Moreover, according to David Landes, contemporary apologists for Islam wrongly dismiss or downplay the economic stagnation and cultural paralysis of the Muslim world today by pointing "to Muslim economic, spiritual, and intellectual openness in an earlier age [and arguing] if they could do it then, they can do it now" (Landes 1999: 414). Landes objects to this reasoning because the level of competition and performance required for success today greatly exceeds what was expected in the past and demands more than what he believes these cultures can produce for the foreseeable future. Landes' assessment rings true. But conditions today call for further analysis, discussion, and encouragement.

The Communications Revolution

In the past, the spread of ideas depended mainly upon geographical proximity and the physical movement of ideas and material goods from more developed to less developed societies. Today's globalized communications change these assumptions. The combined force of contemporary mass media, the culture industries, information technology, and personal communications technology spreads ideologies that range from strict religious authoritarianism to liberal democratic secularism all over the globe. Geopolitical relations and cultural assumptions are in flux everywhere. Religious and ethnic terrorism – one kind of globalization "from below" – is plainly visible yet, as I hope to show in this book, globalization can also spread peace and stability by eliminating "disconnectedness" (Barnett 2005). The key question is this: do current trends in communication and culture only exacerbate the stress or do they offer real prospects for broad human development of the increasingly connected, mobile, culturally aware, individualized inhabitants of the world?

Communication is the quintessential process that underlies all the excitement, uncertainty, and potential. The symbolic materials that populate and energize today's complex webs of human interaction dramatically alter social exchanges and cultural activities of all kinds. Resources supplied by media and cultural globalization help empower ordinary people to express their rights, preferences, and demands. Given all these opportunities, what the world needs to see happen now, in the poetic words of Nobel Peace Prize winner, the human rights activist Shirin Ebadi, is a "globalization of human hearts" (Ebadi 2005).

Many current trends reinforce and illuminate Ebadi's vision. Other developments make her fantasy seem impossible to achieve, if not hopelessly naïve. The 2005 landslide election of religious conservative Mahmoud Ahmadinejad in Ebadi's own country, Iran, the interethnic violence that continues unabated in the Middle East and South Asia, and the cultural crises that confront Europe today surface among the discouraging trends. Still, with the many doubts, limitations, and counter-tendencies fully in mind, I set out to demonstrate in this book how and why the potential of human communication – so greatly amplified by technological and cultural developments – offers real long-term promise for a world of diverse souls who, whether they like it or not, become more and more connected every minute of every day.

Notes

1. As former Director of the London School of Economics and Political Science Anthony Giddens points out, the free market advocates of the nineteenth century were thought to be politically left, whereas "today they are normally placed on the right" (Giddens 1998: 38).
2. All references in the text to the United Nations Development Programme from now on will be abbreviated as UNDP.
3. Some nations of the Middle East – Lebanon, Jordan, and Qatar, for example – are beginning to break with tradition and innovate.

Chapter 2

Human Expression

Interviewed by a CNN reporter a few days after the fall of Kabul, an Afghan teenager explained why young people had been willing to risk confiscations, beatings, and going to jail under the repressive Taliban regime for the simple pleasure of listening to popular music. "Because our souls need such things," he said.

Among their secret activities, Afghanistan's Radical Afghanistan Women's Association (RAWA) – given global visibility during the Taliban's reign by Saira Shah's stunning documentary *Beneath the Veil* – established underground beauty parlors where women experimented with banned substances such as eyeliner and lipstick. Afghan barbers were jailed for giving young men stylish haircuts because, according to the Taliban Ministry of Vice and Virtue, lengthy bangs could interfere with their ability to bow and say prayers properly. In a land where virtually all forms of popular expression and pleasure were subject to draconian punishment, listening to music, applying cosmetics, styling the hair, taking a photograph, and dancing had become acts of serious religious, political, and cultural subversion. The fundamentalist Islamic state of Iran imposes similar restrictions. Restaurants must not serve women wearing makeup; stores may not sell tee shirts emblazoned with pop culture imagery; men cannot wear Western-style neckties at work; no Western music, including classical music, is aired on the state broadcasting system. Music is not allowed in malls, dancing and kissing is not permitted in public, and no partially nude mannequins may appear in store windows. Women can't attend soccer games and must sit in separate areas in mosques and buses. Iran's Farzaneh Kaboli and two dozen of her students were incarcerated for performing folk dances before an all-female audience and released from jail only when they promised to never perform in "public" again.

It seems absurd that prohibitions like these could exist anywhere on Earth in the twenty-first century and be enforced with such (de)moralizing zeal. That's because what's taken away by the culture police cuts to the core of a healthy, integrated human existence. Expression is a primordial necessity. It creates psychological, social, and cultural well-being. As the technological and symbolic resources of the Digital Age become more and more available, opportunities for expanding this positive potential grows immensely. But the potential will always be shaped by cultural circumstances.

The Cultural Politics of Expression

Formalized respect for freedom of expression and the individual autonomy associated with it originated in the Enlightenment in Europe and contributed importantly to the continent's civilizing process over a span of centuries (Chaney 2002: 97). Freedom of expression has since become fundamental to the economic, social, and cultural well-being of Western societies. The Constitution of the United States of America grants citizens great latitude in speech and expression – including the right to have meaningful access to views expressed by others – in its famous First Amendment, a basic principle which has been strongly upheld by the courts over many years.[1] Similar assurances are provided by the political constitutions of the United Kingdom, France, Germany, and many other nation states around the world. Even the People's Republic of China grants freedom of expression in its Constitution, though in practice, of course, individuals suffer tremendously from state censorship.

Cultural values that embody and promote free speech and individual freedom sparked development of the massive entertainment industries that grew so impressively in the United States in the early twentieth century. These industries developed rapidly because

America's culture and economic systems reward creativity, innovation, ambition, and embrace the idea that everyone deserves a fair shot at the "good life." American citizens are constitutionally granted not only the "right to life [and] liberty," but also to the "pursuit of happiness." Most Americans believe they not only have the right to be free in a political sense, but also the right to be happy in general. Life is not to be simply survived or tolerated; it is to be enjoyed – as a *right*.

Many Americans take that right very seriously – some would argue far too seriously. The land of "infotainment," instant gratification, and non-stop fun-fun-fun – where everybody has a "right to party" – certainly can (and should) be criticized for its blatant hedonism, consumerism, and superficiality. But the freedom to have fun has tremendous allure too, as evidenced by the enduring global appeal and impact of American popular culture, even in the face of rapidly growing dislike internationally for many of the country's customs and foreign policies (Pew Global Attitudes Project 2002–5).

The historical contrast between capitalist and communist cultures made it clear that expression diversifies and flourishes best in market-driven contexts. The collapse of the Soviet empire and the student–worker uprising in China at the end of the last century were triggered by the increased presence of communications media of all types and by responses to the symbolic forms they circulated. Young people revolted against communist culture generally – the quotidian and emotional aspects, not just the ideological and political dimensions. Resistance to communist hegemony took shape as powerful symbolic displays: the singing revolutions of the Baltic states; the tearing down of the Berlin Wall; Chinese students and workers who occupied the symbolic heart of the People's Republic – Tiananmen Square – erecting a foam Statue of Liberty, and singing the Chinese national anthem to Red Army soldiers as they were being driven out of Beijing's city center.

Freedom of expression has become a central moral issue in debates about the meaning of human rights. Addressing the World Summit on the Information Society in 2003, United Nations' Secretary General Kofi Annan asserted that "the right to freedom of opinion and expression is fundamental to development, democracy, and peace, and must remain a touchstone for our work ahead." The international body has declared freedom of expression to be an unassailable and wide-ranging right for citizens in all societies. Article 19 of the United Nations' Universal Declaration of Human Rights claims:

> Everyone has the right to freedom of opinion and expression; this right includes freedom to hold opinions without interference and to seek, receive and impart information and ideas through any media and regardless of frontiers. (United Nations 2006)

And here's the most important point: The United Nations' Declaration of Human Rights endorses the highly controversial matter of the expressive rights of *individual persons*, making clear that the organization considers expressive rights to be linked to *individual human rights*. The document speaks of the right for "every*one*" to seek, receive, create, and express ideas through channels ranging from basic movements and utterances of the human body in local contexts to sophisticated manipulations of high technology in global communications. This promise to every single global citizen does not conform to the political demands and cultural traditions of all nations, however. Theocratic and communist state authorities typically regard the concept of individual human rights as a corrupting cultural idea imposed by the West. Despite resistance from some quarters, however, the right of individuals to freely express themselves and hear others do the same is becoming more and more accepted as a universal norm. Even "millions of Muslims have come to enjoy or aspire to [freedom of expression today, and] ultimately spreading and strengthening it may be one of the best hopes for avoiding the incomprehension that can lead civilizations into conflict" (*The Economist*, 2006).

The Need for Expression

Expression is the means by which the inner thoughts and feelings of individual persons are transformed into physical and symbolic representations that appear in acts of human communication. Transformation is the key concept. People phenomenologically convert their private thoughts and feelings into physical signs and actions by using the expressive media available to them – from the naked body to the most elaborate communications technologies. In doing so, they experience great pleasure. The expressive production of signs is self-validating, liberating, and transcendental. In order to comprehend the profound importance of human expression in self-creation and cultural development, it helps to consider the crucial role expression plays in the evolution of social intercourse and in the social psychology of individual persons today.

When Charles Darwin began to focus his work on the evolution of human beings, he noted that certain tendencies appear among human groups the world over, even when they do not come into contact with each other (Darwin 1871/1998). Prominent among these tendencies are primary forms of human expression. Based on his fieldwork and on the writings of his contemporaries, Darwin observed that dancing, music making, acting, poetry, painting, tattooing and other body decorating, gestures, and inarticulate cries of emotion appear universally. Darwin marveled at the complexity and intensity of the universal habits of bodily expression among tribal cultures of his time, the early and middle nineteenth century. The same basic channels of human expression exist today, appearing in everyday life environments but also in more elaborate, celebrated, and commodified forms as the performing arts.

Darwin's theory of the evolution of humans and other animals rests primarily on two powerful ideas: natural selection, where species adapt in ways that promote their chances for survival in competitive environments, and sexual selection (of greater interest to us here), where males and females attempt to attract mates for purposes of sexual reproduction (Darwin 1859/1979). Human expression, in Darwinian terms, originally appeared to induce the most fundamental kind of human interaction – sexual activity that perpetuates the species. Whether we consider the first tribal cultures in Africa tens of thousands of years ago, the indigenous groups that Darwin himself studied 200 years ago, or the modern societies of the current era, humans express their sexual potential for biological reasons. The actual expressive forms and contexts in which these expressive displays appear vary considerably. But many cultural customs and artifacts – ranging from the facial scarring, bodily disfiguration, and canoe art of indigenous tribes to the

steamy music videos, dress styles, and personal web pages of contemporary youth – reflect overall what Darwin argued is the
predominant drive humans have: expressing their sexual potential
to others.

In his classic psychological theory, Abraham Maslow (1943)
agreed with Darwin that human expression and creativity comprise core elements of human motivation and behavior. Expression,
he said, nourishes personal health, stability, and growth. Maslow
believed that the "freedom to express one's self" is a "precondition
for need satisfaction [which is] closely related to the basic needs"
(1943: 383). Sometimes the very survival of the human organism
is at stake. When a baby cries after sensing its mother has left the
room, for instance, or when its body is disturbed by hunger, cold,
noise, or unfamiliar stimuli, the infant alerts caregivers by vocally
and physically expressing fear, thereby signaling a basic survival
instinct (Stewart 2001). In his study of the origins of vocalized
expression, Steven Mithen concludes that our hominid ancestors
soothed and healed each other by humming and singing, making
these expressive faculties part of their repertoire of social skills
(Mithen 2006).

The hierarchy of basic human needs posited by Maslow – rooted,
to be sure, in the intellectual traditions of Western culture – has
become very familiar. Maslow argued that human expression helps
bring about cognitive stability and personal growth as a precondition for need gratification and as the means through which need
gratification occurs. He attempted to generalize his theory of
motivation beyond cultural boundaries without claiming that the
hierarchy of needs applies everywhere in equal measure. Still,
Maslow refused any theory of cultural particularism. He argued
that, "no claim is made that [the category system of basic needs
and preconditions] is ultimate or universal . . . only more ultimate,
more universal, more basic, than the superficial conscious desires
from culture to culture" (Maslow 1943: 390). His aim was to
describe "basic, unconscious goals" rather than "specific, local-
cultural desires" (ibid.: 370).

Still, cultural traditions and values guide all forms of self-
expression. Indeed, the *inability* to express oneself is frequently
interpreted in the West as a symptom of psychological or physical
illness. Therapeutic techniques that employ music, art, dance,

psychodrama, novel, diary, or life-story writing are widely used in psychological counseling and rehabilitation. Even late-stage Alzheimer's patients express delight at hearing their favorite music. Modes of expression are often employed as helpful ways to respond to a crisis. In the wake of the 2001 World Trade Center attack, for example, schoolchildren in New York were encouraged to express their feelings by writing poetry or letters, or by creating art.

Basic biological equilibrium and psychological stability lie at the heart of attempts to gratify human needs at collective levels too. Expressing one's group identity or identities may include public displays of association with sports teams, pop music stars and groups, motorcycle clubs, or consumer products, for example, but they can also reflect deeply meaningful affiliations with religious philosophies and organizations, nations, political parties, and social movements. Religious rituals and national holidays, for instance, represent widely practiced forms of collective expression. Self-mutilation rituals enacted by some Muslim and Christian groups dramatically reflect this collective behavior. Even more extreme are "lamenting" religious groups that turn into warlike "packs" and eventually into a "continually growing crowd" in order to collectively avenge a death (Canetti 1984: 127). The prototypical case is the (patently masculine) response by Palestinian crowds to killings caused by Israeli violence. The fervor of collective religious expression intensifies under threatening conditions, particularly when religious loyalties are stronger than, or interact positively with, nationalist sentiments.

Collective forms of expression often materialize publicly by means of shared forms of gendered self-presentation. Islamic women who wear the abaya, hijab, or burka, for example, project their collective religious and cultural identities over the more individualistic modes of self-expression that are typical of Western styles of dress. When three teenage Sikh boys were expelled from school in Paris for wearing turbans that conceal *kirpans* (small daggers of religious significance), an American Sikh living in the San Francisco Bay area responded, "It's not only cultural, it's religious: it's part of a man's body" (*San José Mercury News* 2006). During the Cultural Revolution in China the androgynous "Mao suit" look and the standard blunt haircut worn by women promoted the imagined egalitarianism of communist ideology above diversity of individual expression. Such collective means of expression, however, do not always reflect voluntary participation or conscious awareness of the effects they create. Extreme covering or de-emphasizing of the female form in the name of modesty, religious conformity, or the collective good, for instance, can also be interpreted as male-dominated cultural requirements imposed on women to control them by limiting their expressive (i.e. social and sexual) potential.

The idea of "freedom of expression" applies much more widely than to the usual associations we give it with freedom of speech. The human body is the only expressive medium possessed by every person on Earth. Culture insinuates itself on that precious resource early in life in healthy and unhealthy ways. Consider one of the most sophisticated and beautiful forms of bodily expression ever imagined – the ballet. The sensuality, athleticism, and artistic expression of ballet make it one of the world's greatest aesthetic achievements and cultural treasures. The female body in motion – the ballerina – expresses the beauty, power, and grace of woman in exquisite ways that have achieved the great admiration of people in many parts of the world – but not everywhere.

Symbolic Creativity and the Expressive Self

> *To be human means to be creative.*
> M. Csikszentmihalyi, *Creativity*, p. 318

Creativity and expression are inextricably linked. Their combined, dynamic force imbues the routine practices and performances of human communication in every aspect of life. Creativity emerges from the human spirit to transfigure a person's thoughts and feelings into meaningful symbolic representations that are expressed to others through various modes of social interaction. The decorative use of jewelry in the southern coastal regions of Africa some 75,000 years ago – the famous Nassarius shell beads of South Africa's Blombo Caves – represents the first documented attempt by humans to employ symbolic resources external to the person for purposes of expressive enhancement, not simply for instrumental purposes

(Blombo Caves Project 2006). The creative blending of familiar symbolic materials into cultural hybrids, or less familiar materials into cultural mash-ups, can foster strong feelings of personal and cultural transcendence. Creativity serves as a distinct, powerful, and productive mode of "human capital" (Cowen 1998: 22).

Creativity and expression make it possible for people to explore and negotiate the most potentially exhilarating and growthful dimensions of life. While it's true that people struggle to maintain basic stability in their lives, by nature they also seek challenges and take risks: "Higher mammals become attached precisely to . . . challenging experiences. People . . . return again and again to scenes which are puzzling: ambiguity and difficulty breed involvement" (Sennett 2000: 178). The same idea applies at macro social levels. For successful societies, "survival no longer depends on biological equipment alone but on the social and cultural tools we choose to use. The inventions of the great civilizations – the arts, religions, political systems, sciences, and technologies – signal the main stages along the path of cultural evolution" (Csikszentmihalyi 1996: 318).

But how does human expression link up with symbolic forms, creativity, and communication? British social theorist Paul Willis' landmark ethnographic study of "why working class British boys get working class jobs," *Learning to Labour* (1977), provides some enduring insights. In the process of carrying out fieldwork in the schools and factories of England's industrial Midlands – the "Black Country" – over a period of years, Willis was struck by two seemingly contradictory themes.

In the first place, the subjects of his research – young, working-class males – proudly immerse themselves in manual labor jobs and later willingly accept predictable unemployment caused by severe industrial decline. Willis' explanation of why these young men continue on this downward spiral made his book a classic in sociology and education. But the second main theme addressed in *Learning to Labour* dominates much of Willis' research and writing since then and is of particular interest to us here. Willis describes how the working-class subjects of his research – the "lads" – creatively negotiate their everyday realities without considering themselves to be "dupes or zombies . . . [there was no] sullen defeat, no cultural inadequacy, no ideological domination." Instead, the young men carry on with energy and style through "the sheer life, intelligence, and wit of their cultural practices" (Willis 2000: xx). The creative, everyday cultural practices of the lads and of British youth in general comprise the focus of Willis' later work – *Common Culture* (1990) and *The Ethnographic Imagination* (2000).

Willis formulates theoretical concepts to describe how people, especially youth, imaginatively engage and take ownership over cultural resources available to them. The first of these is *symbolic creativity*, which he defines as the "multitude of ways in which young people use, humanize, decorate, and invest with meanings their common and immediate life spaces and social practices" (Willis 1990: 2). Lifestyle elements include clothing styles, uses of music and other media, decoration of bedrooms, dance, language and "banter," and romance rituals, among other behaviors. Engaging in cultural activities like these comprise what he calls *necessary work*. As Willis puts it, "In conditions of late modernization and the widespread crisis of cultural values [necessary work] can be crucial to the creation and sustenance of individual and group identities, even to cultural survival of identity itself" (Willis 1990: 2). The individual who engages in this work is the *expressive self* (Willis 2000: 71). The expressive self combs the environment for potential resources useful for fusing symbolic creativity with necessary work.

Positive feelings produced through the expressive displays and communicative performances of everyday life compare with the buzz felt by any entertainer or professional – a musician, actor, dancer, trial lawyer, athlete, or teacher, for instance – before, during, and after a satisfying performance in front of an audience. Authors of expressive displays demonstrate personal competencies and talents of representation through reflexive, creative, transformative "work" in routine communicative interaction. As Dylan Evans writes, "when someone makes up a story, he is calling attention to his own creativity. When someone tells us a joke, he is displaying his understanding of what makes others laugh" (Evans 2001: 78). Some of the most intense pleasures of communication spring from the simple creative breakthroughs that routinely materialize in everyday speech.

The mundane quality of most expressive displays masks their robust significance. Choosing tiles for a new bathroom floor, for instance, is an expressive act. So are planting flowers in a garden; cooking a meal; driving a car (or, more dramatically, a motorcycle); trimming a tree. Expression embodies and articulates multiple meanings. Expressive acts usually have instrumental purposes, but they also exhibit personal and cultural values, tastes, preferences, and styles, whose expression is often considered more important than the functional dimensions. Routine expressive actions embody multiple performative aspects as well. To decorate a home, for example, manifests creative action in deciding on colors, sizes, shapes, and associations among elements – an expressive performance of aesthetic qualities – as well as the actual performing of the physical work. Expression doesn't stop when the creative processes terminate. The product of creative work – a decorated home, for instance – becomes a material manifestation of human expression, a culturally laden communications medium that endures over time.

Instrumentally based, practical satisfactions resulting from the expressive production of everyday life reflect the rewards of what Willis (2000) calls the *use value* of material and symbolic forms. By manipulating available expressive resources, and by framing the ways creative processes and products will be interpreted by others, people assert a degree of control over their environments that then produces a sense of order and safety for those individuals. People sample, fuse, style, pierce, and feel their way through the complex matrices of cultural forms available to them and through their inner states of pleasure and sensation. The profound pleasures generated by expressive displays have great value in and of themselves. Willis refers to this aspect of symbolic creativity and expression as the "sensuous" use of symbolic forms: "the human and the material are brought into sensuous relation through human practices of symbolic work" (Willis 2000: 24). Moreover, these everyday activities don't divide neatly between cultural production and cultural consumption, especially now that communications technologies have become so widely available and easy to use. In many ways, cultural consumption *is* cultural production in a world dominated by "consumer electronics."

Willis' choice of the term "work" to describe human expression and communication makes sense. We work to physically locate material and symbolic materials to use as expressive resources. We then work emotionally when we use the resources. To express oneself is to risk the possibility of unwanted responses: confusion, disappointment, rejection, humiliation, failure. The pleasure that expression stimulates emerges when we overcome a socially conditioned, emotionally felt sense of risk. When we express our thoughts and feelings in a manner we deem successful, even if that judgment is rendered subconsciously, we temporarily reduce the feeling of "communication anxiety" or "performance anxiety." We receive positive feedback from others when we perform well. Natural opiates are released to the brain, stimulating the limbic system, which produces a warming sense of physical pleasure (Dozier 1998).

Emotional Communication

We are apes at our core; all that is unique to humans has been piled on top of our ape heritage.
J. H. Turner, *On the Origins of Human Emotions*, p. 1

When we speak of the risks and pleasures of human expression we are talking about what the American cultural psychologist Edward Stewart (2001) calls the "feeling edge of culture" – emotion. Emotional expression, emotional intelligence, and emotional literacy are vital aspects of life, especially now that mediated communication makes up so much of everyday cultural experience. But the roots and significance of sentiment pre-date even the dawn of human history.

Evolutionary development of emotional potential made the very survival of early primates possible. Among the hominids, the immediate progenitors of modern humans, emotional expression was necessary for "forging bonds of increased solidarity and, thereby, more stable local group structures" (Turner 2000: 20). Emotion later functioned to help bring socially integrated groups of *Homo sapiens* into existence, forming the first true cultures. Emotional communication – gestures and meaningful vocalizations – gave early primates an evolutionary advantage that brought consequences for humans:

Not only did [natural] selection produce an animal capable of controlling emotions and using them to communicate meaning, selection also worked to create an animal able to generate a wide array of emotional states. The complexity of human thought, social interaction, organization, and cultural life is not possible without this ability. (Turner 2000: 85; see also Stewart 2001)

Emotion and communication thus functioned as key adaptive mechanisms for our evolutionary ancestors and continue to do so for humans and other primate groups today. All higher-level mammals possess a range of emotions including suspicion, courage, timidity, grief, shame, trust, and good and bad temperament. Humans, however, have certain crucial characteristics that distinguish them from other primates.[2] Together with an advanced ability to reason, humans differ from other primates because of their high degree of empathy, sympathy, and care-giving behavior. High-level cognitive and emotional skills have evolved among humans because they alone have the ability to express their needs and desires by means of complex verbal and non-verbal codes. In the long term, the unique ability of human beings to communicate with each other and express emotions in sophisticated and productive ways offers real promise for cultivating greater cooperation across cultural groups. The argument I make in this book is based on that very prospect. But the challenge is enormous. Our emotional potential doesn't lead to positive outcomes alone. Another powerful sentiment − fear − stands in the way.

The fear factor and the pleasure principle

> *Pleasure is our perception of the reduction of fear and pain.*
> R. W. Dozier, Jr., *Fear Itself,* p. 164

Fear is the most basic, intense, and mysterious of the universal emotions. Humans originally bonded together as rudimentary cultures and communicated with one another mainly because they feared being devoured by other animals (Stewart 2001). Fear exacerbates tensions among cultural groups too, as today's geopolitical realities make abundantly clear. No one lives without fear and its negative consequences. Why, then, do people sometimes find pleasure in being "scared to death?" How can fear produce both fierce anxiety and acute pleasure? By examining the relationship between fear and pleasure we can understand some of the psychological and physiological underpinnings of the cultural conflicts that have thrown the world into crisis.

Rush Dozier has shown that people manipulate fear to create pleasure, in much the same way that other forms of expression transform inner feelings into pleasures by overcoming risks. We "increase our fear . . . and then enjoy the sensation of our body pushing the fear back down to normal levels through the secretion of natural opiates and other fear-suppressing chemicals" (Dozier 1998: 165). The surge of natural opiates courses through the brain's receptors in the amygdala, immediately producing a bodily sensation: "Each burst of primal fear is followed by a quick reduction of fear, a process we experience as pleasurable" (ibid.: 166). The example Dozier uses is the roller coaster ride, which artificially produces extreme bodily fear followed by a chemical release that stimulates the limbic system when the ride is over. That's why roller coaster riders scream with fright while they whirl around the track, and laugh heartily as they step out of the cars when the ride is over.[3]

The fear–pleasure relationship can be generalized to many situations and is not stimulated only by sudden changes in body chemistry. Religion and culture come directly into play. While many people around the world today fear terrorist attacks, for example, terrorists and other deeply religious people respond to fears of a different type – the threat of dominance by outside groups. Some seek relief from this emotional turbulence by committing violent acts. As Benjamin Barber explains: "Jihad in its most elemental negative form is a kind of animal fear propelled by anxiety in the face of uncertainty and relieved by self-sacrificing zealotry" (Barber 1995: 215). The shock of the increasingly visible West with its perceived moral decadence creates a profound, socially conditioned sense of threat. This feeling stimulates fear and provokes a violent reaction by some, which then stabilizes cognition and produces a type of pleasure at the individual and collective levels. That's why some Middle Easterners celebrate after major terrorist actions against the West or Israel, for example. George W. Bush's rhetoric of war likewise was a primal expression of collective fear turned into military aggression and a political strategy. A major collective release for many Americans came when Bush prematurely announced that "major combat operations" had finished and "we have prevailed" in Iraq. Emotional arousal, tension, and release are central to all these processes (Turner 2000: 52).

Millions of people experience extreme fear in mediated form, especially through television, film, and computer and video games. An entire genre – the horror film – capitalizes on the fear–pleasure reaction. Other genres and media do too: "Hollywood has turned the action film into the artistic equivalent of a roller coaster ride. These movies play on our primal fear of death in the most direct possible ways" (Dozier 1998: 169). Reality television programs in the United States such as *Survivor, Temptation Island, Dog Eat Dog*, and, of course, *Fear Factor* depend on the ability to provoke a sensation of fear among audiences, then release that fear into pleasure. The release is accomplished first by means of a narrative technique – the mediated players ultimately survive – and second, through the psychic distance inherent in the text–audience relationship – audiences feel safe because they experience the fearful images vicariously. The success of fear-inducing media content, however, depends on audiences experiencing their interactions with television and movies as if they are real.[4] That is not an impossible task. Audiences physiologically respond to their mass-mediated social experiences in the same way they do to unmediated actions and events – the "crying at the movies" effect (Reeves and Nass 1996). In a like manner, computer-simulated roller coaster rides elicit the same biochemical activity in the brain as the "real" thing – a sense of pleasure that results from the reduction of fear.

Sensations of mediated fear and pleasure are driven largely by visual cues (Messaris 1994, 1997; Turner 2000). Digital technologies greatly accelerate the emotional effect by the speed, efficiency, and intimacy with which they deliver high-resolution visual imagery and crystal-clear sound. Audiovisual acoustics combine with increased user involvement through constant decision making and interactivity. Sony marketed its hugely successful Playstation, for example, as "the emotion engine" because of the unit's ability to move internal data at vastly increased speed, thereby escalating players' emotional involvement with the games. Speed stimulates the pleasures of expression. When computer users upgrade to faster operating systems or add more rapid access memory (RAM), for instance, they are demanding quicker machine reaction time to their creative impulses and more space within which to exercise their creative potential and express themselves. The positive effects of video games, television, and other electronic and digital media for cognitive development are numerous (Johnson 2005).[5]

Considering the nature and gravity of the geopolitical struggles that are underway in the world today, however, we must stress that pleasure that derives from fear reduction can also perpetuate animosities between cultural groups and encourage destructive behavior. Just as the desired emotional responses by video-game players can be stimulated by mediated experience, so too can the far more serious lashing out by persons who feel their security, values, or well-being are under attack.

The Active Pleasures of Expression and Communication

Go Create!
Sony Vaio advertising slogan

Make Yourself Heard!
Ericsson's European mobile phone advertising slogan

Human beings are natural communicators. Give us more material to work with, and we will create more, communicate more, learn more, express ourselves more, enjoy more. The robust technological and cultural environment of today is like a Moroccan sandwich sold in South London: crammed with delicious ingredients, some familiar to non-Moroccans, some not. But we don't just consume our symbolic worlds like sandwiches; we interact with, play with, appropriate, ignore, ridicule, and re-author them. Human beings construct their very sociality through the creative, undetermined exchange of signs in routine communication. Expression and symbolic creativity are not luxurious "add-on" features of modern life. Their platforms, portals, and potential are central to human existence, whose significance has increased markedly with the roughly simultaneous arrival and rapid expansion of mass media, the symbolic resources that are delivered by the media and the culture industries, the internet, and personal communications technologies, especially mobile phones. These interacting fields of force mark the uniqueness, importance, and impact of the digital era.

The expressive potential of the tools we use to create and communicate today and the pleasures they produce extend pre-existing tendencies. Human beings have long been creating and using "technologies of mood" – beginning with language, music, and visual art – to induce pleasure (Evans 2001). But with so many technologies of mood available today, people now have access to many more channels and codes for innovating and expressing themselves than ever before. The marketplace success of consumer technology depends on the expressive potential of each new product – from the very first home telephones and amateur cameras to the latest sophisticated digital toys and tools. The portability, miniaturization, user-friendliness, and relative affordability of today's mobile phone, MP3 player, and notebook computer (among many other consumer technologies) make it easier than ever to create and communicate.

When communications technology becomes affordable and easy to use it breaks down traditional distinctions between professional communicators and non-professionals. Amateur photographers now operate with the same tools available to professional journalists – a digital camera with auto focus, laptop computer, and an internet connection (Simon 2004). Consumer-grade video cameras and editing software allow anyone to make and share professional-looking productions. At the moment when cameras became standard features of the mobile phone, the expressive art of photography shifted from "flat, illustrative artifact to a means of communication" (Levy 2004: 49). In the process, the mobile phone user became a photographer and visual communicator. Internet users expand their sense of the possible so that today the idea of hosting a website, setting up a web cam, or authoring a "blog" seems perfectly normal to many people. Non-professional internet "power users" take it a step further by writing computer programs, assembling home networks, and hosting their own servers. Simply imagining a global audience for one's creative communications output has become part of the pleasure of contemporary human expression.

People carry out their creative, expressive work in communicational space. In those spaces, everyday culture producers – especially transnational, middle-class youth – design and host an HTML-free web page, choose a customized ring tone, face plate, and voice greeting for their mobile phones and a customized toolbar and desktop image for their laptop computers. They sample, mix, and burn a music CD, make and distribute a digital video, snap and circulate digital photos from their camera phones, download and distribute a DVD. Broadband access, lower cost, and user friendliness of digital video systems have opened up film making to a vastly expanded pool of would-be cinematographers. The people who are doing this kind of symbolic work are not just techno-geeks, pop music freaks, or the sons and daughters of the rich and famous. Anybody with the right equipment, a bit of cash, sufficient motivation, a little training, and some time to spare can do it.

Deep interactivity – the formation and maintenance of meaningful peer-to-peer cultural networks that span the globe – defines the Communication Age. People not only have greater opportunities to consume more symbolic resources than ever before, they have greatly increased the capacity to create and share their expressive output. Interactivity is an indispensable quality of many forms of human expression. Exchanging instant or text messages, playing web-based video games, making internet phone calls, participating in chat rooms, and sharing digital music files, for instance, all mesh contemporary cultural experience with complex levels of social communication.

Industry can barely keep up with current trends. Even the most entrenched, slow-moving communications industries – state-run telephone and telecommunications companies, for instance – have had to respond quickly to the expressive demands of their customers. All the media and culture industries have scrambled desperately to avoid severe economic losses created by ambitious individuals armed with the new media information and communications technologies and the knowledge to exploit them.[6]

Modern communications technology feeds popular creativity while it decentralizes expressive authority. Creative decisions – not unlike those made by people who are paid large salaries in the culture industries – become the purview of the everyday artist, performer, and culture producer. The symbolic creativity exercised by everyday culture producers today combines the "grounded aesthetics" of material and symbolic worlds (Willis 1990) with the "grounded technology" of today's ever-more-mobile and handy communications devices. Although young people often are the most motivated and skilled at this cultural activity, the number of people worldwide responding to the opportunity to actively engage popular culture, the internet, and personal technology is increasing at a great rate.

Mobile expression

New communications technology not only transforms, but also reflects and extends the cultural environments where it takes root and develops. The introduction of any mass medium, information technology, or personal communications device into any cultural context never simply overwhelms local realities. This was evident in my own cross-cultural research on how television and video have become integrated into family life in diverse cultures around the world (Lull 1988), and it has become clear to researchers who study the ways mobile phone technology and the internet have been assimilated.

In an early study of mobile phone use in urban Japan, China, Thailand, Pakistan, the United Arab Emirates, England, and the United States, Sadie Plant concluded that "the mobile is uniquely adaptable, capable of playing many different roles, and able to make itself useful in a wide variety of cultural contexts, social worlds, and individual lives" (Plant 2002a: 77). Mobile phone users employ the device in ways that challenge some cultural traditions and strengthen others. For instance, Japanese adolescents escape the limitations of physical space and the traditions of patriarchy and parental control by using mobile phones to create private, intimate communication space (Ito 2001; Plant 2002a). Mobile phones and the internet help Japanese of all ages maintain and modernize their highly valued social networks, their *uchi* (Takahashi 2003). The mobile phone has been used by Islamist terrorists to wreak havoc but it is also used by Muslim teenagers the world over to make private calls, form friendships, arrange sexual encounters, and conduct other social and cultural activities forbidden by their religion. Reticent British teenagers, especially "taciturn males," find that the mobile phone "makes it cool to talk" (Plant 2002b: 9), though what they talk about typically reflects and reinforces cultural interests that pre-date the arrival of wireless telephony.

The mobile phone functions as the central nervous system of social networks and cultural connections, the axis around which many modern individuals construct their everyday lives. With the addition of still photo and video imaging, capture, and display, built-in browsers for web searching, geo-positioning navigation, and MP3 playback, the mobile phone has evolved into a "remote control for people's lives" (Rheingold 2002: 194). The fundamental human need to interact with others is the primary motivation that underlies all this, as evidenced by the product name Nokia gave to its advanced mobile phone device – the "Communicator." The mobile phone represents the ultimate technological development able to respond to the constant demand for greater range of movement, more frequent and closely managed contact with others, and cultural comfort while in motion.

The mobile phone's oral, print, and visual capabilities are further enhanced by user personalization. The brand, model, features, color, shape, and size of the phone – its audiovisual impact – reflect individual preferences. The mobile phone has become a naturalized part of the human body, serving as the main resource for creating a technology-infused image and lifestyle. The pop culture content of mobile phones demarcates and displays personal preferences and styles. Selection and display of a ring tone form parts of the user's expressive equipment. As the number of features for mobile phones increases, competition among users intensifies. Sadie Plant, in her multinational study, concluded that "the mobile phone is widely used for psychosexual purposes of performance and display" (Plant 2002a: 40). Males are especially likely to compete with their phones by displaying superior technology, trendy aesthetics, and a projected image of cosmopolitan "contact with the wider world" (ibid.: 41).

It is the human need to communicate and express, not the simple presence of fancy technology, that drives the process.

The mobile phone has become so well accepted and is considered so necessary by many people because it helps them interact, simplify their lives, express their feelings, and retrieve content of their choosing in convenient, flexible, and stylish ways.

Cultural Open Sourcing

Open source software is the key technological feature in the development of the internet. And this openness is culturally determined.
M. Castells, *The Internet Galaxy*, p. 38

Open sourcing most often refers to an unrestricted, internet-based cooperative effort among persons, usually unknown to each other, to commonly solve a problem or develop a project through unfiltered, open interaction. These projects frequently have commercial applications. But open sourcing differs from the competitive, hierarchical, proprietary model that drives most industrial research and development. Open source projects unfold with maximum visibility and uncensored online access. No one gets paid for what they contribute and everybody owns the product of the work.

Internet-based open sourcing originated with Linus Torvalds who, as a University of Helsinki student in 1991, used the internet to recruit a global network of persons interested in developing an advanced computer operating system as an alternative to the dominance of Microsoft's program. As Manuel Castells explains in *The Internet Galaxy* (2001), the philosophy that guided Torvalds and his collaborators was based on a "techno-meritocratic culture rooted in academia and science. This is a culture of belief in the inherent good of scientific and technological development as a key component in the progress of humankind . . . within this culture, merit results from contribution to the common good for the community of discoverers" (Castells 2001: 39). Torvalds' work led to development of the free software movement. Communities that have sprung up through the trial-and-error format of open sourcing develop their own standards, rules, decision-making procedures, and sanctioning mechanisms (Weber 2004). Thomas Friedman describes these groups as "self-organizing collaborative communities" (Friedman 2005: 81).

Open sourcing has spawned a global revolution in cultural construction across a range of interests: "The internet offers the possibility of collective, interactive, joint artistic creation through groupware practices that allow people at a distance [to create their art] and produce together, in interaction, and often in contradiction. . . . open source art is the new frontier of artistic creation" (Castells 2001: 199). The scientific and humanistic potential of open sourcing, peer-to-peer interaction, and distributive processing appears to be nearly limitless (Rheingold 2002). The inventing and perpetual revising that open sourcing encourages lends itself to every sphere of the cultural imagination – from multi-site music making, collaborative humor, and theatrical productions to acting out revolutionary political behavior, managing business clients, or building a dirty bomb. Wikipedia has become a popular multilingual, open source encyclopedia with phenomenal impact. A group based in Latvia has even created open source "acoustic space" where artists have unlimited access to sounds retrieved from outer space which they are encouraged to interpret, appropriate, and embellish as "sound structures" (Kunstradio 2005).

Internet open sourcing has greatly influenced the way news is reported, distributed, and evaluated too. The blogging phenomenon – or "open source journalism" (Gillmor 2004: 113) – has sent shock waves through the corporate news industry, accustomed to controlling the flow of public information. Breaking apart entrenched systems of journalism, software development, and art creates new kinds of knowledge with extraordinary potential for enriching the human condition. To this end, information technology guru Douglas Engelbart proposes that there should be absolutely no limits to what "collaborative, knowledge management applications" based on open sourcing can yield. Today's complex human problems, he says, don't lend themselves to individualized solutions. Engelbart calls for an "open hyperdocument system" to create and support "Dynamic Knowledge Repositories" where global collective knowledge and wisdom on virtually any subject area can be generated, stored, and accessed (Engelbart 2005).

The core values of freedom, discovery, creativity, interactivity, equality, and community constitute the organic processes and cultures of open sourcing. They enable broad development of new forms of human expression and cultural experience on a global scale. Crucial to making these advances come to fruition is a shift in the prevalent forms and terms of social power.

Symbolic Power to the People

In a world based upon active communication, hard power – power that comes only from the top down – loses its edge . . . the communications revolution has produced more active, reflective citizens than existed before.
A. Giddens, *Runaway World*, pp. 90–1

Power is such an important sociological concept that political and cultural discussions of social relations and interactions are sometimes reduced to it. Foreign policy, civil rights, gender struggles, party politics, environmentalism, terrorism, and many other realms of modern public life are frequently dominated by discussions of "Who's got the power? How do they use it?" By "power" I refer to four basic capabilities of individuals or groups: (1) the capacity to act and accomplish something; (2) the ability to exercise control over individual or group self-interest; (3) the capacity to influence others; and (4) in certain circumstances, the will and capacity to command or control others.

Top-down, hard power refers to the actions, influence, and control a person or group holds over others. Such power typically actualizes through political, economic, religious, or military authority and practice. Hard power remains incredibly potent today. From terrorist attacks conducted in the name of God to military might flexed in the name of nation, civilization, and "the world," hard power remains a mighty, often destructive, social force. "It's just sheer power," commented retired General Wesley Clark, the former NATO commander and opponent of the Iraq War, as he watched the early hours of the initial "shock and awe" bombing of Baghdad unfold on CNN.

Hard power today functions alongside, sometimes absorbs, and often competes with a far more ephemeral and broadly accessible form of social influence that is deeply interlaced with human expression – symbolic power. John B. Thompson has defined symbolic power as "the capacity to intervene in and influence the course of events, to influence the actions of others and indeed to create events, by means of the production and transmission of symbolic forms" (Thompson 1995: 17). He contrasts symbolic power with economic, political, and coercive power, to which we add religious power.

The ability of groups or individuals to employ symbolic power does not necessarily preclude, reduce, or neutralize the hard power presence or overall effectiveness of elite social groups and dominant institutions. To the contrary, symbolic power often bolsters and strengthens existing hard power relations. We must not misinterpret the role or significance of symbolic power. Greater individual freedom to create and communicate – even in fiercely resistant ways – cannot replace nor does it always reduce hard power influence. Nations, religious groups, multinational corporations, political parties, and military forces all use symbolic resources and communications technologies to upgrade and expand their arsenals of influence. As the bombs were dropping on Baghdad, for instance, authorities in the United States and the United Kingdom were flying in official photographers and videographers for "photo ops" to compete with the alarming images being produced by Middle Eastern news media and circulated worldwide by CNN and many other networks.

Symbolic creativity and symbolic power, however, do not originate with nor do they solely benefit those institutions and persons who are associated with social privilege or hard power capability. Even the most didactic symbolic forms can be interpreted in ways that may have little to do with, or even directly oppose, their senders' intentions. All symbolic forms become resources for radical reading and re-authoring. Furthermore, the communications hardware and software that are widely available today expand the range of opportunities available to non-elites and non-specialists to originate and express their own ideas. People typically initiate these communications within social networks that grow in the process, sometimes to incredible proportions. At other times, symbolic displays spring from organized movements. The media-friendly Orange uprising in the Ukraine and the Cedar Revolution in Lebanon exemplify how organized symbolic power can work contagiously and rapidly on a regional and global scale.

Symbolic forms that routinely circulate via mass media and information technology as popular culture – television shows, music CDs, computer software, movies, websites, and much more – benefit multiple users and have nearly limitless expressive potential. They first serve their institutional originators – the culture, communications, and information industries – by making money and influencing politics and culture. Symbolic forms function in this way as "tangible property" (Soros 2002: 46). This materialization of cultural products as industrial commodities reflects what Paul Willis (2000) calls their "bearer form." In this way products generated by the culture, communications, and information industries don't differ much from the commodities that are cranked out by any other industry. But popular culture also responds to the diverse interests of consumer-users as "intellectual property," helping individuals amass cultural capital. By their very nature the uses and meanings of these symbolic entities, which Willis calls their "cultural form," are far less restricted. Their widespread availability has made them preferred expressive resources for use in routine social communication. They offer special advantages to consumers. Because "the use of a cultural commodity such as a CD or DVD is not extinguished or ingested with use . . . these displays of communicative labor are repeated without diminution" (Willis 2000: 55). Everyday users engage cultural commodities sensually, emotionally, and over extended periods of time.

It's never clear who ultimately "owns" symbolic forms or uses them to greatest advantage in any situation, especially not today. Even in the case of high art, national or ethnic cultures that originally produce such artifacts don't necessarily have a formal, legal, or ethical right of ownership in perpetuity (Appiah 2006). On the street, everyday consumers of popular culture claim ownership over all kinds of cultural forms by interpreting them in highly motivated ways and by using them to their benefit in social interaction. The multiplicity of uses and meanings to which symbolic goods are put dematerializes (Chaney 2002: 80), and rematerializes them. All kinds of people do the producing and reproducing now of art, music, and everything else, often with no intention whatsoever of being faithful to the "original" authors, even when those authors can be identified. Walter Benjamin's (1970) often-repeated claim – that the mechanical reproduction of art dulls the senses and limits the human potential – certainly doesn't explain much in today's world of digital reproduction and global connectivity.

The whole gamut of symbolic forms and technological tools – not just the internet, but the entire panorama of contemporary cultural resources – provides unprecedented opportunities for human expression and for contacting new people and novel ideas. The pleasures of human expression refresh the human spirit and greatly enrich the experience of being-in-the-world. But more than that, expression connects intimately with creativity and the power of the imagination. The freedom to exercise the imagination and to express and share ideas is a core moral idea and basic human right (Appiah 2006: 162–3). As the expressive potential is further unleashed, the capacity to foster greater tolerance grows through the emancipatory processes of communicative exchange.

When oppressive governments attempt to prohibit or restrict the expressive use and sharing of cultural materials, they face an impossible task. Just ask those young men in Kabul listening to, dancing to, singing along with, and burning CD copies of the latest Nazi Jaan and Farhad Daria pop songs. Talk to the thousands of fans in Iran and around the world who watch the videos of Farzaneh Kaboli – the Iranian dancer who was arrested for performing for her female peers – on satellite television. Or chat with hundreds of thousands of young people in Tehran who escape vigilance by Iran's Supreme Cultural Revolutionary Council by going online to exchange opinions about culture and politics. Symbolic resources break down differences and build alliances across cultural frontiers. That's why India's foreign minister arrived in Kabul after the Taliban government fell "in a plane not packed with arms or food but crammed with tapes of Bollywood movies and music, which were quickly distributed across the city" (Nye 2004: 10).

Notes

1. The Federal Communications Commission's (FCC's) "Fairness Doctrine" was an early quasi-legal attempt in the United States to guarantee access to diversity of opinion for radio and television audiences. The Fairness Doctrine was later ruled irrelevant by the FCC when the number of electronic media channels expanded so greatly (especially in cable and satellite TV and radio) that diversity

was deemed to be better achieved through market mechanisms than by government regulation.

2. Still, the emotional differences between man and other primates are but a matter of degree. The chimpanzee, whose DNA overlaps that of human beings by more than 97 percent, shows love and compassion for family members, grief, and a sense of humor. And, like humans, chimpanzees also exhibit extreme brutality, fear, and hatred of strangers, and aggressive competition over territory (Goodall 2000). Precisely *how* emotional communication has evolved to even greater complexity among humans compared to their biological cousins is, of course, subject to much controversy and debate.

3. Surviving roller coaster rides isn't the only way humans in the more developed parts of the world purposefully experience pleasure by surmounting fear. Dozier identifies auto racing, air shows, daredevil stunts, circuses, extreme sports, skydiving, bungee jumping, mountain climbing, hang gliding, white water rafting, and skiing as other behaviors in which people engage enthusiastically to stimulate fear and bring on the pleasure of release from fear.

4. The effect becomes even more intense when the fear-release process occurs interactively. Video games provide a compelling example of how this works. The narrative of almost all successful video games features a struggle to survive. Players voluntarily enter an interactive atmosphere of panic, risk, and mayhem. They must defeat constant threats coming at them from the programmed game environment, and in multi-player games they must also eliminate their human competition. The thrilling, chaotic, frantic struggle to survive creates anxiety based on imaginary fear, which leads to symbolic resolution experienced by the player as relief.

5. While fully appreciating all the expressiveness, creativity, pleasures, and positive effects that mediated symbolic forms stimulate and facilitate, it must be said that the consequences of technological and industrial developments are by no means all positive and inspiring. The hypnotic, addictive qualities of digital media and popular culture clearly often work against the best interests of individuals and their societies. The graphic violence of most video games and action films, for instance, reinforces [male-dominated] aggressive tendencies and desensitizes players and viewers to human suffering. The frenetic, endless repetition of crude lyrics in a subgenre of rap music − "crunk" − and its counterpart in heavy metal stimulates emotional frenzy often centered on themes of hatefulness and hedonism. Extreme materialism, constant immediate gratification, escapism, and blatant sexism are not values or qualities upon which

healthy individual lives and societies are constructed. Moreover, some critics believe that mere exposure to entertainment media and popular culture amounts to a colossal waste of time, energy, and resources. Repeating such experiences over time may create mainly "disposable feelings" or "sensations that feel like, and pass for, feelings" (Gitlin 2001: 41; see also Lull 2000: 264–76).

6. The first substantial indication of just how seriously internet piracy impacts the music industry surfaced when the Grammy Awards were handed out in Los Angeles in 2002. According to an official from the Record Industry Association of America (RIAA), popular music sales for the previous year had declined by more than 10 percent, the biggest drop in more than a decade, a trend that has continued.

Chapter 3

Programming Our Personal Supercultures

Pulitzer Prize-winning *New York Times* journalist Thomas Friedman titled his neoclassic treatise on globalization *The Lexus and the Olive Tree*. He used symbolism evoked by these images to draw a contrast between two main tendencies in contemporary geopolitics and economics. The Lexus represents global integration, modernity, risk, and progress. Friedman describes how Japanese automobile makers use robotics technology to profitably manufacture luxury vehicles like the Lexus for sale to the global market. The olive tree, on the other hand, stands for locality, premodernity, safety, and stagnation. Olive trees "represent everything that roots us, anchors us, identifies us, and locates us in this world . . . a placed called home" (Friedman 2000: 31). But excessive attachments to home can also paralyze, divide, exclude, and destroy, the author points out, as we have seen so tragically for years in Israel and the Palestinian territories.

Another metaphorical pairing that demonstrates the contrasting tendencies of globalization is represented by the differences, but also by the dynamic interplay, between "roots and wings" (Zachary 2000). Much like the olive tree, roots refer to local cultural conditions and the human propensity to remain immersed within them. Wings signify the simultaneous strong tendency to explore cultural worlds beyond that which is already familiar. It is human nature to embrace the local but it is likewise instinctive to explore novel cultural territory, and not just for economic purposes. Moreover, individuals and societies have both roots and wings. Roots and wings complement and reinforce each other in many ways, and people are becoming ever more adept at juggling them effectively.

Today the cultural "frames and horizons" of individual persons are proliferating as many of the "constraints and controls that typically structure everyday life" are diminishing so that difference, variety, and the extraordinary have started to feel normal for many people (Chaney 2002: 69, vii, 147, 151). People experiment with culture more than ever before, and they do so very creatively. Consequently, as has often been said, distinctions typically made between local and global, near and far, virtual and real, and fact and fiction have become far less clear or meaningful. At different paces and with different faces, cultural diversification and fragmentation are increasing all over the world.

Cultural Experience

Current trends do not signal that culture or meaning have melted into air or disappeared any other way. "Mainstream," "dominant," or "official" cultures continue to exert tremendous influence over everyday life. But because nearly everyone on Earth today encounters and responds to a proliferating presence of new cultural resources and opportunities that extend far beyond their native territories, the cultural templates and methods people use to organize their worlds and create their identities are fluctuating to such an extent that the very meaning of culture is changing.

Two fundamental phenomena simultaneously expand and diversify cultural experience while they shape consciousness and alter the circumstances of daily life for individual persons and societies. First is the explosion in the amount and variety of cultural materials that are now visible and accessible to people worldwide. For many, that's a very positive, even necessary, development. But as cultural representation becomes more robust and diverse, cultural fragmentation necessarily follows. That fragmentation challenges individuals to rethink their cultural assumptions and activities and defies those in society who try to manage the cultural lives of others. The idea that outside influences are "destroying" culture is often promoted most vigorously by those who believe they have something valuable to lose in the exchange.

The second major cultural change has developed in conjunction with the first – the individualization and personalization of cultural experience. We are accustomed to thinking of culture in broad terms – British culture, Brazilian culture, corporate culture, indigenous culture, and so on. Many of the cultural resources that are widely available today, however, have less to do with geographic territory, ethnic traditions, or material objects. Available cultural resources have become increasingly mediated, symbolic, and mobile. Individuals today assemble their multicultural selves by making ambitious and creative use of the multiplatform panorama of resources. People have always looked outside their traditional cultures for inspiration. But today the scope, speed, and consequences brought about by this kind of personal cultural engineering stand out from any other historical period.

All of this requires work. As Anthony Giddens points out, "Where tradition lapses, and lifestyle choice prevails . . . self-identity has to be created on a more active basis than before" (Giddens 2000a: 65). Individual persons are becoming the primary agents of their cultural self-formation – a process that involves constant searching, interpreting, experimenting, evaluating, deciding, sorting, and assembling of cultural resources in ways that lead to personally relevant and satisfying experiences and identities. To do this cultural work effectively people need to develop new and challenging "symbolic skills" (Giddens 2000b). These skills require expertise in practical areas such as multi-tasking, time-shifting, flexible social scheduling, and, even more important, cognitively based "relevance switching" (Rheingold 2002: 77).

Culture, culture, Superculture

Terry Eagleton (2000) cleverly differentiates "Culture" from "culture." The classic idea, Culture, is rooted in geography, ethnicity, history, and tradition. The second meaning, culture, refers to the full range of diverse cultural resources that are available to people – not just that which descends from Culture. Culture and culture do not negate each other and culture is not a zero-sum game in any case. We live in both. Culture with a capital C continues to be relevant, even necessary, to individual persons and groups as "ways of life" that are passed on from generation to generation. People continue to invest in, maintain, and rely on shared visions of the world and the expected array of everyday activities, rituals, and identities that animate and preserve those visions. But many of the traditions we commonly associate with Culture are in flux today. And at the same time a flood of cultural resources not associated with Culture has become readily available, even to some degree for people who live in the less economically developed parts of the world or under authoritarian rule. To understand how people really live in the current era, the changing nature of cultural experience must be explored. The notion of "personal superculture" is one effort to explain this contemporary cultural experience.

The personal superculture of any single person is the dynamic sum of cultural experiences and identities the person creates for himself or herself from all the cultural ideas, images, and objects with which the individual comes into contact. Personal supercultures are self-customized matrices and networks of relevant human, material, and symbolic cultural elements. They are intricate cultural multiplexes that promote self-understanding, belonging, and identity while they grant opportunities for personal safety, security, growth, pleasure, and social influence (Lull 2001). Personal supercultures – which I hasten to make plural because individuals develop their own particular supercultures – represent the inevitable outcome of contemporary cultural activity. We invent our personal supercultures from the particular mix of resources made available by Culture and culture, even subconsciously. The Swedish social anthropologist Ulf Hannerz describes these dynamics:

> our particular biographies, involving the places and countries we have visited or lived in, the books we have read by authors from anywhere, the television programs we zap between, the websites we visit, the people we have known, may come together in coherent perspectives as best we can. Each of us may stand at a particular intersection in that total network of the global ecumene. If there is an "integrated whole," it may be a quite individual thing. (Hannerz 2001: 64)

Hannerz acknowledges that while individual persons draw from some commonly held cultural resources in the "total network of the global ecumene," in the final analysis we all construct "particular biographies." These biographies – active, unfinished, highly synthetic projects – constitute the distinct supercultures of individual persons. "Autobiography" may be the more appropriate metaphor to reflect the process by which individuals write cultural content and accents into their multicultural selves.

The "supers"

From superstores and super babies to Superman and the Super Bowl, there is no shortage of supers in this world. In common language, "super" can modify nearly any noun – a market, a baby, a man, a football game – to signify that whatever thing, person, process, or event the prefix modifies greatly exceeds its expected reach or magnitude. Such is the potential, and increasingly the reality, of contemporary cultural activity.

The modifier "super" pervades the social and applied sciences, including media and cultural studies. Michael Real (1989) was among the first to employ it in order to describe the sharply widening scope and impact of telecommunications media ("super media") in the late twentieth century. Digitization takes the reach and influence of electronic media to unprecedented levels – not only in terms of technical capacity and clarity, but in the ability to maximally push audience emotional involvement. Todd Gitlin (2001) obsesses over what he calls "super saturation" – "the torrent of images and sounds [delivered by super media] that overwhelms our lives." Heightened emotional reactions can also be expected when humans turbo-charge nature to produce "super stimuli" through techniques such as artificial lighting and coloration effects, amplified sound, Viagra, deep-tissue body massage, drug-enhanced states of perception, even spicy food (Evans 2001). "Super computers" – hundreds of thousands of computers configured together – provide exponentially expanded levels of informational compass and access, interfacing, processing, and productivity. In all these cases the prefix "super" indicates that the concept it modifies exceeds normative expectations to the point where the original idea has been changed so significantly it must be understood in a new way. Personal supercultures thus exceed normative cultural experience in volume and variety, are composed of bits and pieces that come from a multiplicity of local and distant sources, contain relatively parochial and relatively public elements, and take material as well as symbolic form. The concept "personal superculture" is broad and eclectic at the same time. It encapsulates the two defining, coterminous characteristics of cultural activity today: expansion and personalization.

Culture in common

> . . . these days Boise, Idaho is very much like Manhattan as far as audiences go. Between shopping malls, cable TV, and USA Today, everyone has the same kind of experiences. Everybody knows about the same things.
>
> Popular American comedian Bobby Slayton

As individuals construct their impermanent personal cultural profiles and engage in diverse contemporary cultural experience, they increasingly draw upon non-localized cultural forms and networks of communication. Doing so, it is striking to observe how much cultural knowledge people have in common, particularly in their own nations and civilizations. We've all been introduced to Osama bin Laden, Air Jordan, Tony Blair, and the bacon, lettuce, and tomato cheeseburger – certainly in the West, and increasingly around the world. Public performers like Bobby Slayton are so sure of that fact – at least within cultural groups sharing common citizenship, language, or ethnicity – they assume that a mutually held base line of cultural knowledge exists. Their professional lives depend on it. Ordinary citizens make similar assumptions as they navigate through their daily routines and social interactions.

The "non-places" of "super modernity" (Augé 1995) also condition standard cultural expectations. Non-places offer the comforts of anonymity and predictability. They are physical spaces that have become familiar on a global scale – international airports, big box stores, ATM machines, cinema multiplexes, franchise restaurants, shopping malls, and the like. For middle-class members of nations around the world, non-places paradoxically help people feel safe and culturally competent. People feel in control when they understand the physical environments and sociocultural rules of the places and non-places they inhabit.

Contemporary cultural experience thus clearly reflects a common awareness that derives from exposure to the familiar themes, personalities, and products that are represented by the news media, entertainment industries, internet, religious institutions, governments, political parties, schools, and the non-places of supermodernity. How these cultural resources are interpreted, positioned in relation to other resources, and used, however, are not generic processes. Personal supercultures ultimately are just that – personal. Individual persons construct their supercultures by responding to their particular needs and advancing their special interests. The personal superculture does not refer solely to a common block of cultural images available to everyone, although some cultural forms arriving from a distance are quite familiar to people everywhere. A person's superculture dynamically represents that individual's particular matrix of meaningful cultural meanings and experiences – some of which are widely shared, most of which are not.

Cultural Technology in the Communication Age

> *Nothing can replace personal contact, and human nature isn't changing. But a medium – or is it a place? – that transcends the traditional limitations of time and space, enabling connections on an unprecedented scale, is fertile territory for innovation.*
>
> Dan Gillmor, former technology writer for
> the *San José Mercury News*, 2002

> *The mobile phone is the key device of the postmodern age. In the same way as computers with internet connections . . . it is perfectly suited to the ideology of an individualistic society committed to networking.*
>
> T. Kopomaa, *Birth of the Mobile Information Society*, pp. 121, 125

The internet best symbolizes the striking changes now taking place in contemporary cultural activity across the board and around the world. Nothing compares with the way the internet makes cultural resources visible, accessible, and useful for personal endeavors and social interactions, encouraging individuals to create and manage multiple links with distant cultural resources and people, adding new elements to their personal supercultures.

Worldwide popularity of the internet has been apparent since its inception in the 1980s. By 2006, some 73 percent of American adults were using the internet, with more than 60 percent going online any given day (Pew Internet and American Life Project 2006). The estimated percentage of the world's total population that had gone online by then reached 15 percent, with the heaviest use concentrated in North America, northern Europe, and the Far East (Internet World Stats 2006). Broadband access has exploded in countries like Iceland, South Korea, Holland, Denmark, and Canada (InfoWorld Media Group 2005). Rich countries have the most significant internet penetration, although China with its enormous population and favorable disposition toward technology trails only the United States in absolute number of users and will soon become the world leader. Despite fluctuations in the global economy, internet use continues to proliferate almost everywhere.

What accounts for such tremendous growth? Social networking and opportunities for creative expression are the main motivations that inspire internet users. Researchers at Carnegie Mellon University concluded that from the beginning the web's "killer application . . . is interpersonal communication" (HomeNet 2003; see also Cole et al. 2003). The production of user-generated web content – a truly remarkable trend – complements and reinforces the social dimension. Online communities such as MySpace, Xanga, and Facebook, for example, give people a chance to meet each other, express their opinions on personal, social, and cultural topics and trends, and creatively present themselves to their imagined publics. File-sharing sites like Flickr and YouTube facilitate the easy exchange of photographic images, video, and comments on other users' postings. Yahoo's My Web allows people to search each other's files of cultural preferences for things like music and restaurants.

Internet users log on mainly to create and sustain conversations and relationships. They do so via email (still the most frequent online activity overall, though declining for young users), chat rooms, blogs, and instant messaging (the preferred mode for young users). The Carnegie Mellon researchers found that pleasurable activities (communicating with family, friends, and strangers; tracking sports and popular culture; listening to music; playing games; and pursuing specialized interests) are far more pervasive – in terms of time spent online – than gathering information for professional or educational purposes. People go online for pure entertainment reasons – a "place to hang out" much like the mall (Pew Internet and American Life Project 2006).

As alluded to above, internet users have also gone from being passive consumers of content to active content creators and distributors. Considering the scope and significance of what's going on, Paul Saffo, Director of the Institute for the Future, says that a "revolution without bystanders" is underway. He contends that common activities such as blogging, eBay sales, and posting on sites like Flickr, YouTube, and Second Life is the routine work of everyday culture "creators," not consumers or producers (Newsweek 2006). Reporters from *Newsweek* described the evolving nature of the internet in a cover story:

> Less than a decade ago, when we were first getting used to the idea of the internet, people described the act of going online as venturing into some foreign realm called cyberspace. But that metaphor no longer applies. MySpace and Flickr aren't places to go, but things to do, ways to express yourself, means to connect with others and extend your own horizons. Cyberspace was somewhere else. The Web is where we live. (Levy and Stone 2006)

The effusive, combined presence of mass media, popular culture industries, and the internet coincides with the unprecedented diffusion of personal communications technology, especially the mobile phone. These multiple forces interact in technological convergence and social practice to dramatically expand cultural options and create new opportunities for people to express themselves and communicate with others. Web access by mobile phone, for instance, makes available the internet's cultural spaces, which themselves often reflect the content of traditional media, while facilitating the flexible one-to-one communication advantages for which the phones were originally intended. Whether seeking personal contact or cultural stimulation, mobile phone users surf and zap just like someone searching the web or flipping between TV channels, "making continuous choices, thus creating a personalized selection of the programming" (Kopomaa 2000: 108). The mobile phone expedites constant contact with the "network." In Timo Kopomaa's words:

> Our ability to manage everyday life depends on our ability to connect to networks . . . The network is the reflection of an individualizing and disintegrating world, a world inside ourselves. Portable communication devices, which permit uninterrupted contact with the network, have become part of ourselves. (Kopomaa 2000: 21–2)

Many analysts rightly conclude that the internet – particularly when performance is accelerated by broadband access – has radically transformed lifestyles for those in a position to take advantage. But to better comprehend how cultural life is changing today, we should interpret the internet and the smart mobile phone as but the centerpieces of a spectacular, empowering mix of communications technology that includes cable and satellite television, digital and analog video recording devices, satellite radio, audio compact disc players and burners, digital video disc players and burners, personal digital recorders like TiVO, MP3 players, digital still and video cameras, personal digital assistants (PDAs), and personal entertainment organizers (PEOs). These devices supersede or function alongside earlier technological advances like fax machines, telephone-answering machines, and remote control devices for home entertainment centers, all of which also expand user options, diversify cultural experience, influence social relations, and alter perceptions of time and space. We witness today not only the much-heralded convergence of technological components and functions but also a melding of normative social behaviors facilitated by communications technology and a general blurring of distinctions between social life and technology.

People who integrate the internet into their daily routines are more likely to be connected to other communications technology and to other cultural media as well. The Pew Internet and American Life Project (2006) reports that people who read newspapers, watch TV, and use mobile phones and other personal communications devices are more likely to use the internet than those who are less engaged. A cosmopolitan involvement with the world predicts internet use too, according to the same report. Individuals who are socially content, trusting of others, outgoing, and believe they have control over their lives are the most enthusiastic internet supporters.

Cultural Programming

In the early 1970s, the American sociologist Herbert Gans came up with what he hoped would be a workable plan to help meet the cultural needs of ordinary people. Because most people have cultural tastes that don't fit well with elite or "high culture" offerings, and because he believed people shouldn't be simply subjected to the "lowbrow" fare typically served up by the commercial media of the time, Gans called for a national public media policy in the United States that would transmit a wide range of cultural offerings via radio and television. The proposed policy was termed "subcultural programming," which the author claimed "would enable audiences to find content best suited to their wants and needs, thus increasing their aesthetic and other satisfactions, and the relevance of culture to their lives" (Gans 1974: 133). Subcultural programming "accepts the right of taste publics to make their own aesthetic choices," Gans said (1974: 140). The ultimate result of this policy, according to Gans, would be a "user-oriented culture." Gans's utopian plan to meet the diverse cultural needs of the American public through subcultural media programming put the primary responsibility on the government and culture industry producers.

Part of the solution for creating more diverse cultural programming – not just in the United States – has been found since the time of Gans's proposal through the multi-channel capacity of cable television, direct satellite telecommunications, the internet, and the proliferation of niche markets. Even multimedia configurations like web-based television channels that program for a very narrow audience are succeeding because the internet's reach can make a viable audience even for very specialized content. We live today in a global cultural environment of near limitless proportions. The locus of much cultural activity has shifted from programming decisions made by governments and media institutions to choices made by individuals.

Similar to the way directors of radio and television stations select a mixture of program elements to create a sound, look, or texture appropriate to a particular format or image, individual persons now take the initiative to program their ongoing autobiographies – their personal supercultures. People routinely meld traditional cultural influences – religion, language, food, music, and so on – with the clamoring diversity of cultural resources arriving from afar. Individuals determine the "use value" (McCracken 1990; Willis 2000) of all available cultural resources by synthesizing and condensing particular resources into personalized patterns of meaning and utility. They put those resources to work in the ways and on the schedules that they believe are most convenient and beneficial.

Thomas Friedman describes the transformation from structural to individual cultural influence as "in-forming." He means that individual persons now have access to the resources necessary "to build and deploy [their] own supply chain of information, knowledge, and entertainment. In-forming," he says, "is about self-collaboration" (Friedman 2005: 153). Cultural invention, scheduling, editing, and transmitting – activities traditionally associated solely with professionals in the media and culture industries – are being practiced now by ordinary people too. Non-specialists are becoming increasingly more comfortable and competent in their roles as cultural programmers and distributors.

The Cultural Self and Self Culture

As self cultivators, we are clay in our own hands, at once redeemer and unregenerate, priest and sinner in the same body.
T. Eagleton, *The Idea of Culture*, p. 6

As . . . mediated experiences are incorporated reflexively into the project of self-formation, the nature of the self is transformed. It is not dissolved or dispersed by media messages, but rather is opened up by them, in varying degrees, to influences which stem from distant locales.
J. B. Thompson, *The Media and Modernity*, p. 233

When people assume more individual responsibility for constructing their complex cultural lives, they learn new cultural practices and communication skills while modifying others. Self-cultivators are cultural entrepreneurs. They program their lives by searching through the range of cultural resources – local and distant, direct and mediated, material and symbolic, familiar and exotic – to which they have access. Not everyone is positioned equally to respond to these cultural challenges and opportunities. Gender, religion, nationality, socioeconomic class, age, and ethnicity all strongly influence opportunities for access while they filter and frame how individual persons react to unfamiliar cultural forms. People selectively appropriate new materials into their cultural worlds. In this era of accelerated media transmission, widened cultural globalization, and escalated human mobility, individuals everywhere have to work diligently in order *not* to regularly confront a rush of cultural materials arriving from outside their home territories. Media globalization provides constant attractive stimuli that permit, even encourage, "escape from one's locality, one's national space, and sometimes from one's family" (Rantanen 2005: 150). But encounters with cultural forms originating outside one's own traditional sphere can also provoke an opposite response – revulsion and rejection.

The consequences of any of these cultural transactions don't just impact the individual person – the "cultural self." Entire societies are affected by the growing trend toward individualization. This is the "self culture" that Ulrich Beck and Elisabeth Beck-Gernsheim (2002) have in mind. They are concerned that national cultures like Germany change fundamentally, in some ways for the worse, when the solitary pursuits of individuals assume overarching cultural prominence. Of course, it's also true that protecting a collective national identity – especially in highly patriarchal societies – serves the interests of political-cultural authorities who may feel threatened by the uncertainties and contradictions of the encroaching individualism.

Evolving self-cultures in modern Western nations are characterized by an increasing number of single-person households, more divorces, and greater overall privatization of space and time. Print media, personal communications devices, personal entertainment media like MP3 players, and the internet reinforce these tendencies by encouraging private consumption of information and culture. In such a world, people are tempted to free themselves from tradition, turn their lives into "works of art," and organize their personal lives in ways that fulfill their individual aspirations (Beck and Beck-Gernsheim 2002: 43). Realizing this potential requires sufficient cultural autonomy, social guarantees, and personal confidence, which do not distribute evenly across social categories. Consequently, the German authors ask, "Does talk of a 'self culture' perhaps correspond to how the winners see things, when the silent losers go downhill with the violence born of despair?" (ibid.: 47). And while current trends may enrich the cultural lives of a great many individual persons in a society, eventually what happens to the communities where they live?

Encountering Culture

Cultural knowledge can be gained through: (1) direct sensory experience; (2) oral histories and interpersonal contact; (3) print media; (4) photographic and cinema technology; (5) electronic media; and (6) digital technology. The last three channels in particular dramatically increase the reach and impact of cultural transmission and open up attractive and convenient avenues for cultural exploration.

Does it matter which channels people use to gather cultural information and make decisions that influence their cultural pathways? Some critical observers believe the distinction is crucial. John B. Thompson (1995) distinguishes between the meanings and consequences of what he calls "lived experiences" and "mediated experiences" in self-formation. He concludes that mediated experiences represent relatively new ways for engaging the world. They generate events that lack the direct involvement of lived experience, which he refers to as the firsthand "encounters" of everyday life. Mediated experience, from this perspective, produces "non-reciprocal relations of intimacy with distant others" which can lead to debilitating consequences such as the pathologies exhibited by some star-struck fans of media celebrities (Thompson 1995: 225). Although Thompson does not take a fully alarmist view of what he calls the "sequestration" of lived experience, he nonetheless worries about the confusion that the transformation from lived experience to mediated experience signals for individuals and societies.

The cultural triumph of electronic media concerns some social researchers too. Television viewing has replaced much time formerly spent on "social activity outside the home, especially social gatherings and informal conversations," according to Robert Putnam, author of a study on trends in American public life (Putnam 2000: 237). Putnam sees problems with the amount of viewing in which people engage, the privatization of leisure time, and with the very way people watch television – remote control in hand ready to change channels at any moment. Of all the distractions available to Americans, Putnam found television to be the most consistent and significant predictor of civic disengagement.

Concerns about the erosion of public life also focus on the internet, which not only cuts into unmediated social interaction, but into the amount of time people spend watching television (Cole et al. 2003). Making a case against the internet as a medium that ultimately acts against people's best interests, however, is much more difficult than making the same argument against television which, often in too dismissive a manner, has long been blamed for a wide range of psychological, social, and cultural ills. The internet offers many more opportunities to initiate cultural experience, interact, and communicate. It blurs distinctions commonly made between direct and mediated experience. The more we get used to it, the more natural it becomes. The studies conducted at Carnegie Mellon University (HomeNet 2003) about online experience reveal that going online has a generally positive effect on communication satisfaction, social involvement, and psychological

---

Universal values and concepts

Transnational cultural media

Civilizations

Nations

Regions and everyday life

Figure 3.1 The cultural spheres

well-being. The most important factor is the relationship between offline and online experience. In sum, the "net benefit depends on whether [online] relationships supplement or substitute for offline relationships" (HomeNet 2003). For most people who regularly use entertainment and information technology, however, "mediated experience" today *is* "lived experience." Under any circumstances, voluntary immersion in mediated experience – with all its positive and negative consequences, real and imagined – continues to grow dramatically.

The Cultural Spheres

In the concrete reality of today's world, places and spaces, places and non-places intertwine and tangle together.

M. Augé, Non Places, p. 107

Cultural experience does not simply present itself, nor do we create it, in serial fashion. "Real" or "lived" cultural experience is in many ways no more authentic than or superior to "mediated" or "virtual" encounters. Cultural realms have become intricately embedded in each other. The cultural spheres, which I will now discuss briefly, are the places and spaces of cultural inspiration. Everyone in the world – to varying degrees, with varying motivations, and with varying consequences – engages the cultural spheres. They function as windows and access points composed of material and discursive cultural elements that originate from near and far and everywhere in between (Figure 3.1). The spheres are fluid, dynamic, and enmeshed in the ways they are represented, perceived, interpreted, and negotiated.

Universal values and concepts

The speed and reach of electronic and digital media expose certain basic values and concepts very broadly. These themes are not uniformly represented nor are they commonly interpreted from place to place or person to person. But their meanings are not undetermined either. The fundamental meaning of freedom, justice, autonomy, and equality, for example, are promoted quite clearly in the most well-known document that aspires to promote shared values – the United Nations' Universal Declaration of Human Rights. Universal concepts of expression and emotion, psychological needs, and standards of aesthetics and beauty also emerge independently or are commonly recognized as they travel within or from one cultural group to another. It is the discursive presence and utility of universal values and concepts – not their essential truth or ability to generate interpretative consensus – that gives them great purchase as cultural resources on a global scale.

Universal values and concepts often spread in mediated form. The "spectacular narratives" of films made by Steven Spielberg and George Lucas, for instance, are based on myths "intelligible to everyone, independent of their culture, educational level, national history, economic development, or political system" (García Canclini 1995: 111). The archetypal dilemmas, dramas, and fantasies of these directors' films resonate with local myths, values, and ideals to guarantee cross-cultural appeal. At other times broadly shared human values like "individual rights" arrive in more contested form. Popular American TV police dramas (e.g. *Law and Order, CSI, NYPD Blue*), for example, demonstrate that even individuals who are accused of crimes should have legal rights and be given due process under the law (Almond, Appleby, and Sivan 2003: 79). Such values clash with actual cultural practices in many parts of the world, but still provoke interest because they correspond with a shared sense of the fundamental tenets of human rights and social justice.

Transnational cultural media

People all over the world are exposed to an unprecedented amount of cultural imagery that emanates from international sources. Complaints of "cultural imperialism" and "media imperialism" continue to be made because the powerful icons of global capitalism – McDonald's, Blockbuster, Nokia, rap and rock, Nike, Coca-Cola, Hollywood films, Microsoft, Disney, and so on – are more visible than ever. The ubiquitous nature of cultural entities such as these interact with the places where they are encountered and consumed – strip malls, pedestrian shopping streets, multiplex cinemas, outlet stores, fast food restaurants, and so on – which themselves have become the prominent non-places of supermodernity (Augé 1995).

Reductionist views of transnational cultural activity like this, however, fail to explain the complex and contradictory processes that characterize how people actually engage cultural forms arriving from afar (e.g. Lull 2000; Tomlinson 1991). The question that never seems to be sufficiently answered by the harshest critics of global cultural activity – unless we assume that most people simply don't know what's good for them – is why archetypal international media and cultural products like McDonald's or Disney find such enthusiastic acceptance outside their countries and cultures of origin. People everywhere willingly, creatively, and repeatedly seek cultural imagery, ideas, and materials from outside their home environments. Retail marketplaces where material and symbolic cultural goods and services are sold often respond to the consumer in much more efficient, beneficial, and respectful ways than do the government agencies, political parties, labor unions, and other social institutions that are supposed to sensitively respond to and represent their interests (García Canclini 1995). Furthermore, it isn't just cultural commodities, brand names, logos, entertainment media, and commercial hype that travel internationally.

Non-governmental organizations, educational and cultural exchange programs, terrorists, religious missionaries, sporting teams and clubs, tourists, political treaties, and trade agreements, among many other phenomena, regularly introduce cultural values and styles across national borders.

Civilizations

> *America is successful and wealthy because of its values, not despite them.*
> *It is prosperous because of the way it respects freedom, individualism, and*
> *women's rights and the way it nurtures creativity and experimenta-*
> *tion . . . Americans gravitate toward societies that share those same values,*
> *and they recoil from those that don't*
>
> T. Friedman, *Longitudes and Attitudes*, pp. 176–7

> *When the darkness comes upon us and we are bitten by a sharp tooth, I*
> *say: Our homes are flooded and the tyrant is freely wandering in our*

homes . . . And over weeping sounds now we hear the beats of drums. They are storming his forts and shouting: "We will not stop our raids until you free our land . . . "

Osama bin Laden reciting a poem in a video broadcast by
Al-Jazeera, December, 2001

The very term "civilization" is problematic. It is sometimes used to distinguish between cultural groups – some are fully civilized, some are not. The term can over-privilege the role of science and technology as principal markers of human achievement. It can mask significant differences between cultural groups that are said to form part of the same civilization. Still, when used as an analytical framework that broadly reflects and sorts differences in cultural orientations and tendencies worldwide, civilization becomes a useful categorization system that facilitates analysis and comparison.

That was a key point in Samuel P. Huntington's *The Clash of Civilizations*, wherein the author argues that eight or nine world "civilizations are the ultimate human tribes" (Huntington 1996: 207). It's easy to criticize any analytical framework that groups the world's six billion diverse people into a few basic categories (e.g. Western, Latin American, Islamic, Buddhist, Hindu, Orthodox, Sinic, Japanese, African), and Huntington was by no means the first scholar to do so. Moreover, Huntington makes no crude argument of cultural determination based solely on civilizational differences. His work has often been simplified and then summarily rejected for political purposes – often, it seems, by people who haven't carefully read the book.

What is particularly useful about the concept of civilization is not how pure or predictable civilizations are, nor how they sometimes compete internally or externally. More important is how they encourage and facilitate cultural flows and connectivity among people who share common traditions and traits. Flows and connectivity among members of the same civilization serve as vital resources for cultural construction across geographical and geopolitical boundaries. When fundamental sources of cultural capital such as language, history, musical styles, and religious heritage are held in common, people are more likely understand, appreciate, and feel comfortable with each other. They enjoy what Joseph Straubhaar calls "cultural proximity" (Straubhaar 1997). Straubhaar and others have shown that most people prefer to stay within their own cultural groups the majority of the time for mediated cultural experiences, too. The quantity of exchange of symbolic cultural materials among nations that make up civilizations – Latin America, East Asia, or the Islamic world, for example – is striking.

All civilizational liaisons develop within broad geopolitical patterns, which also influence how relations play out between and among nations. In the wake of September 11, for instance, British Foreign Secretary for the Blair government, Jack Straw, said that UK support for the United States "is instinctive. We are part of the same family." The culturally similar UK and the USA share an official political position in the "war on terrorism," of course, including the invasion of Iraq. But underlying cultural affinities often persist even in cases where strong political differences exist at the government level. The cultural relationship between Mexico and Cuba provides a good example. The two countries share considerable history, values, and a common language, which explains much of their cultural affinity. Even in the face of threats made by the United States about Mexico's supposed responsibilities concerning the boycott America has imposed on Cuba, the intra-civilizational link between the two Latin American countries, situated as it is within a wider geopolitical context, encourages continued cultural interaction.

Mass media, information and communications technology, and the culture industries make it easy for people from specific cultural groups to have access to culturally and linguistically familiar content. Such tendencies are readily apparent in California, for example, where ethnic communities unite around film, video, religious artifacts, sports, popular music, news, and much more from their countries of origin. A Mexican, Chinese, or Vietnamese immigrant to California these days, for example, need not be overly concerned about assimilating into English-speaking, northern European-based American culture because the Mexican, Chinese, and Vietnamese communities themselves, and the civilizations they represent, have become prominent features of the North American cultural landscape. Urban life, modern transportation, mass media, popular culture, and information and communications technology mediate and transform cultural groups, but never in just one direction.

Notwithstanding what they have in common, immigrant communities reflect a broad spectrum of cultural orientations and preferences. Diversity lives inside diversity, and not always in harmony. The typical case has the older generation clinging to tradition while young adults, adolescents, and children explore novel cultural experiences and develop multicultural lifestyles and identities. Electronic media and popular culture play central roles in these developments. Consider the television viewing habits of North African immigrant families in France. Parents and elders typically watch Arabic-language channels on the main television set in the living room while their children prefer French-language stations and international (mainly American and British) channels including MTV, CNN, and TNT (Hargreaves 1997). As Morley (2000) and others have observed, however, the Islamic activists among them almost always come from the younger generation. Inter-civilizational experience socializes most young immigrants into mainstream cultural life in their new surroundings, but it also provokes turbulence among radical young male immigrants. We saw that tension play out, for example, with the two British Islamist groups who terrorized the London transportation system in 2005, the failed plot of Canadian Muslims in Toronto a year later, and the horrendous plan by a large group of British Muslims that same year to blow up airliners with liquid explosives. All the key figures in the 9/11 attack were young men who had spent considerable time living in Europe or the United States.

Nations

The nation is not something given in nature, and for whatever remote connections they may have to earlier ethnic communities, nations are a product of relatively recent history. They have all been built from a diversity of cultural fragments.

A. Giddens, *The Third Way*, p. 131

The musicians, the sound crew, the lighting crew . . . they're all Mexicans!

Mexican pop singer Aleks Syntek in a concert attended mainly by Mexican Americans at a club in Dallas, Texas; comment made in Spanish

Nation states are political entities that ideally represent the interests of individuals and groups who live within geographical boundaries given legitimacy through formal recognition that is granted by other nation states. The nation state organizes life for its members and cultivates identity and loyalty. When functioning at its best, the nation state offers stability, opportunity, and security. At worst, it limits and oppresses people.

Nations function as enduring political entities that impose certain demands (e.g. legal restrictions, taxes, tariffs), provide services (e.g. social welfare programs, military protection, passports), and expect loyalty. Success of the economy (living standards, particular products, exports) forms a sizeable part of national identity. National history, ideology, and culture become familiar to citizens and others through contact with a standard set of symbolic forms. These include flags, colors, anthems, religious traditions, folkloric and popular culture, political rhetoric, textbooks and school curricula, media systems, currency, postage stamps, monuments, museums, tourist literature, even national animals, flowers, and food.

Keeping diverse people united under one flag, history, ideology, religion, or language challenges even the most politically stable, economically strong, and culturally traditional nation states. Consider the cultural situation today in the United Kingdom. With the rise of Islamic militancy and illegal immigration from Muslim countries to Europe on the rise, British authorities responded by tightening asylum laws and proposing a change in the oath of allegiance for immigrants years before the London bombings. In the revised oath, the government asks diverse, newly arrived immigrants to formally declare cultural loyalty to the Western-style democratic values that characterize the history and dominant culture of Great Britain, and to promise to uphold the laws supporting those values. Another case in point is China, where the government now requires exclusive use of the simplified version of Chinese written characters (rather than the pre-communist era complex characters used in Taiwan), and prohibits anglicized words like internet, WTO, or Titanic: "We have 56 ethnic groups who speak 100 spoken languages and we have 30 written languages," said a Chinese government official. "Things are already complicated enough . . . everyone should be able to speak the same dialect.

That's very important for national unity" (*Straits Times*, Singapore, January 17, 2001). The Chinese government's attempt to restrict religious practices further demonstrates how state authorities try to manage culture in order to maintain ideological control. All these efforts have become much more complicated today with the rapid adoption of communications technology and the manifold increase in the circulation of all variety of symbolic forms.

The importance of nation as a bounded geographical place, a political construct, and a shared social space – a "home territory" (Morley 2000) of ontological security and comfort – should not be underestimated. People depend on the nation state individually and collectively for its social and political power and for its ability to provide a (relativized and contested) sense of belonging. At particular junctures – votes taken by the United Nations Security Council, Olympics and World Cup competitions, the physical crossing of borders, negotiation of trade agreements and military treaties, attempts at political asylum, and currency exchanges, for instance – nation becomes the dominant structure through which decisions are rendered, actions taken, and loyalties demonstrated. Despite all the inevitable internal contradictions and conflicts, most people of the world still speak rather freely and proudly of nation in philosophical and practical terms. National pride is especially prevalent and important for citizens of developing countries (Pei 2003: 32).

Regions and everyday life

> *Despite globalization, people are still attached to their culture, their language and a place called home. And they will sing for home, cry for home, fight for home, and die for home.*
> T. Friedman, *The Lexus and the Olive Tree*, p. 250

We began this chapter by referring to Thomas Friedman's *The Lexus and the Olive Tree*. In that book he positioned the risks of globalization against the instinct to stay safe at home. Greg Zachary's *The Global Me* made a similar contrast between the "wings" of globalization and the "roots" of the homeland. The last two cultural spheres discussed here – regions and everyday life –

refer to the olive tree and the homeland roots. As people fashion their cultural activities and identities, they look first at what is close at hand. They continue to rely on shared geographic, ethnic, and cultural places and spaces – the material and symbolic cultural resources they believe to be truly "their own."

Consider how language is spoken in the English countryside, for example, where accents can signal differences that are considered by some to be important enough to lead to late-night fights in pubs or worse. The actual cultural differences between these groups often are slight, representing subtle peculiarities that trace back centuries, sometimes just from one side of a river to the other. But language demarcates cultural difference and people (mainly men) will sometimes kill each other over subtle cultural differences. Ethnic Pashtuns cross back and forth across the border between Afghanistan and Pakistan, ignoring a distinction that matters less than ethnicity – the political demarcation of nation states. The tendency toward regional primacy in culture and cultural politics can be seen in post-Franco Spain as well, and not only in the fiercely contested case of Catalonia. Regional cultures historically have been preserved and circulated through oral traditions and now endure by means of print, electronic, and digital media.

While "life at home" today includes various influences that arrive from a distance, our cultural worlds – our personal supercultures – will always incorporate and reflect cultural resources and practices that physically surround us most closely. The significance of our most familiar environments and habits, therefore, must never be considered simply as the backdrop for construction of more elaborate and sophisticated cultural activities and identities. Precisely because the most parochial aspects of everyday life are so omnipresent and routine, they profoundly and uniquely influence thinking and power relations at every social and political level (Chaney 2002; Heller 1984).

Social actors draw creatively from all the cultural spheres – universal values and concepts, transnational cultural media, civilizations, nations, regions, and everyday life – to construct their cultural worlds. The spheres are dynamic. They act like clouds or "fronts" (Gonzalez 2001), continually reconfiguring themselves internally and in relation to the other spheres.

The Cultural Mix in Action

. . . an international student from Cameroon who speaks fluent English and French as well as African languages and local dialects, has a different purchase on the global ecumene than the monolingual English undergraduate whose only travel abroad is to the rave enclaves of Ibiza or Corfu.
A. Sreberny, "Globalization and Me," p. 300

Being an individual does not exclude caring about others. In fact, living in a highly individualized culture means you have to be socially sensible, able to relate to others, and obligate yourself in order to manage your everyday life
U. Beck and E. Beck-Gernsheim, *Individualization*, p. 211

Learning a language, eating Thai food, marrying someone from another country, or flying off to Reykjavik on a Crazy Iceland Clubbing Package can all expand a person's cultural awareness and appreciation, certainly, but they are hardly equivalent experiences. Although the cultural experiences of poor people are also becoming much more diverse than before, individuals with economic capital have more freedom than others to think outside their inherited cultural boxes, to "play" with culture, and to develop complex tastes and identities that draw from all the cultural spheres. They "live through layers of affiliation, putting on another layer or taking one off, depending on the setting" (Zachary 2000: xi), as they pay "continuous partial attention" (Friedman 2002: 22) to the cultural options they feel they need or enjoy.

The postmodern person is not an atomized individual. Although people today have much greater individual freedom than ever before to search, select, and connect according to their own needs and tastes, that freedom is exercised in profoundly social ways. The sense of inner security that people need to stay healthy and manage their daily lives does not disappear in the face of increased cultural fragmentation and individualization. To the contrary, people put new technological and cultural resources to work in ways that make them feel socially engaged and culturally comfortable. Young people especially have no problem embracing traditional values while taking advantage of unfamiliar cultural resources. As communications technology becomes more sophisticated and cultural resources more diverse, the potential for creating multiple personal rewards and pleasures increases. While individuals seek the comfort of common ground with others, they also search for differentiating experiences that distinguish themselves from others.

Not everyone's pleased. Observing the cultural changes, the sociologist Zygmunt Bauman argues that the era in which we live accelerates what he considers a disastrous "consumerization of a precarious world and the disintegration of human bonds" (Bauman 2000: 165). It's no secret, for instance, that many of the cultural resources that people browse, borrow, buy, and steal today turn large profits for the media and culture industries. Critics have rightfully condemned the questionable ethics and clear excesses of media and popular culture. Bauman may be right that some people have abandoned some of their committed friendships for more ephemeral social attachments. Certain changes brought about in the fast-paced, postindustrial world of what Bauman calls "liquid modernity" are cause for concern.

The terms "cultural programming" and "personal supercultures" reflect current realities: individualization has become an increasingly widespread characteristic of cultural life. As Barry Wellman argues, today it is the "person . . . who has become even more an autonomous communication node" and the "portal" of cultural behavior (Wellman 2002: 233, 238). Individual persons, however, do not want to be isolated. As people increasingly assume the role of cultural creators, they continue to connect, coordinate, and socialize with others. The social qualities of email, instant messaging, blogs, chat rooms, file sharing, and contacts generated by search engine references, for instance, provide unlimited opportunities for people to connect with other individuals and groups.

Expressions like "virtual tribes," "online communities," and "peer-to-peer" interaction were early attempts to characterize these social processes. Extending ideas that spring from Manuel Castell's notion of the "networked society" (Castells 1996), Barry Wellman describes the nuances of "networked individualism" and "personal communities" that don't depend on fixed geographical locations or traditional forms of social interaction (Wellman 2002). David Mateo's notion of "collective individualism" nicely illustrates the intricate nexus that links individual persons with cultural groups. Through ethnographic field research, Mateo shows how young people creatively use the internet and mobile phones to form alternative communities in culturally unstable, post-Pinochet Chile. It is the unique social space of the rave, according to Mateo, that best exemplifies how modern individuals fuse their empirical worlds with their cultural imagination and their sense of personal independence with their need to connect and commune with others (Mateo 2004).

Superculture Revisited

In the 1960s, the economist and social theorist Kenneth Boulding introduced a term he thought accurately described the remarkable cultural developments that had taken place on a global scale after World War II. Observing that spectacular innovations such as skyscrapers, jet aircraft, electronic media, intercontinental hotels, genetically modified foods, and birth control pills were appearing all over the world and changing the consciousness of people everywhere, Boulding referred to the modern trends collectively as the "global superculture" (Boulding 1969, 1978).

The global superculture, Boulding thought, was not simply the product of homogenizing capitalist hegemony or cultural imperialism – two key discourses of the time. Fully aware of, and critical of, the social and environmental dangers posed by rampant technological development, Boulding still considered the tangible achievements represented by the global superculture as spectacular evidence of the ultimate triumph of scientific knowledge. Boulding believed that by combining the power of theoretical science, world religions, international trade, non-governmental organizations, and the material resources that were circulating at the time, a "world system" could be built that would profoundly benefit all mankind (Boulding 1989). He envisioned a massive unleashing of scientific and human energy that could put an end to war, promote greater understanding between diverse peoples, and save the environment.

The terms most often used to describe the era in which we now live – the Information Age, the Communication Age, and the Digital Age – make clear where scientific priorities have gone since Boulding pondered global conditions in the 1960s. The key developments that have taken place since then – the transformation from heavy to light industry, from durable goods to information, from labor-intensive to service-based economies – have brought about extraordinary cultural changes. Scientific knowledge and cultural materials mature and move around today with greater speed and far-reaching consequences than even Boulding could have imagined. But now, just as was the case 40 years ago, the most pressing issues we face concern the moral determination of people, not the substantive products of their collective genius.

Fears that were expressed about spread of the "global superculture" last century emerged from the belief that modern scientific and cultural developments were too distant, cold, and anonymous – too "corporate" – to respond to real human needs. Much of the criticism today centers on the other end of the process. Greater cultural individualization doesn't seem to offer much hope for creating a more sensitive and harmonious world. Or does it?

Incorporating an expanded range of ideas and resources into one's own cultural experience can reinforce a spirit of discovery, foster tolerance and respect for difference, and ultimately promote cultural enlightenment for individuals and the world at large. That's because the mindset that underlies all the dramatic changes that are taking place today is one of *cultural sociality*. All forms of creativity, connectivity, and cultural production – even the more mobile and mediated experiences that are common to the digital era – involve integration with others, a need for approval, and the making of group identities and communities. It is the inherently social nature of the new forms of cultural construction that ultimately offers the greatest chance for our common humanity to finally prevail.

Chapter 4

The Push and Pull of Culture

September 11 and its continuing violent aftermath have motivated people everywhere to reflect intensely on the meanings and implications of their cultural realities and futures. This reflection takes place at a time in history when "Culture" as a normative social force that inscribes values and regulates behavior is being confronted by the pervasive decentralization of life experience and the dramatic rise of the individual as a personal cultural decision maker.[1] As Ulrich Beck has pointed out, "The ethic of individual self-fulfillment and achievement is the most powerful current in modern society. The choosing, deciding, shaping human being who aspires to be author of his or her own life, the creator of individual identity, is the central character of our time" (Beck 2000: 165).

Processes of individualization that emerged as cultural characteristics in Western societies have intensified greatly in the current era and the trend is spreading rapidly elsewhere. The diversity and amount of cultural information to which people have access today encourages unprecedented personal cultural experimentation and self-reliance. But a seemingly contrasting development – cultural retrenchment – is also taking place. The remarkable rise of the individual in globalization has changed but not erased collective Culture as a stable, guiding source of belongingness, security, and identity. At the same time that individuals the world over put an ever-increasing array of cultural resources to work for personal purposes, groups of persons who identify with nation, religion, ethnicity, tribe, and race often confront today's uncertain and threatening times by displaying their collective will and cultural capital.

These seemingly antithetical tendencies in contemporary cultural experience represent the classic "dichotomy between the autonomous agent and the socialized self" (Agre 2001: 6) and make up what I call the "push and pull" of culture. This expression – push and pull – has many uses in the English language and Western culture. In the present context "push" refers to those cultural influences that become part of our cultural lives more or less implicitly and not necessarily with our knowledge or consent – the demands of culture. Many push aspects of culture are inherited: primary languages, religious or spiritual orientations and practices, basic social values, types of food, and so on. They are the non-volitional elements of our dominant cultural consciousness and praxis – features of life over which we originally had little control, whose contours make up our basic orientation to the world, provide primordial stability, and whose influence can never be completely extinguished, no matter how hard we may try later in life (Lull 2000: 132–3). The product of these influences is the acculturated individual and the societies in which they live.

The "pull" side of culture, on the other hand, refers to the dynamic nature of contemporary communication and the role of the self as an active agent of cultural construction – the do-it-yourself cultural programmer discussed in the previous chapter. Pull represents the volitional side of cultural formation and is characterized by the "flexible self" (Willis 2000) who actively seeks increased personalization of cultural experience through individual creativity and choice – culture-on-demand. Pull culture is more space than place, more dynamic than static, more engaged than removed. Pull represents the provisional self under constant construction.

The push-and-pull dichotomy directs attention to the precarious balance between collective and individual needs, each of which has been sharpened considerably by the contrasts and contradictions of the Communication Age. I have appropriated the specific meanings of the associated terms "push" and "pull" from the world of information technology and marketing. Push refers primarily to the idea that certain events can be introduced into the awareness of people without their asking or consent. In terms of the internet, for example, junk email and instant messages, spyware, and unwanted pop-up ads that appear on a personal computer are push intrusions. So is the channeling of a search engine request to a sponsored link, junk text messages sent to a mobile phone, or a telemarketing call received at home.

Pull signifies the user-driven side of the model. Extending our example of internet communication, in a pull experience the user tells the browser what information he or she wants to retrieve from the digital environment. The user logs on, sets preferences, and then searches, selects, and socializes according to his or her schedule and priorities. This active engagement can be initiated personally by the user in real time or programmed into a computer by the user to automatically retrieve the desired content. Users maintain basic control over the process. In many respects today's information technology and telecommunications devices offer "not only the feeling of being able to control the complexities of modern life, but also a real possibility to do so" (Kopomaa 2000: 5).

Push and pull are not pure or dichotomous tendencies. In Silicon Valley parlance, "true push" means that websites and other sources immediately send data to the user's home computer whenever an event occurs – a change in market prices, for instance, or the arrival of sports results. "Managed push" refers to sender initiatives that are based on known or estimated user profiles and preferences – the "TiVo model." Yahoo, for example, calls its web service "the internet that logs on to *you*." The best solution for the high-tech communications industries in general has been to make individual preferences easily accessible. As Thomas Friedman observes, "Companies like Google, Yahoo!, Amazon.com, and TiVo have learned to thrive not by pushing products and services on their customers as much as by building collaborative systems that enable customers to pull on their own, and then responding with lightening quickness to what they pull" (Friedman 2005: 156).

Overall, the locus of much cultural activity today is shifting from structure and tradition (push) to individual persons, their chosen resources, and social networks which are composed of varying degrees of proximity and mediation (pull). The technological advances brought on by modernity and globalization make the speed and efficiency of the pull side of cultural activity extremely attractive and rewarding for individuals and, in many respects, for the societies in which they live. Innovation and creativity lead the way. As George Soros points out, the cultural freedoms that people enjoy today clearly have "liberated inventive and entrepreneurial talents and accelerated [further development of the] technological innovations" that helped open or widen the creative spaces in the first place (Soros 2002: 4). The global transition toward greater cultural loosening and self-determination is by no means limited to advances made in information technology. Information and cultural materials travel like never before and people everywhere have more opportunities for access to diverse information and culture than they have ever known.

Certainly not all prominent contemporary thinkers are as encouraged as George Soros is with current cultural developments, and in truth Soros himself has no Pollyanna-ish position on this issue either. Warning signs about the cultural consequences of globalization appear everywhere. Globalization creates tremendous uncertainty and trepidation, especially for those who believe they have been victimized or abandoned by it. Some observers fear the severe degradation of cultural integrity and the breakdown of community. Zygmunt Bauman, for example, argues that the uncertainties of the present have become "a powerful individualizing force [so that] the idea of 'common interests' grows ever more nebulous and loses all pragmatic value" (Bauman 2000: 148). Even Ulrich Beck, whose generally even-handed analysis of individualization will be discussed later, suggests that, "God, nature, and the social system are being progressively replaced, in greater and lesser steps, by the individual – confused, astray, helpless, and at a loss" (Beck and Beck-Gernsheim 2002: 8).

Sociologist Robert Putnam found considerable empirical support for the conclusion that Americans – widely known for their individualistic lifestyles – have become extremely disconnected socially and disengaged from civic life in the current era. He argues that Americans' immersion in contemporary entertainment and communications media has reached such a degree that the bonds necessary for a "happy, well educated, healthy, and safe" society are seriously eroding (Putnam 2000). The name of the book reporting these findings, *Bowling Alone*, illustrates the trend. Americans used to bowl with friends in teams. Now many prefer to bowl alone. The trend toward increased individualization in many aspects of life, especially for the middle class (but not only for them), can be observed around the world. Cultures will continue to differentiate common human experience, however. It's more difficult to imagine Mexicans "bowling alone," for instance, than their neighbors to the north.

These trends should not be read only in a negative light. Precisely the same conditions that may cause some people to disconnect from each other and from tradition also facilitate robust, creative, individual cultural initiatives and activities. These conditions include:

* unprecedented degree of access to cultural forms;
* global connectivity;
* temporal and spatial flexibility;
* creativity and hybridity;
* immediacy of experience;
* digitization of communication and cultural forms;
* expanded range of personal communications options.

We live in Cultures but we initiate "cultural experiences" and we lead "cultural lives" that don't just reflect our primary cultural locations. The push and pull refers to the dynamic and dialectical nexus between Culture and culture, between the cultural life of the group and that of the individual. Figure 4.1 summarizes the key contrasts.

What happens to families, tribes, nations, and civilizations – the primary traditional cultural units – as cultural experience becomes more and more individualized? How do people form stable communities and meaningful identities in a world where tradition confronts a "permanent revolution" of market forces that, in some crucial ways, "undermines traditional structures of authority and fractures local communities" (Giddens 1998: 15)? Is it true that increasingly commercialized culture "strokes our solitary egos but leaves unsatisfied our yearning for community" (Barber 1995: 243)? How do contemporary societies strike the proper balance between social guarantees and personal freedoms? To what and to whom are people loyal these days?

Push	Pull
Culture	culture
collective	individual
public	private
non-volitional	volitional
security	risk
slow-paced	fast-paced
gradual change	rapid and flexible
macro	micro
closed	open
community	habitat
uniformity	diversity
social norms	personal wants and needs
production	consumption
coherent	fragmented

Figure 4.1 The push and pull of culture

The Push of Culture

Individual persons today chase their dreams with unprecedented energy and latitude but they still need to connect, communicate, and commune with others. From birth, the human organism gravitates toward the safety and stability provided by a relatively predictable, orderly, and constant flow of everyday life. This instinct never disappears. Adults depend on predictable structures, norms, and behavior for survival and stability too, especially when they believe their individual or collective living situations have become abnormally uncertain, threatening, or uncontrollable.

Familiar cultural structures and traits act as commodious resources for physical survival, psychological stability, and identity. These primordial elements include ancestry, collective memory, ethnicity, race, religion, everyday customs, rituals, language, core values, geographic territory, and trusted institutions – "blood and belief, faith and family" (Huntington 1996: 126). People rely on the push side of the cultural equation to maintain the integrity and viability of the familiar in an increasingly uncertain and dangerous world. In this sense, Culture can be said to represent the general interests of an entire group. That's why Culture never functions solely as an unwanted, dominating, limiting force that is imposed on individual persons. To the contrary, most people depend on Culture for great comfort, even for survival.

Loyalty and dependence on Culture become strongest when the group competes with or feels threatened by outside forces. The terrorist attack on America stimulated a strident appeal in the United States by President George W. Bush and other government officials to interpret 9/11 and subsequent military activity in cultural terms. The cultural conflict was rhetorically enhanced by invoking a universal moral standard ("good" v. "evil," "free" v. "oppressed," and so on), which was later used by Bush to rationalize United States military action, including the invasion of Iraq. The "war against terrorism" permitted wide military license in defense of nation and Culture.

The religious-ethnic-territorial conflict between Israel and Palestine has been the most persistently visible example of extreme group affiliation and cultural dependency. Although some diversity of opinion can be found on each side, Culture is perceived overall by most Israelis and Palestinians as a preordained, divine, and necessary source of belonging, protection, identity, and expression. The political positions are fueled by such extreme cultural-religious self-righteousness that for many believers on both sides any competing interpretations of religious history or territorial claims to the "holy land" are simply out of the question. Proposed compromises between the two sides have been made mainly as practical measures to forestall the vicious cycles of killing, not to settle irreconcilable religious issues. When ethnoreligious groups clash, collective Culture matters more than anything. Faith becomes Culture. Any diversion from the ideology of the dominant group that reduces or relativizes cultural integrity or survivability is thought to be unacceptable.[2] In such contexts, even mundane exercises of cultural individualization (the pull tendency) can be interpreted as unpatriotic or disloyal.

Although uncertainty and threat greatly sharpen allegiances to and dependencies on Culture, the less chaotic and treacherous activities and routines of everyday life are likewise patterned according to the expectations and sanctions of ideological orthodoxy. As David Chaney points out, even the most familiar cultural structures "tell us that there is a distinctive way of doing things [that is] imbued with moral force" (Chaney 2002: 8). The ongoing, shared life of cultural groups (the *durée* of social activity: Giddens 1984) reinforces and shapes the idea that Culture has ethical qualities, long-term viability, and practical utility. Moreover, "these ways of doing things persist through generations; they will generally hold without discussion or question, and they display a level of group life that precedes individual experience" (Chaney 2002: 8). Cultural institutions introduce, reinforce, and perpetuate the group's characteristic values, rituals, and patterns of behavior as normal and expected.[3] These cultural values, practices, styles, and identities are contained within and emerge from a collective memory system – an empirically elusive cognitive architecture widely sensed by cultural members. While not historically invariable or genetically determined, these "internal cultural patterns" migrate across time and space from generation to generation (Sowell 1994: 229; see also Lull 2000: 152–5). The most compelling explanation of the persistence of cultural traits across time has been made by evolutionary biologists, especially Richard Dawkins' concept of "memes" (Dawkins 1976)

Diaspora

> *Kamal would sometimes act as self-titled censor: Anything that questioned the Islamic faith, according to Kamal, would be unacceptable. He would switch off the station.*
>
> El-Nawawy and Iskandar, *Al-Jazeera*, p. 16;
> discussing a Muslim immigrant watching
> the Al-Jazeera television network via digital satellite in Canada

> *The guy from Germany (Dirk Nowitzki) cheers the guy from China (Wang Zhizhi) and the American crowd goes nuts!*
>
> Matt Pinto, Portuguese-American announcer for
> the Dallas Mavericks professional basketball team that also
> included players from Mexico, France, Canada, and Iceland

Cultural reproduction persists even when individual cultural members become deterritorialized from their geographic and ethnic origins. Diasporic communities play particularly important roles in this type of cultural maintenance when cultural commodities and personal communications hardware are readily available, and where freedom of expression is permitted or guaranteed by law. The Iranian community residing in southern California, for instance, can rely on two Farsi daily newspapers, several magazines, three television outlets, and two radio stations broad-casting in Farsi and English, nightclubs, mosques, all-Iranian Rotary clubs, student organizations, and countless websites among other channels, sites, and rituals that have all been established to facilitate social life and cultural transmission. The Iranian diaspora in California depends heavily on non-mainstream media and popular culture forms (Naficy 1993), as does the South Asian diaspora in the United Kingdom (Gillespie 1995), Vietnamese who have relocated to California (Lull and Wallis 1992), Mexicans living in Los Angeles (Uribe 2003), various Asian communities that have formed in Australia (Cunningham and Sinclair 2000), and countless other deterritorialized groups who construct new versions of their Cultures around the world.

Immigrant groups create their multidimensional cultural worlds *with* and *against* the dominant cultures where they relocate. Many of the cultural values and practices immigrants bring with them change in ways that reflect their new situations. But immigrant groups also (consciously and unconsciously) position themselves in some respects against the host culture; that's why diasporic groups tend to hold on to their cultural values tightly and often become even more traditional and culturally conservative than those who remain in the homeland. Immigrants become situated within and subject to multiple push influences: the force of their original Cultural groups and the hegemony of their new Cultures. Of course, diasporas profoundly influence their host Cultures too. The unprecedented degree of human migration and mobility today accelerates and directs cultural change in multiple directions simultaneously.

One consequence of today's patterns of intense global human migration is the creation of multicultural societies composed of groups representing very different cultural histories, values, and practices. In many respects nations and economies which embrace and encourage multiculturalism, even in circumstances where dis-similar ethnic and religious groups co-mingle, can reap tremen-dous economic and cultural benefits from the energy, creativity, and productivity that diversity generates, especially in this era of technological development and heightened global economic com-petition (e.g. Cowen 2002; Zachary 2000). Waves of technological innovation and subsequent economic prosperity for many decades in northern California's Silicon Valley may still best exemplify how cultural diversity has led to impressive economic productivity in the United States. In such complicated situations, however, the culturally disparate groups are also held together by an effective overarching push structure.

In many cases immigrants in complex societies have fled dysfunctional political systems or distressing economic conditions so that the new cultural territory, while unfamiliar and threatening in some respects, offers fundamental advantages and reasons to stay. As he departed his post as mayor of New York City several months after 9/11, for instance, Rudy Giuliani praised American culture as an equitable "system" that is based on political democracy, freedom of religion, a market economy, the value of human life, and the rule of law. New York City's ethnic mix is composed of roughly equal numbers of whites, Hispanics, and blacks, with significant Jewish, Asian, Arabic, African, and other Middle Eastern minorities. The city's schools enroll students who have migrated to the United States from nearly 200 nations and speak more than 100 languages. "We're everyone," Giuliani said. "This [political-cultural structure] is what holds together people of different religions, ethnicities, and languages." Giuliani is right that New York and the United States in general is home to an extraordinarily diverse population who live in remarkable harmony.

Some argue that world history proves that no political system can hold a culturally diverse society together over the long term, however, especially when strong cultural differences among population subgroups conflict (e.g. Huntington 1996). That argument is frequently made today by opponents of legal and illegal immigration, affirmative action, official languages, and other race or ethnicity-based policies. They claim that national political and cultural stability can't survive when competing subgroups put their interests ahead of the wider community or when the values of the newcomers threaten the foundations of historically successful host Cultures. Illegal Mexican immigrants in the United States were told by their leaders to put away their Mexican flags during the enormous street demonstrations in 2006, for instance, and to hoist the red, white, and blue for the television cameras to see. Violence that broke out among Bosnian Muslims, Croats, and Serbs in the former Yugoslavia represents archetypal recent examples of how national unity that is constructed for pragmatic or political reasons among rival ethnic and religious groups cannot easily endure. Sectarian violence following the invasion of Iraq in 2003 shows the same cultural consequences. Political–cultural separatist movements all over the world – Canada, Kashmir, New Zealand, Chechnya, and Sri Lanka among other places – all attest to the "cultural incompatibility" argument.

Push cultural tendencies have multiple and contradictory consequences. Push offers cultural members safety, security, identity, and a sense of belonging. It supplies a ready stockpile of material and symbolic resources and a general framework for interpreting the world. But powerful cultural systems can also inculcate rigid, divisive, non-cosmopolitan values among cultural members and be used as pretexts for religious, ethnic, racial, political, or cultural discrimination against others inside and outside national borders. As Phil Agre succinctly points out, "people understand new things through the prism of what they know, and the distortions introduced by the prism are often severe" (Agre 2001: 6). So while the push of Culture organizes life and offers stabilizing influences and other benefits, it also limits freedom, opportunity, and well-being – consequences that have become especially relevant as human beings move around the planet in such great numbers.

Nation as contested push

Despite highly visible, emotional outbursts of patriotism provoked by violence and war, any idea that the most common formal structure facilitating the push of culture – the nation state – functions smoothly as a unified, totalizing force in the age of information, communication, and globalization can be quickly put to rest. Nation and nationalism must always be considered in cultural and historical context. India serves as an unambiguous example. Strong disparities in religious status among Hindus and between Hindus and Muslims, as well as in gender roles, economic status, and educational level sort Indians into sharply differing social positions and hierarchies. Regional differences in language and ways of life, along with divided loyalties produced by geopolitical and religious tensions between India and Pakistan, further exacerbate the cultural variation and social differences. The Satellite Instructional Technology Experiment (SITE) in India in the 1970s has become a classic example of how difficult it can be to overcome cultural differences within a nation state, even when social benefits for the varying groups seem clear. Despite an enormous expenditure of foreign aid, investment capital, and the expertise of the United States' National Aeronautics Space Administration (NASA), India's federal government failed to effectively reach the outlying population with vital programs in health and education transmitted by what was then a highly advanced telecommunications satellite system. And today, despite the United Nations' efforts to get Indians (and citizens of all countries) connected to the internet, many people resist the idea not just for lack of money, but for the same reasons they refused to participate decades ago in the development programs emanating from New Delhi by satellite television – differences in cultural values, customs, language, religion, and a general distrust of the central government.

The combined influence of culture and class runs deep in the perception of nation. To continue with the example of India, anthropologist Pramila Jayapal (2000) found in her research that many parents in the outlying regions of India simply don't want their children (especially not the girls) to develop computer skills, or, in many cases, to obtain anything more than a basic education, if that. Parents fear that exposure to high technology will entice their children to leave the countryside for the city. Jayapal also cites a recent survey done by the Society for Integrated Development of the Himalayas wherein the trend she observed was found to be very widespread in the region. Education and the advent of computers are considered by many rural dwellers as threats to the treasured cultural fabric. Many parents believe that education alienates children from traditional cultural beliefs and creates a sense of indifference toward land, family, and customs.

That attitude is not new among the rural poor around the world, of course. But it assumes particular relevance in discussions about the consequences of today's economic and cultural globalization, especially the belief of most developmental experts that an inability to take advantage of available digital opportunities will only widen the global socioeconomic gaps *within* nation states. In developing countries, social unrest, disintegration, and malaise tend to revolve around extreme differences in socioeconomic conditions. The lower classes struggle to survive while the middle class builds domicile-fortresses to guard against threats and inconveniences posed by the anonymous poor nearby.

Nation states are interpreted by their own citizens in terms of national history and current conditions, which, while never disconnected from past and present transnational influences, greatly shape political realities in specific ways. Indeed, nations' internal problems can no longer be attributed mainly to colonial histories or to the conditions and demands of the global economy. So, for example, while the forces of globalization have influenced national development in Chile in recent years, those developments can only be understood in terms of the dramatic terrain of post-Pinochet national politics and culture, which spans approximately the same time frame. The attempt by Chilean legal authorities to punish Pinochet was an effort to put an end to an era in national history and start anew. That dream was cultural as much as political, as was revealed in a speech by Michelle Bachelet soon after she was elected president of Chile: "We are becoming a country in which we can all look each other in the eye and recognize ourselves as part of the same Chile!" (Bachelet 2006). But identity politics are never so logical or linear. The fierce anti-Pinochet sentiment of the past gave Chilean youth, intellectuals, and progressives a compelling issue around which to organize and identify. In another part of the world, the "Third Way" approach to development of social capital in the United Kingdom called for the creation of "British street café culture" and national community service to counter an increasing lack of trust among Britons of differing racial, cultural, and social groups and classes. Cultural initiatives underway in many other nations have likewise been designed to clarify, recreate, or energize national Cultures.

Culture and nation are frequently equated. But, as Terry Eagleton points out in *The Idea of Culture*, "people who belong to the same place . . . do not thereby form a culture; they do so only when they begin to share speech habits, folklore, ways of proceeding, frames of value, a collective self-image" (Eagleton 2000: 37). Culture, he rightly argues, is not the same as synchronous living. The fixity, shared understanding, and appreciation of Culture, especially national Culture, have become even less stable in a globalized world of international business, tourism, foreign employment, legal and illegal immigration, military interventionism, nation building, and increased privatization of the public sphere. Cultural loyalties, customs, rituals, and identities have become less and less confined to or determined by geographical territory or human surroundings. The conditions that inscribe and reinforce the foundations of most national Cultures – common languages, religions, histories, and relations with other nation states – have become far less taken-for-granted. National Cultures today are held together more by their capacity to effectively expose people to a system of common symbolic referents than by their ability to exact social compliance. The push of culture therefore increasingly refers to *the shared experience of exposure to particular signs in a crowded and highly competitive symbolic environment.*

The Pull of Culture

In his comprehensive treatise on the origins of human emotions, Jonathan H. Turner (2000) shows how the propensity toward individualism, autonomy, freedom, and mobility observable in contemporary human behavior is clearly evident throughout the evolutionary history of apes and humans. Individualism, autonomy, freedom, and mobility comprise the dynamic essence of the "pull" side of contemporary cultural experience. Strong and natural human tendencies toward gratification of individual physical and psychological needs, the flexible pursuit of differentiating personal interests and preferences, and the making of increasingly diverse cultural choices constitute the core processes of individual cultural programming and the creation of personal supercultures.

The trend toward greater individualism, autonomy, freedom, and mobility in contemporary societies is associated with core Western values, and with capitalism and commercialism, all of which have greatly permeated and shaped modernization and globalization. The impact of these ideological and cultural influences increased significantly in the late twentieth century. Consequently, many basic cultural orientations and practices, including those related to the most intimate sensibilities and expressive outlets of the culturally situated human body, are changing. Youth almost always lead the way. Millions of young urban Chinese, for instance, are more likely now than ever before to exercise autonomy from family and state to determine their sexual partners, preferences, and activities. The popularity of arranged marriages in the Far East and South Asia is declining overall. Individual fashion and style – such as Chinese women's liberation from Maoist uniformity, the hip-hop look of modern urban youth in Manila, and the "tea hair" fad among individually expressive Japanese youth – have found highly symbolic cultural places in contemporary Asian cultures. Cultural changes that appear on the human body are never just cosmetic; they disrupt tradition, open up cultural options, and eventually create new cultural norms and social practices.

Individualism, autonomy, freedom, and mobility have characterized most Western societies since the Enlightenment. Fueled by the dramatically accelerated pace of life in recent years, these values have expanded to great lengths in the West. The typical Westerner understands that he or she belongs to and has responsibilities to sociocultural communities of various types, but also operates as a highly motivated, relatively independent agent for the cultural self. One key indicator of increased individualism overtaking cultural tradition, for example, is the tendency for contemporary couples to co-habit and produce children but not marry. Nordic couples are particularly likely to forgo the religious and civil formalities of marriage. In Iceland more than 60 percent of children are born out of wedlock; in Norway, about half. More than 30 percent of children today are born to unmarried parents even in strongly Catholic Ireland. Several Western countries now recognize same-sex marriage. Even in the religious United States, the latest census statistics show a dramatic increase in the number of unmarried couples living together.

The scope and scale of cultural resources available for personal use and the cultural variety and flexibility they produce have expanded tremendously in Western cultural settings. In the West cultural entrepreneurship is itself a cultural value. People creatively appropriate, personalize, and indigenize cultural materials ranging from the abstract to the didactic, for reasons determined largely by them. The expanded and improved range of available resources and options has facilitated more cultural freedom overall, established new cultural precedents, and encouraged greater acceptance of diverse lifestyles. Some cultural choices that are made in the relatively freewheeling spaces of modernity and postmodernity are extremely serious, even life-changing. Other cultural decisions, however, have more to do with taste or style than necessity. British historian Eric Hobsbawm nicely describes the difference. He says that relative to the difficult cultural choices faced by many others around the world, middle-class Westerners have less demanding decisions to make. When choosing what food to include in their meals now, for example, comfortable Westerners "only need to decide whether they want a sandwich with French bread or *focaccia*, with cooked or smoked ham, and with fresh or dried tomatoes" (Hobsbawm 2000: 85–6).

Individualism

Individualism as it materializes in the hyper-commercialized context of middle-class lifestyles sometimes reaches the point of absurdity, unconscionable luxury, or dangerous selfishness. Instant personal gratification and self-fulfillment through consumer activity is especially characteristic of contemporary American culture. The range of personal cultural options is extraordinary. From beds that feature compartmentalized firmness and individually controlled temperature zones to "personalized watercraft" (noisy jet skis), personalized ring tones for mobile phones and toolbars for personal computers, individual viewing screens on the back of airplane seats, "myspace.com," the "Army of One," "My MTV," the iPod, and "Windows ME," in many ways the United States has become above all else an over-amped, over-hyped, over-stimulated world of "It's all about me" and "I want it all now!" The link between cultural individualism and capitalist economics that makes all this happen was succinctly captured in a line from the script of a US television commercial sponsored by the American investment firm, Brown and Company: "I believe in the market. I believe in me."

In many ways the always-on interface between cultural individualism and personal communications technology – especially the mobile phone, MP3 player, and wide availability of wi-fi hot-spots – exacerbates the tendencies toward self-centeredness. Cut loose from the traditional constraints of time and space, the individual person is able to self-decontextualize and communicate at will. The power of the individual as a sociocultural agent has become so extreme that an entirely new business-technology model, founded on the principles of emerging "individual human communication behavior," the "I-centric Communication System," has been formed (Arbanowski 2003).

Thomas Friedman argues that since the fall of the Berlin Wall the marriage of high technology with economic globalization has largely erased geographic boundaries in the production of many goods and services, creating lucrative opportunities for new corporate players, especially companies located in India and the Far East. The world, in Friedman's familiar phrase, has become "flat" (Friedman 2005). But, as Friedman and others have also observed, it isn't just nations and companies that take advantage of the flattening. Individuals, too, have unprecedented opportunities for influencing the world as "super empowered individuals" (Friedman 2002). Winners come from all directions. Personal empowerment of individuals is taking place at every level from the most global and public (Osama bin Laden, for example), to the most local and private (the everyday life of ordinary people everywhere). Information and communications technology make it all possible.

Without question, individuals have more cultural freedom and opportunities than ever before. But that freedom also demands a social price. People rely upon and become identified with their roles as individual consumers of material and symbolic goods and services: the fascination with buying logos rather than sustainable goods is a prime example. The social consequences of this mindset can be harmful. As the late Herbert Schiller speculated in his last book: "If present trends continue, all human interactions will be on a pay-for basis. This denies the social nature of human existence and elevates self and selfishness as the primary motivators of people. In such an order, common or national endeavors have little chance of acceptance, and agreeable human associations disappear" (Schiller 2000: 197).

As the mass media, information technology industries, and culture industries assume ever-greater presence and significance in everyday life, trends toward increased individualism, autonomy, freedom, and mobility become more acute. Proliferating cable and satellite TV channels, satellite radio, video-on-demand services, internet sales, micro-market segmentation, and niche media advertising – including addressable advertising techniques that target individual homes, rooms in homes, screen names, and cell phone numbers – all reinforce and intensify individualism. These realities are not simply imposed on people. Individuals set their cultural preferences and carefully choose their experiences.

Individualized reception of news and entertainment from contemporary multi-channel media leaves people "utterly alone," according to Robert Putnam, relieving them of the necessity to coordinate the timing or meaning of their cultural experiences with others. Putnam uses the analogy of "parallel play" in child development to show the potential dangers of individualization. It's normal for young children to play in a sandbox, Putnam explains, with each child focused on his or her own toy or territory, completely ignoring the other children. Healthy children eventually outgrow parallel play. Putnam argues that immersion in television (not to mention GameBoys, PlayStations, personal computers, MP3 players, Walkmans, and mobile phones) leaves adults at an "arrested stage of development, rarely moving beyond parallel attentiveness" (Putnam 2000: 244). Adult parallel play increases as media content becomes more abundant and diverse, appealing to individuals according to their own linguistic and cultural frameworks and biases, a development he believes undermines the quality of civil society (Putnam 2000: 216, 217).

Mobile media help create and reinforce the tendency toward increased individualization in modern societies. The mobile phone facilitates "always on" connectivity while simultaneously separating the user from fixed physical locations and time frames. Precisely because mobile phone users send and receive voice and text messages from unfixed locations at unfixed times, the technology fundamentally changes how space and time are perceived and gives users near limitless room for creative applications. The dynamic that functions at the center of the complexity – a seemingly infinite number of personal, social, and cultural uses of the technology – is propelled by the potent combination of the mobile person and the mobile phone. The lifting out of the person from the physical environment temporarily "de-spatializes" the user from local entanglements while facilitating other interpersonal involvements through "tele-socializing" (Kopomaa 2000: 116). Individual persons decontextualize and recontextualize themselves as they apply the practical force of their mobile phones to create desired outcomes. Spontaneity and surprise are valued. The mobile phone fits perfectly into lifestyles where "all there is to do is 'see what happens'" (Augé 1995: 3).

Despite the negative consequences of individualism, the individual person should not be considered as simply a product of Culture or just a follower of traditions or trends. The expansive transformation and mediation of time and space underway today, changes in the most common routines of everyday life, improvement in modes of transportation, arrival of the mobile phone, and the unprecedented availability of symbolic forms and cultural resources brought on by modernization and globalization all significantly sharpen and accelerate the potential for individuals to act independently and creatively. Of course their actions never materialize under conditions of free will or complete range of motion. The rise of individualism itself can be understood in part as a structured (but not determining) process; each person is slotted by society's institutions into roles and responsibilities that carry heavy demands which individuals themselves increasingly face alone (Beck and Beck-Gernsheim 2002).

Does greater cultural autonomy imprison or liberate individual persons and societies? Some observers fear that the demands placed on individuals in contemporary Western societies, and more frequently throughout the world, have become overwhelming and detrimental. In the Western-style "individualized, privatized version of modernity the burden of pattern weaving and the responsibility for failure falls primarily on the individual's shoulders" (Bauman 2000: 8). Modern Western subjects in liberal democratic societies are "expected to use, individually, their own wits, resources, and industry to lift themselves to a more satisfactory condition and leave behind whatever aspect of their present condition they may resent" (ibid.: 135). Bauman finds this expectation of self-reliance, especially in today's uncertain and threatening world, to be morally unacceptable and impractical. Vulnerability of individual persons to the structures that surround them has long been a primary concern of leftist politicians, labor unions, civil rights advocates, and some sociologists. Indeed, sociology's "credo states over and over again that the individual is the illusion of individuals who are denied insight into the social conditions and conditionality of their lives" (Beck and Beck-Gernsheim 2002: 15).

Zygmunt Bauman's gloomy contention that people are fundamentally ill-equipped to assume major personal responsibility for the challenges that face them in modern life, or that they shouldn't have to do so in the first place, seems oddly out of place today. The individual now is "making a surprising return" in social theory and in practice, "not simply as consumer or audience member, but as an active creator of his or her own life" (Sreberny 2002: 294). Most contemporary observers certainly would agree, however, that the increasingly individualized ways of being in the world brought about by modern global standards of living and technological change continue to pose great risks and heavy challenges (Chaney 2002: 23, 140). In any encounter with twenty-first century modernity, people must display "initiative, flexibility, and tolerance of frustration" in the sociocultural "evolution that has been unleashed by the ongoing individualization" that is clearly on the upswing (Beck and Beck-Gernsheim 2002: 4, 31).

"A life of one's own"

In two key writings, Ulrich Beck has described the contours of what he considers to be the primary characteristics and consequences of individualization. Both push and pull aspects of individualization appear in the formulations (Beck 2000; Beck and Beck-Gernsheim 2002). The main features of Beck's argument are summarized in Figure 4.2.

The phrase, "creating a life of one's own," captures the essence of the trend toward greater individualization. Intensive individualization is encouraged by Western modernity and the institutional structures it has attempted to put in place on a global scale. Western societies routinely sort citizens into singular social categories in economic and civil terms (chief executive officer, head of household, team captain, valedictorian, group leader, person

- Individualism makes life in a differentiated society coherent and meaningful.
- Laws and policies make individuals, not groups, the recipients of benefits.
- Individualism is not a standard concept; it depends on institutional architecture and resources.
- Life is condemned to activity with risks, possible failures, individual blame.
- Life is nomadic, elusive, mediated, transnational, global, networked.
- "Self-thematization" of personal biographies takes place.
- Local identities strengthen as a consequence of globalization.
- Cultural and personal hybridization is pervasive.
- Life is experimental.
- Life is reflexive: active self-management is necessary for stability and progress.
- The individual is positively valued.
- Life is "radically non-identical."
- Individuals are more flexible and adaptable to change than social institutions.
- "Altruistic individualism" develops as part of the phenomenon.

Figure 4.2 Creating a life of one's own (summarized from Beck 2000)

responsible, etc.) in a process Talcott Parsons labeled "institutional-ized individualism" (Parsons 1978: 321). Such structured distribution of behavior and identity does not determine the consequences of the sorting, however, nor does it come close to explaining the whole of individualization. Personal expression and creativity are at work. These human properties are not simply derived from or determined by social structure. Individualization develops actively and upwardly from personal engagements with cultural forms and from the symbolic work of identity formation that often conflicts with dominant institutional roles and expectations (Willis 2000).

New Cultural Horizons

Just as the dominant values of Culture never fully determine the consciousness of the individual, individual agency does not function with any complete "autonomy of spirit" either (Eagleton 2000: 4). The personal interests and activities of the sociocultural individual do not develop independent of, nor are they necessarily positioned against, the interests and activities of the sociocultural collectivities in which the individual is located. Individual persons engage the world with specific motivations and interests but they continue to function within, and often reinforce and support, the ideologies and customary ways of living cultivated by their Cultures. People need individual *and* collective cultural experience. The push and pull of culture therefore refers to the undetermined, yet structured and inter-articulating spectrum of social and cultural activities in which individuals (who never act completely alone) and collectivities (which themselves subdivide into multiple social groups) participate with varying degrees of awareness, motivation, and consent.

Culture frames, limits, and empowers all at the same time. Any theoretical formulation that positions structure against agency in an all-embracing way is untenable on sociological and cultural grounds in any historical context but is completely unreasonable in today's effusive and undetermined information and communication environment. The deeply resonating synergy between structure and agency has become more dynamic than ever now that structural constraints in most contemporary societies have been loosening up. At the same time ordinary people have become more and more culturally active and independent. The "push and the pull of culture," therefore, does not refer to a bipolar categorical *system* of cultural direction or influence. The two dimensions do not function independently in any case; they are deeply embedded in each other. We often pull that which is made known to us through push, for example.

It's more productive to think of the push and pull of culture as an ongoing, interactive, undetermined, mutually constitutive *process* of human interaction. Even from a psychological point of view, it couldn't be any other way. Push and pull tendencies do not become manifest in individual human consciousness as cognitive opposites and the discomforts people may experience moving between them need not be considered counterproductive or harmful. To the contrary, a robust array of collective affiliations and more individualized identities contribute to healthy cognitive balance and stability. The complexity and hybridity that routinely appear in the material and symbolic world of cultural representation also exist in the nuanced templates of individual human cognition and in routine patterns of situated social interaction.

The variety of cultural transformations now underway promise unprecedented fulfillment of the human potential in many ways, yet individual accomplishment and satisfaction alone cannot provide an adequate moral or pragmatic base in the long run for cultivation of a healthy and well-functioning society or, for that matter, for the development of healthy, well-functioning individuals. The same communications technologies that connect individuals and promote their personal and shared interests also contribute to the decline of social responsibility in key respects. One need only think of the loud-talking mobile phone user stumbling and bumbling through a crowded public area or negotiating a turn in a vehicle without bothering to extend the courtesy of signaling. As we develop new ways to connect and communicate, we also create new ways to ignore and inconvenience each other. Many common contemporary cultural involvements appear "abstract and cold-blooded" and lack the traditional "degree of emotional involvement we have with the family, the nation, or the little brown church in the wildwood [not to mention the little mosque or synagogue down the street]" (Boulding 1969: 348).

Even the generally well-intentioned, popular celebration of cultural diversity and the creation of government policies to support multiculturalism – acting together with the vicissitudes of market segmentation and media saturation – can disrupt national solidarity and distract citizens from solving the social problems they face in common (Gitlin 1996). Modernity and globalization fuel a double withdrawal: individual persons frequently become more isolated in key respects from their local micro-social environments while they also become more distant from their dominant cultural frameworks. To build viable communities and a global civil society amidst the push and pull of culture, diverse individuals will have to dedicate themselves to "a new balance between individual and collective responsibilities" (Giddens 1998: 37). That commitment will be realized, however, only when people everywhere believe they have a meaningful stake in its development and consequences, and give the same consideration to others.

Notes

1. Again, I will follow Terry Eagleton's (2000) useful stylistic device of capitalizing Culture when referring to the concept in the familiar, macro sense of dominant, traditional, or national culture.

2. Nationalist cultural sentiments arise in less dramatic situations too. Privatization of the public cultural sphere – replacing public television stations with commercial enterprises in Latin America, for example, or turning over the national railway and underground system to private interests in England – unsettle populations who come to view national institutions such as these as cultural treasures. Selling off land, buildings, and businesses to foreign buyers and elimination of agricultural or industrial subsidies can likewise create great cultural unease. Immigration policies and practices provoke political and cultural unrest, especially when immigrant cultures differ sharply in values and appearances from the host group (Morley 2000).

    National flags appear in abundance on holidays and during international competitions such as the Olympics or the World Cup. In England during World Cup competitions, the St. George's Flag – associated historically with the political far right – is displayed by many as a way of claiming cultural territory, not just in support of the English side in global football matches, but as a statement about English cultural sovereignty.

3. Cultural assumptions are questioned most strongly when taken-for-granted, everyday behavior is disrupted. For example, the assassination of Foreign Minister Anna Lindh in Sweden in 2003, like the killing of Prime Minister Olaf Palme 17 years earlier, caused Swedes to question the order and security of their national culture. Lindh and Palme traveled Swedish streets without bodyguards. It came as a shock to many Swedes that Lindh had apparently been killed by a "Swedish-looking man," according to media reports, much as the chief suspect in Palme's death was also Swedish. In Palme's case, the Swedish suspect was arrested only after several Turkish immigrants, considered by many much more likely to be the assailants, had been cleared of charges.

Chapter 5

Globalized Islam

*In the course of the twentieth century it became abundantly clear in the
Middle East and indeed all over the lands of Islam that things had indeed
gone badly wrong. Compared with its millennial rival, Christendom, the
world of Islam had become poor, weak, and ignorant. In the course of the
nineteenth and twentieth centuries, the primacy and therefore the dominance
of the West was clear for all to see, invading the Muslim in every aspect
of his public and − more painfully − even his private life.*
B. Lewis, *What Went Wrong?*, p. 151

*People turn on their TVs, everybody has satellites, computers. The world
sees what's going on. And there is a young Arab population that is very
frustrated if their governments don't lean out toward them and give them
opportunities for a better life.*
King Abdullah II of Jordan on *Hardball*, MSNBC,
December 10, 2004

Largely because of the reach of global media and information
technology, the more developed and the less developed countries
and cultures of the world now all live in the same neighborhood,
but it certainly is no global village. It's more like Rio de Janeiro,
Brazil, where poor people peer down on guarded luxury apartments from their shacks in the hillside *favelas* directly behind. Or
Riyadh, Saudi Arabia, where the fast-moving luxury cars of oil-
rich sheiks kick up dust in the faces of poor country men and
women who crowd the busy streets.

Ideological conflict between Islamic and Western cultures
remained quite dormant until recent decades. The relative isolation
of the Muslim world had kept the population largely unaware of

tremendous progress in science, technology, and the arts being made in other parts of the world during the twentieth century. Westerners, on the other hand, had long been taking advantage of opportunities in the East "even in the period when the West was inferior in every material and cultural respect" (Lewis 2002: 35). But technological advances in transportation and communication, particularly in the past 30 to 40 years, have greatly diminished the isolation of the Islamic world. The internet, satellite television, the flow of international popular culture, tourism, trade, and business and student travel have made foreign ideological and cultural systems much more visible to Muslims in the Middle East and Asia than ever before. At the same time the Muslim and Arab nations and cultures have become more visible and relevant to the rest of the world.

Adaptation to cultural nuance and change is always difficult, particularly for people whose dominant worldview emerges from an ideological base made up of uncompromising religious conviction that is reinforced by broad cultural values, romanticized regional histories, pervasive religious rituals and everyday practices, and stringent hierarchies of authority and social power. The presence of American, British, and other Western nations' military forces in the region, and the bellicose actions of Israel in Lebanon and the Palestinian territories, have only sharpened the differences and deepened the animosities. The combination of historical factors is inflammatory:

- Jews occupy Palestinian territory; Hindus occupy Kashmir; Russians have taken over Chechnya.
- Americans and Britons invaded Iraq twice and took over the country.
- The United States tacitly supported Israel's destruction of civilian areas in Lebanon.
- America and the UK maintain a long-term military presence in Saudi Arabia, Kuwait, Egypt, Turkey, Qatar, and Afghanistan.
- Western cultural flows spread over Arab/Islamic territory much more than the reverse; the United States exports more media content than any other nation on earth.
- Arabic satellite television outlets routinely transmit inflammatory images from Palestine, Lebanon, Iraq, Afghanistan, Iran, Syria, and Pakistan.

One response to these developments has been motivated by interpretations of the Koran. These interpretations assert that the "infidel's" military, political, economic, and cultural presence in the Middle East violates the religious sanctity of geographic territory that Muslims believe divinely belongs to them. The very existence of Israel, of course, represents the most egregious violation, and hatred of Jews and the Jewish state is "overwhelming" in the region (Pew Global Attitiudes Project 2006). Cultural loyalties to religion, ethnicity, and tribe within the Muslim world inspire the believers to rise up to expel the foreign presence. This is the territorial or proprietary argument made by those who think that a religious and cultural invasion of sacred land has taken place.

The Muslim world prides itself on its long and distinguished history, its cultural traditions, and especially its religious identities. But today modernization, Westernization, and globalization have made it more and more difficult for Islamic believers – particularly those deeply committed to the prevalent idea that Islam is a superior religious culture – to rationalize the enormous, increasingly visible gap between themselves and the modern world. Understanding that a widespread feeling of moral superiority exists among Muslims is key. A profound sense of moral and religious supremacy (*al-taghallub*) brought about by divine revelation is a hallmark of the religion – "if this point is missed, Western observers will fail to grasp how Muslims feel about the current world order" (Tibi 2002: 57, 61).

Although all monotheistic religions claim ultimate moral authority, Islam is particularly strident in its declaration of superiority. The Koran plainly and repeatedly states that Islam is "the religion of truth" which "prevails" and is made to be "superior over all other religions" (Suras 9:33, 61:9, 48:28). This belief in religious dominance also derives from the chronological history and geographical proximity of Judaism, Christianity, and Islam. Islam is considered superior by many of its adherents because it is the most recent of the major monotheistic religions, all of which developed in the same part of the world: "The Christians claimed that they had fulfilled the Jewish law and therefore supplanted it with a new and final revelation. The Muslims in turn claimed that they had built on the wisdom they had inherited from Jews and Christians with a new and truly final form of commitment to

Allah" (Wallerstein 2003: 102). That mentality was on display in a WTO meeting in Davos, for instance, when the Saudi Arabian ambassador to the United Kingdom answered a question about why his country doesn't allow churches. The ambassador said that churches and temples are unnecessary in Saudi Arabia: "Christians and Jews ought to be content to worship in mosques because Islam accepts both Jesus Christ and Moses as prophets" (The Davos Report 2004: 7).

To dedicate one's life to God in an extreme way encourages the Muslim to feel morally superior. Loud public calls to prayer that begin every day before dawn, the prone-position prayer rituals five times per day, repeated readings of the Koran (often in a language that is not understood by the reader), required pilgrimages, numerous holy days, fasting, highly restrictive dress codes, and the incessant mention of Allah in routine everyday conversation persistently reinforce the unassailable importance of Islamic ideology and identity for its believers. But now, science, technology, secularization, openness, diversity, and democracy – the foundations of modernity and globalization – threaten Islamic religious authority and cultural values. Pervasive, powerful, and dynamic Western culture has collided with premodern cultural conditions and religious certainty in ways that have shaken the cultural confidence of Muslims everywhere: "much of what traditional societies hold as 'given,' as inscribed in nature and therefore immutable, has been revealed to be ephemeral and alterable" (Almond, Appleby, and Sivan 2003: 229).

Religious fundamentalism emanating from the Middle East combines with ethnic nationalism and longstanding tribal identities and loyalties in the face of the encroaching modernity to create what Bassam Tibi (2002) calls "ethno-fundamentalism." Such sanctioned intolerance can easily lead to ethnic violence and revenge. As Irshad Manji puts it: "Like seventh century Bedouins, who anticipated a vendetta against them at every turn, desert-inspired Islamists immediately suspect, even hate, the 'other.' This means Jews. It means Westerners. It means women" (Manji 2003: 139). All signs point in the same direction. Secular culture – especially its perceived degenerate consumerist, materialist, and sexual dimensions – is taking over the world and threatens Arab and Islamic territory and beliefs.

The pressing dynamics of globalization come into play in a very competitive way: "the more [the world] becomes diffused, the more it produces a backlash by people who feel overwhelmed by it, homogenized by it, or unable to keep pace with its demands" (Friedman 2002: 4). The apocalyptic tone of much religious preaching and the growing terrorist violence are primary compensations made by the "losers" in the global cultural comparisons (Landes 1999: 492). The Muslim Brotherhood movement, originating in Saudi Arabia in the early twentieth century and especially active in Egypt today, is a particularly strenuous attempt to promote religious and cultural unity across geopolitical boundaries. The movement was inspired by a verse in the Koran, which says, "The believers are truly a single brotherhood, so establish reconciliation between your brothers; and fear Allah" (Sura 49:10). Some of the rhetoric flowing first from Egypt – including a claim that the Holocaust was myth and that Israel supported the 9/11 attack – also emanates today from Iran, Syria, and elsewhere. Global communication helps facilitate the Muslim Brotherhood's sense of common purpose: ". . . what brings Arabs together is a notion of joint destiny. As with the human nervous system, a single pinprick can be felt throughout the rest of the body" (El-Nawawy and Iskander 2002: 20).

The Islamic Cultural Body

Go out any evening in Jeddah (Saudi Arabia) and you can see . . . young men all over, in malls or cruising in cars, ogling veiled women or surfing the internet in search of some cyber-contact with females.
                                    T. Friedman, *Longitudes and Attitudes*, p. 356

The body may be the most important site of cultural struggle. It is, literally, our "self." As the late Lebanese anthropologist Fuad Khuri (2001) made clear in *The Body in Islamic Culture*, the physical human body – as it is interpreted through generalized, heterosexual masculine experience – plays a crucial role in the guiding philosophies of Islamic and Arab societies. A tremendous difference in perspective and experience exists between Muslim cultures and Western cultures concerning the body. This glaring discrepancy has yet to be sufficiently analyzed as a primary cause of the cultural discord between Middle Eastern and Western cultures. The differences become manifest in even the most basic social and sexual attitudes and practices. Today, under the constant gaze of media globalization, these contrasting cultural values and practices have become much more visible than before.

The paragraphs that follow describe some of those values and practices. As is the case throughout this book, support for the observations and analyses that I make draw from a range of sources including the Koran, and from a variety of scholarly authorities, many of them Muslims. The examples and comments that follow do not in their totality depict any particular Islamic person, family, sect, or nation. I refer to conditions that exist in various parts of the Muslim Middle East in order to illustrate main tendencies within Islamic ideology and culture. The basic values and cultural practices that make up Muslim nations are remarkably consistent from place to place (Inglehart and Baker 2000; Inglehart and Norris 2003; World Values Survey 2006). Cultural patterns are important analytical tools. As the following composite view demonstrates, the overall attitude taken toward the body in the Islamic world, especially toward the female body, reflects a way of thinking that is wholly out of step with global modernity. Clearly, the key issue is gender relations. But what's being considered is not solely a matter of sexual discrimination; the cultural values described here have greatly influenced all aspects of human development in Muslim societies.

In the Koran women are considered – along with gold, silver, branded horses, herds of domesticated animals, cultivated land, and sons – to be the rightful possessions of men (Khuri 2001: 40; Sura 3:14). Women are to be enjoyed by men. Muhammad married one of his twelve wives, Aisha, when she was six (Muhammad was 50 at the time), consummating sexual relations with her when she was nine years old. Because there is a biological limit to the number of children a woman can bear, but almost unlimited possibilities for men, "female exploitation begins here" (Dawkins 1989: 142). Polygamy and institutionalized pedophilia are hallmarks of historical Islamic sexuality and persist discursively and often in social practice today. Osama bin Laden is one of 55 children born to one of the 22 wives that were taken by his father

Muhammad, for example. But intractable versions of the forbidden fruit principle are also in full effect when it comes to sexual relations for Muslims. The Koran identifies women as a source of temptation, and one common interpretation provides men justification to control them physically – even "banish to the couch and beat" them if they become too "rebellious" (Sura: 4:34). Women "are humiliated from birth . . . their very existence is a disaster, their body a sin" (Landes 1999: 413).

The mere presence of women in public unaccompanied by men is problematic and sometimes forbidden. They often become subject to intense harassment outside the home. For instance, when some young men driving cars in Saudi Arabia spot a woman passenger in another car (women are not allowed to drive there), they sporadically chase the vehicle, pull up alongside, and hurl comments at her in what is recognized culturally as a courting ritual (Yamani 2000: 110). The Saudi government ruled in 2004 that women may not run for political office or vote in national elections. They need their husband's permission to study, travel, or work. They can't unveil for photographic identification, appear on television, mix with men in public, or leave home without cloaking themselves in abayas.

Gender discrimination in the Arab Muslim world stems from a culturally conditioned fear of the human body and shame associated with bodily functions. Fear and shame of the body, of course, is not peculiar to Islam. Like the holy books of the other doctrinal religions, the Koran was written by men for men. It repeatedly and clearly emphasizes that the divine necessity for (male) bodily and spiritual purity supersedes whatever pleasures of the flesh women can provide. The male body should not be contaminated by outside or evil influences. In Islam the "human body is a source of shame that must be concealed and guarded" so that "intercourse or even touching women, like sickness and travel, generates a polluted state to be purified" (Khuri 2001: 38, 41).

All bodily fluids, especially semen and vaginal secretions, are considered to be so inherently unclean that extensive purification rituals are required after sexual contact, particularly if (male) orgasm has been reached (temptation–orgasm–cleansing). The washing custom required in this and other situations borders on obsessive–compulsive behavior. Yet body rituals are connected to basic tenets of Islamic faith and to the full range of standard religious practices. They are not to be questioned. As Irshad Manji points out, "the entire exercise of washing prescribed parts of the body, reciting specific verses, and prostrating at a non-negotiable angle, all at assigned times of the day, can degenerate into mindless submission – and habitual submissiveness" (Manji 2003: 18). The prayer ritual demands extreme body conformity – total subjugation and concentration by the individual and compulsive group behavior by the collectivity – "prayer packs" which grow into "crowds" on Fridays (Canetti 1984: 142).

Gender segregation related to worship is fundamental. Men and women pray separately.[1] Menstruating women can't touch the Koran or enter the mosque. Hundreds of thousands of boys in the madrassa schools of Pakistan and elsewhere today are being prepared for life completely isolated from females. The Taliban in Afghanistan greatly restricted women's movement in public because the Ministry of Vice and Virtue feared that just the sound of female voices or the sound of women's shoes on the street provokes impure thoughts. The Taliban banned kite flying, "because someone climbing a tree to remove a kite might end up watching, even inadvertently, an unveiled woman in an adjacent house or garden" (Roy 2004: 260). Homosexuality, of course, is subject to extraordinary punishment. People with AIDS are not tolerated and often commit suicide because "premarital sex, adultery, homosexuality, and intravenous drug use are not supposed to happen in the Muslim world" (Kelley and Eberstadt 2005: 45).

Sexual pleasure for women does not receive attention in Islamic scripture, except as a shameful feeling to be punished. The female Islamic body must be hidden away. Islamic women routinely cover themselves from head to toe, even in the home in certain contexts, and are routinely accompanied in public by male family members to shield against the male gaze. Female-requested divorce and abortion are not permitted. Male doctors cannot perform routine medical examinations and procedures on females. Thousands of women are victimized by "honor killings" every year in Islamic countries when relatives believe they have brought shame to the family or community (sometimes for the slightest indiscretion having to do with the body; National Geographic News 2002).

Female genital mutilation – an exceedingly dangerous practice whose sole purpose is to eliminate women's sexual pleasure and insure loyalty to the husband – is still practiced in many Islamic countries (and imported to Europe, the United States, and elsewhere). Muslim women have been discriminated against for such a long time that their degraded condition today seems natural and even preferable to many Muslims, including women, although many if not most of them would not explain it that way, often pointing to Muhammad's first wife, Khadija, as a strong, even dominating influence on the prophet.

An Islamic court in Nigeria had to decide in 2003 if a Muslim woman should be stoned to death for having sex outside marriage. The gang rape in Pakistan in 2002 of a young Muslim woman was meted out as punishment for her younger brother's alleged sexual relations with a woman outside marriage. A Kurdish Muslim girl was killed by her father in England for dating a Christian Lebanese boy – 10 years after the family had settled in the UK. Even the ardent defender of Islam, Edward Said, recognized that such religiously sanctioned and justified behavior makes the Muslim religion "seem" backward and cruel (Said 1997: xv). Fortunately, all these cases received considerable international media attention. The Nigerian woman was exonerated, the Pakistani woman has become a symbol of women's rights in the Muslim world and an inspiring social activist, and the case of the Kurdish girl in England exposed the widespread but little discussed problem of honor killings in Europe's Islamic diasporas.

Given such extraordinary sexual repression, it's no wonder that female tourists in Islamic countries are warned (and sometimes required by law) not to show any skin in public. It might help us understand why some of the 9/11 terrorists spent nights at a lap-dance club in Florida before heading north on their religious mission, or why every single one of the Saudi operatives on 9/11 was unmarried and had no "normal" sexual interaction with women (Friedman 2002: 337). In an impinging world of people and images that is dominated by the liberal cultural codes of the West, many Muslim men – denied the conventional, enjoyable, human, non-sexual experience of viewing the female body – are simply unprepared to handle the sight of a woman who does not follow the rule of absolute physical "modesty." Even photographs of models in Western fashion magazines sold on the streets in the Middle East "present an almost irresistible temptation to men" (Appiah 2006: 83). And, as adults, most Muslim women will never experience the water of the sea, the rays of the sun, or a summer breeze directly on their skin. The primary assumptions that drive this physical repression are that males cannot control their sexual impulses and that women have no independent control over their bodies.

The sexual inexperience and frustration of so many young Muslim men contributes something unique to Islamic versions of the global "crisis of masculinity" (Willis 2000), most notably for working-class males. Traditional male identities are under attack from several directions. The information and knowledge-based economies of late modernity have changed the nature of work for men so that men's traditional roles, sense of gender superiority, and bodily forms of expression have been challenged by the global transformation from heavy to light industry, from machinery and assembly lines to computers and office suites. The contrast in the Middle East is especially stark because national economies in the region – except for the extraction of oil deposits – have barely become industrialized. In every evolutionary stage from tribal, agricultural, or industrial economies, the male physical body has been problematized as a site of gender and cultural identity. The male response to the loss of cultural power can be violent. Cultural and religious rage, domestic violence, and, in the extreme case, terrorist acts (especially the Islamist's trademark of slitting the victim's throat) are utterly masculine forms of expression that serve as outlets for the pent-up frustrations that males face in the increasingly uncontrollable cultural environments they inhabit.

Islamic beliefs and scripture are often used today to legitimize Arabic *machismo*. Tribal values and traditions interact with interpretations of the vague, contradictory, and unprovable content of the most polysemic and revered of all published texts – the Koran and the hadiths, the Torah, and the Bible. The flow of global popular culture creates even more problems. Imagine how the purveyors of cultural tradition in Islamic countries respond to the trends in popular culture that circulate today.

The visible visual body

The revolt against modernity is a rebellion against cosmopolitanism and its urban culture and urbane entertainment.

B. Barber, *Jihad v. McWorld*, p. 211

The body is considered to be so threatening in Islam that throughout the centuries even the creation or display of images depicting humans (and animals) has been forbidden. Calligraphy was invented in the Middle East to avoid representing bodily shapes too literally. For Muslims, there should be no object of worship other than God himself. That includes Muhammad. The extreme reaction to the political cartoons published in Denmark brought global attention to how seriously Muslims object to symbolic representations of their prophet. The blowing up of the ancient stone Buddha in Afghanistan by the Taliban just before the American and British intervention was motivated by Islamic authorities' desire to eliminate competing religious iconography and to eradicate any spiritual human semblances rendered in art. Historically, religious repression of images has not been unique to fundamentalist Islam. Christianity and the "unique role of God" were challenged by the "cult of image" movement in Byzantine times, for instance, where "images, saints, and idols . . . were worshipped in their own right as autonomous gods" against the dictates of the Church (Cowen 1998: 194).

By contrast, global popular culture figures are not only highly visible today, they are exceedingly visual. They can be seen in sensual motion all over the world. The visible female form in motion arouses men because their sexual responsiveness is in large part visually based. Confident, independent-minded, fun-loving, attractive, physically comfortable, sexually adventuresome women that routinely appear in Western television, film, and popular music generate tremendous global appeal. Imagine how Muslims, especially men, respond to these images. To get an idea of how serious the cultural gap between Islam and the West really is, consider the following account. In *The Looming Tower*, a fascinating political and cultural analysis of Al-Qaeda, Lawrence Wright describes the experience of Sayyid Qutb, one of the founding fathers of today's Islamic fundamentalism, when he studied at an

American university in the 1940s. As he set foot on campus, Qutb was completely unnerved by the American girls' lack of self-consciousness about their bodies and their relaxed attitude toward sexuality. He wrote: "A girl looks at you, appearing as if she were an enchanting nymph or an escaped mermaid, but as she approaches, you sense only the screaming instinct inside her, and you can smell her burning body, not the scent of perfume but flesh, only flesh. Tasty flesh, truly, but flesh nonetheless" (Wright 2006: 12). The author writes that Qutb began writing diatribes against the West, including justifications for the killing of non-Muslims, shortly after his experience in the US, and reports that Mohamed Atta, who piloted one of the jets into the World Trade Center, had a similar pathological disgust for women. Ironically, as Sam Harris points out, "the most sexually repressive people in the world today – people who are stirred to a killing rage by reruns of *Baywatch* – are lured to martyrdom by a conception of paradise that resembles nothing so much as an al fresco bordello" (Harris 2005: 127).

Will cultural habits change in the increasingly globalized Islamic world? Certainly not in the short term. Cultural traditions everywhere perpetuate themselves as the "organizing medium of collective memory" (Giddens 1994: 64), so any cultural change will be slow. Although some young Muslims in the Middle East and other parts of the world have already managed to partly shed or sidestep the ultra-conservative trappings of traditional Islam, in many cases "the younger generations in Muslim societies have remained almost as traditional as their parents and grandparents, producing a continually-expanding cultural gap [compared with other young people around the world]" (Inglehart and Norris 2003: 68). Mai Yamani's report from Saudi Arabia concludes that Islam is the primary axis on which young people – including middle-class youth with regular access to the internet, satellite television, and global travel – construct their identities. She concludes that, "The vast majority of the new generation perceives Islam as the stable and unchallenged base of their identity and guide for everyday life" because it "allows for other competing allegiances [like family and nation] to be subsumed into the larger category" (Yamani 2000: 134, 13).

Gender equality, political democracy, and economic prosperity

How do these conditions affect the political and economic well-being and future of the Muslim world? Only a small percentage of countries populated by a Muslim majority are elected democracies, a fact which has led Samuel Huntington (1996) and others to argue that the primary cultural distinction to be made between Islamic countries and the West rests on differences between their political values and systems. According to this line of thought, relative tolerance and egalitarianism develop far more effectively in nation states that are governed by a stable political democracy.

Other scholars argue for a different causal ordering. They claim that it is a culture's degree of gender equality and sexual liberation – not its democratic politics – that "proves time and again to be the most reliable indicator of how strongly that society supports principles of tolerance and egalitarianism," which then leads to economic development (Inglehart and Norris 2003: 64). Huntington himself later agreed that the role of women and religion in society creates the sharpest divisions in the world today (The Davos Report 2004: 6). A comprehensive study of comparative gender equality in 58 nations found the five Nordic countries rank at the very top of the list, and four predominantly Muslim countries (Jordan, Pakistan, Turkey, and Egypt) appear at the very bottom (World Economic Forum 2005). Without question, the gender gap in Islamic cultures perpetuates cultural characteristics that stymie the development of democratic institutions and dampen economic vitality. Fortunately, mass media and the internet expose the unfairness and offer the possibility of reform. As Irshad Manji argues, "when intentional discrimination against women, religious minorities, and assorted 'others' is dragged into broad daylight . . . Muslims will inevitably be better prepared for the transition to democracy" (Manji 2003: 181). Shining a light on structural injustices like these creates "cultural transparency," an idea that will be discussed in the next chapter.

The principle of gender equality took a long time to evolve into social practice in the West. Of course, comprehensive gender equality has not been achieved anywhere. But the ideals of Western gender relations – including creation of political and cultural space for the discourses, politics, and activities of various feminisms – lie at the heart of Western modernity and have influenced cultures everywhere. Gender equality is one of the most visible "good ideas" of modern thought that globalization spreads widely – so widely, in fact, that even the residents of many Middle Eastern cities today feel the impact. Men must deal with the changes:

> In their new world they see . . . the disorienting effects of modernity; most unsettlingly, they see women, unveiled and in public places, taking buses, eating in cafés, and working alongside men. They come face to face with the contradictions of modern life, seeing the wealth of the new world but also the tradition and certainty of the old. (Zakaria 2003: 140)

That effect becomes even more extreme when those men and their families migrate to the West.

Islam in the West

> *My brother is a good bloke, fully Westernized.*
>> Comment by the brother of a Muslim man from Tipton,
>> England, captured in an Al-Qaeda stronghold and taken to
>> Guantanamo Bay prison. As he defended his brother on
>> British television, he held up a Rockport USA tee shirt as
>> proof that his brother could not be a terrorist.

Despite a general belief held by many Muslims that they cannot live a good life in the land of infidels, and notwithstanding a long, grinding history of Islamic resistance to modernity and multiculturalism, some 12–20 million Muslims now inhabit nations of the European Union and about seven million live in the United States and Canada. The demand for low-wage physical labor in Europe, coupled with scant economic opportunities in their homelands and liberal Western policies granting political and religious asylum, have stimulated the enormous migrations. Many Muslim immigrants have adjusted successfully to life in the West. Those who have become European citizens are voting more than before, taking up initiatives to improve their conditions, and finally, in the wake of the London bombings and later terrorist arrests, a considerable number have also begun to denounce Islamist terrorism.

Other Muslim immigrants have not adjusted well and many have no intention to fit in. The challenge experienced by these deterritorialized immigrants living in the modern liberal environments of Western societies fuels a shared feeling of hopelessness and anger. The tendency to cling to old ways dominates. The *Guardian* newspaper in London – which is extremely sensitive to the needs and predicaments of immigrants, especially Muslims – reported in late 2004 that only about 40 percent of Muslims living in the United Kingdom say they should do more to integrate into mainstream British culture. More than 20 percent of them believe integration has gone too far already. Some 80 percent in the survey said they believe the war on terrorism is a war on Islam (*Guardian* 2004). Another large survey conducted by the *Guardian* (2005) right after the London bombing that year revealed that despite the tendency for respondents to provide acceptable answers to questions, a strong minority of Muslim voices in the UK (19 percent) would not condemn the bombings and about half of them said they were surprised the bombers were British. Questions about loyalty emerge from the other side of the ethnic divide, too. A Pew Global Attitudes survey conducted just before the 2005 London bombing showed that "Western publics believe that Muslims in their countries want to remain distinct from society," a state of affairs those citizens view negatively, although majorities in Great Britain, France, Canada, and Russia say overall that they have a "somewhat favorable or very favorable view of Muslims" (Pew Global Attitudes Project 2005).

All the main figures in the 9/11 attack on America had resided for considerable time in Europe and others have made pilgrimages from there to the Middle East to do their holy work. Omar Sheikh, the murderer of Danny Pearl, an American journalist working in Pakistan, may be the best known of these. The anger that possesses these young men develops in part from their personal contact with secular European modernity – officially tolerant and pluralistic, yet cold, isolating, and judging in practice. They have also seen first hand the objective socioeconomic conditions in which many Muslims live in Europe (high unemployment, low wages, linguistic, religious, social, and cultural segregation), and have learned the bitter truth of even more drastic comparative living conditions between Europe and the Middle East. These interacting factors have discouraged and radicalized some men who then became "easy pickings for militant preachers who knew how to direct their rage" (Friedman 2002: 164).

The liberal political and cultural environment of Europe with its guarantees of free speech and assembly has given even the most radical voices among the Islamic extremists living there much room to disseminate their fiery messages of piety and duty. Those emotionally arousing influences interact combustibly with the living conditions experienced by much of the Muslim population in Europe, strong cultural differences that persist between many of the immigrants and the rest of the population, intergenerational discord, a widespread identity crisis for young Muslim adults, and the sudden global attention given to Islam and Muslim extremism after 9/11. Today, uprooted Muslim populations – especially young people residing in Europe – actually "are more prone to assess what Islam means to them" than those who live in environments that embrace the religion's assumptions and everyday practices (Roy 2004: 105). As European "born again" Muslims living outside the traditional cultural confines imposed on their peers in South Asia, North Africa, and the Middle East, young people can create "decontextualized, neofundamentalist" religious-cultural-political spaces and ways of defining themselves (Roy 2004: 51, 258). This encourages Islamic youth living in Europe – often feeling marginalized and disrespected – to use their publicly per-ceived "otherness" as a resource to construct alternative, reactive cultural identities (ibid.: 45).

Because so many Muslim immigrants have not assimilated well into European societies – for reasons having to do not only with cultural attitudes held by immigrants, but also because of discrimi-nation meted out by many of their hosts – the existence of distinct and largely separate communities representing two different (and competing) civilizations may be creating a continent of divided "cleft societies" (Huntington 1996). Some attempts have been made by European governments to address this problem. Measures have been taken, for instance, to encourage greater assimilation through increased investment in social services for immigrants, education, and cultural recognition. But protectionist cultural movements and nationalist political candidates also abound throughout Europe. Rejection of the proposed European Union constitution by voters in France and Holland reflects growing unease with the idea of opening the doors to immigrants from Turkey. The Dutch were angered when Theo van Gogh, whose documentary film *Submission* revealed the abusive treatment of some Muslim women, was murdered by an Islamic man acting out of religious conviction. The French government's decision not to permit conspicuous religious symbols in public school was interpreted by some as a means to confront the sectarian influence of Muslim culture in France. Danes and other Europeans were surprised and discouraged by the response of Muslims there to the political cartoons depicting Muhammad.

There can be no downplaying of the important differences that exist between religious and secular philosophies of political governance and daily life. Here is an area where cultures *do* clash frequently. It begins with the very concept of the nation state, which is widely perceived within the Muslim world, especially in the Middle East, as an imperialist strategy imposed by the West to discredit, manipulate, and limit Islamic religion, culture, and law. As Bassam Tibi explains, compared to the political nation state, "[t]he political culture of Islam is more authentic in the eyes of the people in this region since it predates nationalism and the nation state and rests upon powerful religious tenets" (Tibi 2002: 117). The United Nations, in this scenario, is regarded as just another Western-dominated imperialist institution that compounds the problem. When votes are taken in the United Nations' General Assembly, the "Islamic bloc" typically votes in unity. No other major religion commands such conformity. That's because "in the Western world, the basic unit of human organization is the nation [which] is then divided in various ways, one of which is religion. Muslims, however, tend to see not a nation subdivided into religious groups but a religion subdivided into nations" (Lewis 2003: xx).

Those within Islam who envision a global Muslim civilization "posit a world in which the Muslim religion and the Islamic state are co-created and inseparable" (Barber 1995: 206), with far less room for secularism than in any other major world religion. The Islamic Republic of Iran most clearly symbolizes how Muslim religious authority can dominate the public sphere. Iraq's political parties are founded on warring factions of Islam. The new Iraqi constitution declares that, "no law may be legislated if it contradicts the fixed beliefs and rulings of Islam." Taliban fighters operate years after their supposed annihilation in Afghanistan. The judge in the apostasy case in Afghanistan deemed Abdul Rahman's conversion to Christianity "an attack on Islam," as calls for his execution rang out from the nation's mosques. Islamic law was adopted in the North-West Frontier Province of Pakistan in 2003, allowing tribal forces sympathetic to remaining Taliban elements to continue to "crush the evils of society" in the name of God. Islamic warriors have imposed Shariah law in Somalia and banned movies, music, and imported TV programs. Shariah law has been brought back to Indonesia's Aceh Province, the area that was so devastated by the tsunami in 2004, to allow public canings at mosques and the harassment of non-Muslim foreign aid workers. All these political developments represent what Michael Ignatieff calls the "battle between the civic and the ethnic nation" (1993: 248). They reveal "discernible patterns of religious militancy by which self-styled 'true believers' attempt to arrest the erosion of religious identity, fortify the borders of the religious community, and create viable alternatives to secular institutions and behaviors" (Almond, Appleby, and Sivan 2003: 17). A powerful challenge to such religious and cultural authority in the Middle East has arrived recently, however, as media globalization rapidly spreads its influence.

The Opinion, and the Other Opinion

What the printing press did for the Protestant reformation – relax the stranglehold on knowledge – indie TV channels can do for Islam.
I. Manji, *The Trouble with Islam Today*, p. 169

There is a new Arab street in the Middle East, built on Al-Jazeera and internet chat sites.
F. Zakaria, *The Future of Freedom*, p. 152

Beginning in 1996, a powerful new force emerged in the Middle East that has made an enormous impact on the culture and politics of the region. Originally transmitting emotionally evocative images of Israeli soldiers and tanks in the occupied areas of the West Bank, bodies of Palestinian victims killed in the endless bloody struggle in the "holy land," grieving Palestinians wailing in the streets, the destructive successes of Palestinian terrorist "martyrs," sympathetic interviews with leaders of Hezbollah and Hamas, and much more, the Arabic-language satellite television channel Al-Jazeera ("the island"), based in Qatar, began to draw huge audiences throughout the Middle East. The overall audience has swelled to more than 50 million viewers throughout the Arab world today and spawned the arrival of more than 100 other satellite channels in the region (Miles 2005). Even Al-Qaeda has started an internet-based television channel, The Global Islamic Media Front, in order to counter the democratizing influence of Al-Jazeera and other satellite channels.

The range of issues covered by Al-Jazeera as well as the competence and professionalism with which the network operates have grown tremendously. But it is Al-Jazeera's journalistic philosophy that matters most. The network's motto, "The Opinion, and the Other Opinion," signals an extremely important development in Middle East political culture. Any "other opinion" certainly has not always been welcome or even tolerated in Islamic countries where all institutions, including the media, have been subjected to strict religious or state control. Just the idea that divergent opinions have merit and should be given public exposure represents a huge step toward creating a modicum of political and cultural democracy in the Middle East.

Employing reporters and editors trained in the journalistic styles of the BBC and CNN, and developing programs that feature Western formats and production aesthetics, Al-Jazeera has "galvanized the world's 1.2 billion Muslims . . . with expert knowledge and understanding of Arab politics and audiences" and a fresh approach to news reporting (El-Nawawy and Iskandar 2002: 32). Although Al-Jazeera first gained fame by transmitting dramatic, sympathetic images and accounts of the Palestinians' struggle against Israel, and later became known as the preferred television outlet for the messages of Osama bin Laden, the network also quickly gained attention for its willingness to stir unprecedented debate and controversy. Operating relatively free from direct government and religious control, Al-Jazeera has respectfully interviewed top American and Israeli political figures, critically discussed the role of women, sexuality, and polygamy in Islamic countries, openly analyzed the economic backwardness of the region, debated the pros and cons of secularization and privatization of the Muslim world, exposed cases of abuse and torture by police, and directly criticized Arab leaders – topics never before discussed in depth or complexity by Arab media. By introducing a free-form talk show format that encourages audience participation, viewers are exposed not only to novel content, but to more complex and introspective ways to think about social and cultural issues. By expanding content and introducing more diverse and democratic presentational formats, Al-Jazeera and other media outlets in the region are cultivating productive new ways for Middle East publics to reflect on the political and cultural issues that concern them. The presence of French, German, English, Danish, and American channels also broadcasting in Arabic in the region add even more streams of fresh information to the media mix.

The global TV war

Al-Jazeera and the other Arabic-language networks have been able to compete effectively with the more well-known international networks in coverage of the Palestinian–Israeli and Hezbollah–Israeli conflicts, the Afghanistan War, and the Iraq War. With their cultural, linguistic, and political advantages, the Arab networks scooped the international media by being the first to broadcast Osama bin Laden video tapes (El-Nawawy and Iskandar 2002), and by transmitting exclusive live images of the visually spectacular bombing of Baghdad. Because CNN and other international outlets had been expelled from the country, the international news networks had to depend on the Middle Eastern networks for live video feeds from Iraq, over which they added their verbal descriptions and interpretations.

Despite claims by the Americans and British that "smart" bombs were hitting military targets with precision and that civilian deaths were minimal, the overall visual impression, especially in the first week of the war, was that much of Baghdad was in flames. While the destruction of human life was great, the actual number of Iraqis killed and wounded actually mattered less in terms of regional and world opinion than did the incalculable emotional impact of the images of violence and suffering that were telecast around the clock. The symbolic force of those images provoked great concern all over the world about American hegemony and military power and the willingness to use that power under the aggressive command of President George W. Bush.

Satellite TV coverage of the Iraq War extended and amplified other deep-seated visual impressions. It blended with images transmitted on state-run television stations in the Middle East in 1979 of Iran's Islamic revolution and the American hostage debacle. It meshed with the long and tortuous visual history of the Palestinians' struggle against Israel, with images of anti-American protestors in the streets of Pakistan and other Islamic countries, and with scenes of prisoners from the Afghanistan War apparently being humiliated at the American camp at Guantanamo Bay and later at Abu Ghurayb, among other incidents. These images accumulate to confirm a widespread perception in the Middle East that Americans and the West don't respect Arab and Islamic culture and religion in general (Newport 2002: 1, 3). The effect of these realities is further magnified by the emotional expressiveness of Arabic cultures, the extreme subjectivity inspired by immoderate religious beliefs (such as the majority of the Muslim population in the Middle East disbelieving Arabs were responsible for 9/11, or the idea that God himself was under attack by infidels), and a ready willingness to believe in conspiracy theories (El-Nawawy and Iskandar 2002: 60).

The ability of Al-Jazeera and television generally to stir passions and civil unrest has to do not only with specific images being transmitted or the cultural groups that are involved. The very nature of the visual medium – especially its insistent emphasis on sensational events and emotionally evocative close-up images – can create a dynamic, swept-away experience for viewers. A few hundred protestors on the street can appear on television to be a majority. The heart-rending shot of a badly burned or disfigured child can represent universal (or ethnic) pain and suffering. The most compelling of these kinds of images become sought-after media commodities that are shared among networks worldwide, where they are repeated and recycled like the hottest songs on a contemporary hits radio station or a megastar's video clips on MTV.

Al-Jazeera itself became a victim of the Middle East conflicts, and not just once. Maintaining the only authorized network bureau in Kabul during Taliban rule in Afghanistan, the Al-Jazeera network office there was hit by American aerial munitions during the retaliatory strikes in November 2001. The United States claimed the bombing of the network was an accident. But lightning apparently struck twice when the Al-Jazeera office in Baghdad, and the offices of the competing Arab network Abu Dhabi, were also hit by the United States military during the Iraq War, killing Al-Jazeera correspondent Tareq Ayyoub. The Americans called the strike "self-defense" and an unfortunate accident – a claim that has been strongly disputed with visual evidence supplied by documentary filmmaker Jehaine Noujaim in the story of Al-Jazeera – *Control Room* (2004). With the support of the Americans, the Iraqi interim government in 2004 temporarily closed down Al-Jazeera's Baghdad office, accusing the channel of inciting violence, hatred, and racial tensions. A report later that year in London's *Daily Mirror* claimed that President Bush threatened in a memo to Prime Minister Blair to bomb Al-Jazeera's headquarters in Qatar, a story that was denied by the White House or passed off as "humorous, not serious" (Maguire and Lines 2005).

Al-Jazeera's coverage of the Iraq War, including startling images of the American "shock and awe" bombing of Baghdad and other cities, served to greatly inflame anti–American feeling around the world, but it also showed detailed evidence of the excesses and abuses of Saddam Hussein's regime that were uncovered in the aftermath of the physical destruction. As the American forces closed in on Baghdad, Muhammad Saeed al-Sahhaf, Iraq's Information Minister in the Hussein government, said, "I blame Al-Jazeera for supporting the Americans." At the same time American Secretary of State Colin Powell was chastising the network for giving voice to Al-Qaeda by broadcasting "inflammatory remarks to stir up Muslims." Because both sides have felt the power of the network's influence, Arab and American officials have each tried to sway and silence Al-Jazeera. But in the globalized media environment of today, trying to prevent Al-Jazeera or any other network from airing incendiary content is "as pointless as trying to stop the tide," and in the case of the United States, such censorship also "runs counter to the value of openness that America wants to symbolize" (Nye 2004: 108).

The opinion, and the other opinion, are indeed being heard and seen in the Middle East and increasingly around the world. What Al-Jazeera has accomplished may not rival the degree of objectivity characteristic of news media operating in Western democracies (which, of course, are themselves influenced by commercial and political interests). But the network has opened up new spaces for public debate and discussion of issues and events in the rigid societies of the Middle East. Recent programs have included harsh criticism of Islamic history, principles, and practices. Boosted by privileged access to Iraq during the war that was denied to Western and other international networks, Al-Jazeera encouraged the daring, growth, and success of the other Arab-region satellite TV networks that were allowed to remain in Iraq. Now fixtures in the region, Al-Jazeera and the other Arab satellite television channels "have made it completely legitimate, even normal, to argue publicly about political and cultural issues" in the "new Arab public" (Lynch 2006a, 2006b).

The fast, flexible, and fluid nature of media globalization made the appearance and impact of Al-Jazeera and other independent-spirited satellite TV networks of the Middle East possible. Digital communications technology allows even small media outlets to cover events in the field and transmit their reports widely. Agreements have been struck with international networks including the BBC, CNN, MSNBC, NHK, and many other national networks to share video feeds with the Arab outlets, helping to launch Al-Jazeera and the others to global recognition and respect. Middle-class audiences in the Middle East, having tired of their didactic and dull state media, were ready for fresh sources of news and entertainment packaged in slick Western style, but presented in Arabic by Arabs. Al-Jazeera hosts websites in Arabic and English that function as multi-mediated, intertextual platforms for the dissemination of news and opinion, as well as sources of revenue. The entire programming schedule of Al-Jazeera is available in the United States as a feature of the "Arab Elite Pack" on Dish Network TV, and throughout Europe – where the market for Arabic programming is even greater – on various subscription television services. Al-Jazeera also introduced an English-language international channel in 2006, featuring respected commentators such as David Frost, Riz Khan, and David Foster, which became available immediately to an audience of more than 40 million households worldwide.

The New Imagined World of Islam

God has hit America, and He has destroyed its greatest buildings . . . and thanks be to God, America has been filled with fear from north to south and east to west.

Osama bin Laden on Al-Jazeera shortly after 9/11

Terrorism addresses political, economic, and cultural grievances by forcibly sending messages that wouldn't otherwise circulate efficiently in the global marketplace of ideas. It expresses cultural feelings through creation of sensational symbolic displays that are guaranteed to capture media interest because of their visual power and narrative allure. In the wake of 9/11, militant Islam was transformed into a highly visible cultural force that repelled many, puzzled some, and attracted others.

The symbolic consequences of Islam's proliferating global profile have been extraordinary. Two months after the 9/11 attack the Pew Research Center for the People and the Press (2001) reported that the image of Muslims in the United States had improved significantly in national public opinion from before the attack, rising from a 45 percent to a 59 percent favorability rating.[2] The Koran was selling in record numbers and much popular attention was given to Arabic music, dance, history, and culture. The personal image most associated with 9/11 – Osama bin Laden – became an unspeakable villain for some people but also a media celebrity with tremendous star power. As images of bin Laden were being circulated worldwide by Western law enforcement authorities as the world's most wanted criminal, vendors in Middle Eastern countries were making money hand over fist selling posters and tee shirts featuring bin Laden as an Arabic action hero and modern-day Robin Hood. He has surfaced as one of globalization's highly visible super-empowered individuals (Friedman 2002), achieving even greater global name recognition than the prophet Muhammad in whose name he claims to be fighting.

Islam was gaining considerable momentum as an influence on world culture and politics inside and outside the Middle East many years before the recent wave of terrorism. The Islamic resurgence that began in the late twentieth century has been propelled by a host of internal and external developments and influences. A substantial part of the increased global presence of Islam is demographic. Arab Muslim countries more than doubled their population toward the end of the last century and will double again by 2020 (UNDP 2002b: 35–8). The nature of everyday life for Muslims has changed in recent decades, largely because of the demographic shift. Massive population increases and urban migrations that took place throughout the Middle East toward the end of the twentieth century have "reconstituted" traditional rural society together with its conservative norms in the big cities. At the same time the Islamic "traditional social system is also gravely threatened by innovations such as education and modern employment, as they apply to both women and men" (Kurtz 2002: 53). These demographic and cultural developments interact with powerful influences brought on by domestic modernization and the impact of globalization. It is the ever-increasing "intensified communication and media consumption, and expanded interaction with Western and other cultures [that] undermines traditional village and clan ties and creates alienation and an identity crisis" (Huntington 1996: 116). Urbanization, social uprootedness, and increased levels of literacy, education, and access to communications technology have threatened Islamic religious tradition and authority to a degree never experienced before.

Instrumental modernity

A defining characteristic of the Islamists' attack on America and the West is "instrumental modernity" (Tibi 2002: 199) – the selective appropriation of global resources for ideological and cultural purposes. The technology necessary to produce paper – the medium used to print the Koran and thereby spread the influence of Islam centuries ago – was found in Asia. Today's religious warriors use computers and mobile phones much like Muslim leaders in the past commandeered handguns and artillery from the West (Lewis 2002: 13). In a well-known historical development, the Ayatollah Khomeni of Iran made audio cassettes from exile in Europe to stir the revolutionary fundamentalist movement in the late 1970s. Since then the technology arsenal has grown enormously. The 9/11 hijackers practiced on flight simulator devices, used credit cards to buy their tickets, booked their homicidal flights online, and operated hand-held navigational devices to get exact coordinates on the World Trade Center towers. Al-Qaeda terrorists have long used satellite telephones, internet sites, financial wire transactions, and encryption software to coordinate their activities worldwide.[3] Physical location has become less important for the nomadic Al-Qaeda's work: "With laptops and DVDs, in hide-outs and at neighborhood internet cafés, young code-writing jihadists have sought to replicate the training, communication, planning, and preaching facilities they lost in Afghanistan with countless new locations on the internet" (Coll and Glasser 2005). The London metro bombers used mobile phones to detonate their explosives, the same plan imagined by those who attempted a year later to blow up airliners leaving from Heathrow Airport. As intelligence techniques have improved, the Islamists have appropriated other Western inventions – disposable cellular phones and one-time email accounts among them – to avoid being traced. Even the most peace-loving Muslims use the internet to share information globally about one of the most important pieces of information the culture embraces – the precise location of the crescent moon signaling the beginning of Ramadan.

The immigration of Muslims from their countries of origin to the West combines with the unique influence of modern communications, especially the internet, to create a new kind of Islam. One result of these historical conditions is the attempt to found a "virtual ummah," in the words of Olivier Roy (2004: 183) – a global, hegemonic Islam growing out of the Muslim diasporas of Europe and elsewhere that is free from the cultural constraints of the immigrants' homelands and free from the dominant cultures of their new lands. The virtual ummah resonates with the basic principle of Muslim unity – dar-ul-Islam – "where good Muslims convene; it is not a territory; it is an 'environment'" (Roy 2004:

158). The idea that religion should dominate over ethnic and cultural differences is a general principle of Islam, and a requirement of world domination by Islamic mythology. Ironically, this kind of ubiquitous Islamic influence can only germinate and grow outside Islam's home territories.

The communications problem

Communications media have also posed problems for religious and cultural authorities throughout history in the Islamic world. A language revolution took place in the late eighteenth and early nineteenth centuries in the Middle East when some books from the West were translated into Arabic and other regional languages and made available (to a relatively narrow field of readers) with the development of printing press technology (Lewis 2002: 45). Two succeeding communications media spreading from the West – telegraphy and newspapers – further disturbed the cultural isolation of Middle Eastern Islamic nations.

Islamic religious leaders, much like Christian clergy of a previous era, have characteristically considered advances in communications technology to be cultural intrusions capable of spreading heresy. The most extreme tendencies derive from teachings of the puritanical Wahhabi sect originating in eighteenth-century Arabia, which fervently rejected any innovation that religious leaders believed did not directly advance Islam. The founder of the Saudi Arabian kingdom two centuries later, Abdel Aziz, became the target of a revolt "because he was introducing modern technologies like the telephone" and was associated with the "infidel" British (Zakaria 2004a: 31). Typewriters had to be registered in Iraq as recently as the 1990s (El-Nawawy and Iskandar 2002: 68).

Today's global communications media and information technology make it easy for movies, video, television programs, popular music, sports, fashion, and many other cultural artifacts and influences to penetrate national borders and challenge cultural traditions. In many respects these cultural interventions have weakened the political and cultural control of Arab leaders. Further complicating matters, most developing countries depend on cost-effective foreign sources of media programming and also end up imitating the officially despised but successful formats and program ideas coming from abroad. The global appeal of TV reality shows is a particularly notable general trend. A striking specific example is *Man Sayarbah el-Million?* ("Who Wants to Marry a Millionaire?") transmitted throughout the Arab world via satellite by the Middle East Broadcast Centre (MBC) of Saudi Arabia. Soap operas, like the progressive "Auntie Noor" on Egyptian TV, also do well, as does an Egyptian version of *Sesame Street* in Arabic. A spin-off of the UK's *Pop Idol* (and America's *American Idol*), *The Arab Idol* drew more than 40 million viewers in Lebanon, Syria, and Jordan – to become the most popular program ever broadcast on Arab-region television.

As the years have gone by, most Muslim and Arab authorities have accepted the inevitable presence of communications media and eventually found ways to use them to strengthen their religious, cultural, and political power. The change began with early-morning electronically amplified calls to prayer that resound from loudspeakers on mosques, penetrating the most private recesses of everyday life. Fundamentalist leaders of all the major religions have learned how to harness the symbolic power of communications media, information technology, and the culture industries to reinforce and expand their influence. Televangelism, direct mailing, video and audio cassettes, commercial advertising, mobile phones, blogs, email, and web pages are put to use by religious groups to advance their institutional, and often very profitable, "spiritual" interests (Almond, Appleby, and Sivan 2003: 125). An evangelical Muslim from Egypt – Amr Khaled – has become a regional religious superstar with personal appearances and an extremely popular website. Even the forward-leaning Al-Jazeera network features a famous TV sheik – Yusuf al-Qaradawi – whose traditional views on religious, cultural, and political issues influence the Middle East and beyond.

Gaps in human development have become manifest not only in material terms on a global level, but in symbolic and expressive terms as well. The consequences of this turn of events for the Islamic world are complex and contradictory. Media and cultural globalization facilitate both increased Westernization and increased Islamization. Striking discrepancies in comparative living standards, religious philosophies, economic and cultural exchange ratios, and differences in political and military power have become plainly evident for everyone to see – including, for the first time in history, inhabitants of the Middle East. As Bernard Lewis points out, "In earlier times such discrepancies might have passed unnoticed by the vast mass of the population. Today, thanks to modern media and communications, even the poorest and most ignorant are painfully aware of the differences between themselves and others" (Lewis 2003: 17). The larger implications of this phenomenon throughout the world – cultural transparency – are explained in the next chapter.

Notes

1. Men and women pray in separate parts of the mosque because "Some early adherents of Islam showed up late for prayers so they could stay in the back and ogle the women's behinds, even penning bawdy odes to the sight," reports Abou El Fadl, a professor of Islamic law at the University of California-Los Angeles. According to the lore, this behavior caused Muhammad to recommend that men pray at the front of the mosques and women at the back (*New York Times* 2006).
2. Favorable impressions of Islam have fallen off considerably in recent years. A CBS poll conducted in 2006 had Americans rating Islam next to last among organized religious groups. Scientology was the only religion that got a lower rating (CBS News 2006).
3. Modernity and globalization supplied the airplanes, mobile phones, Toyota pick-up trucks, encryption software and so on, but it also brought the video cameras that caught the "home video" chats of bin Laden and other Islamic militants which have been used in the effort to capture the perpetrators of 9/11.

Chapter 6

Cultural Transparency

Webster's New World College Dictionary names its "Word of the Year" for the expression that best captures something distinctive and important for the preceding 12-month period. The word that was selected by language experts for 2003 means "openness to scrutiny from the outside." In today's clandestine and manipulative world of high-stakes politics and cut-throat business, the honored term that was chosen represents honesty and ethics. The Word of the Year was "transparency."

Transparency typically refers to the ability of social forces outside the circles of established power to monitor political and economic systems and, when appropriate and possible, to pull back the curtains of secrecy and expose abuses of corrupt governments or unscrupulous corporations to a wide public, usually through media or internet reports. The Enron, WorldCom, Xerox, Arthur Anderson, and Global Crossing scandals in the United States are examples of the kinds of transgressions that transparency can make public, as was the attempted SARS epidemic cover-up by the Chinese government. And when the Chinese government banned media coverage of widespread anti-Japan protests in 2005, cell phones, email, text messages, instant messages, blogs, online forums, and streaming video "inflamed public opinion and served as an organizing tool for protesters," according to the *New York Times*. Reporters for a "celebrity watch" internet site exposed the police cover-up of Hollywood actor-producer Mel Gibson's anti-Semitic rant when he was busted for drunk driving in Malibu, California.

What was revealed in all these cases is much more than a parade of embarrassing facts. *Transparency is systematic scrutiny — an ongoing, penetrating condition of openness, surveillance, and vigilance that makes the actions of powerful persons and institutions visible and holds them publicly accountable.* In his insightful book *The Transparent Society*, David Brin says that transparency functions like a surge of biological T-cells traveling through the human body detecting errors in the corporeal system. But this powerful social safeguard, Brin argues, can only develop with the ceaseless initiative of active, independent-minded, opinionated people. For that reason "the relentless drumbeat of messages extolling individualism, eccentricity, and suspicion of authority must continue" (Brin 1998: 135, 330–1).

Multinational corporations that invest and operate in developing countries have today become subject to an unprecedented degree of scrutiny regarding their labor and environmental practices, gradually leading to more sustainable decisions. As economist and globalization expert Jagdish Bhagwati points out, "with the growth of the NGOs, with CNN and the BBC everywhere, the ability of multinationals to do something legal but offensive in terms of widely shared morality is seriously diminished" (Bhagwati 2004: 130–1). Global cash flows of all kinds are also being exposed today in ways that deny "criminals, terrorists, and conspiratorial elites the power to hide away – and hide behind – mountains of untallied cash" (Brin 1998: 98). The very assumption that operating in the shadows is good for business no longer makes sense in a more open and publicly networked world. To the contrary, argues Dan Gillmor, a pioneering thinker on these issues, "with few exceptions, I'd suggest that the more transparent a company is, the more likely it will succeed" (Gillmor 2004: 58).

Transparency increases efficiency and honesty, serving society well. Examples of this in the United States include release of the on-time arrival records and lost baggage statistics among commercial airlines, accident rates for individual automobile models, denial rates for home mortgages reported by race, sex, income, and census tract, data on the release of toxic materials, graduation rates of college athletes, and home addresses of sex offenders (Brin 1998: 252–3). The internet, especially blogs, operates as a global fact checker on every public claim and has increased the circulation of information on every imaginable topic.

Transparency is a grand concept composed of many details. Closed circuit television cameras surveying troubled neighborhoods throughout England, for example, have reduced crime significantly since their introduction in the 1980s. Their ubiquitous presence has been helpful for conducting investigative work against terrorists, too. When a second group of Islamists tried to strike the London transportation system in July 2005, video cameras positioned inside train stations provided clear images of the perpetrators, leading to their later arrest. Timothy McVeigh, the anti-government radical who blew up the court house in Oklahoma City, Oklahoma in 1995 was tracked down with the help of a video camera operating at a McDonald's restaurant where he ate lunch the day of the bombing.

To help deter future acts of terrorism, and to inform the public of what has happened in any specific case, the footage is also released to news media who circulate the images globally via television and the internet. Terrorist organizations discovered that negative consequences can arise even when they voluntarily make their actions visible. The videotaped beheadings of Western captives in Iraq posted on Islamist websites slowed when Al-Qaeda realized the images were hurting their cause among fellow Muslims. The very spectacle of 9/11 and images of subsequent terrorist acts have made unforgettable contributions to the pool of symbolic resources available for global public consumption. Fiction plays a role in cultural transparency related to terrorism too. Salman Rushdie's novel *Shalimar the Clown*, for instance, brilliantly exposes the immorality and futility of religious insurgencies between Muslims and Hindus in Kashmir (Rushdie 2005).

The most powerful governments in the world have become particularly vulnerable to the damage that visibility and transparency can bring, even during wartime. As civilian neighborhoods in Lebanon were being pummeled by Israel during the sudden hostilities in 2006, for example, Lebanese President Emile Lahoud told international TV networks, "I hope the US population sees these images so they won't want to stand with Israel completely." Even with the barriers to investigative reporting posed by military and corporate censorship, the human suffering, complexity, and contradictions of the Iraq War surfaced from the cumulative barrage of media images and reports. The massacre of Iraqi civilians at Haditha and elsewhere in Iraq – and similar incidents in Afghanistan – further neutralized the moral posturing of American foreign policy that was already reeling under President Bush, who himself had become embarrassingly transparent.

Military prisons managed by the Americans also became sites of global disgust and debate. The Abu Ghurayb prisoner abuse scandal was composed of key elements that feed transparency – a digital still camera operated by a soldier, an internet uplink from Iraq downloaded by a personal contact in the United States, release of the images to the commercial television industry, and the global circulation of those images via television, the internet, newspapers, magazines, and other media. The other controversial prison, Guantanamo Bay, became "the most scrutinized detention center ever," according to US Defense Secretary Donald Rumsfeld. That scrutiny led to reform in the treatment of detainees and to plans to shut down the facility altogether. The fatal shooting of an injured, unarmed Iraqi by a US Marine inside a mosque in Fallujah in 2004 appeared on the photo blog of an NBC reporter, Kevin Sites. The burning and desecration of two dead Taliban fighters by US troops in Afghanistan in 2005 showed up originally on an Australian TV station and was picked up by news outlets around the world. Like the unforgettable images of terrorism, all these troubling events and more contribute mightily to the supply of symbolic resources that fast become part of the global consciousness.

The growing number of highly competitive mass media outlets, the cascading spread of the internet, the capabilities of new communications and information technology, aggressive Western-style journalistic practices, and the spirited watchfulness of human rights groups and non-governmental organizations (NGOs) make political, economic, and military systems more transparent and accountable to the global public than ever before. One of the most active NGOs, Transparency International, promotes the idea of "a world in which government, politics, business, civil society and the daily lives of people are free of corruption" (Transparency International 2004).

The question that concerns us in this chapter is how transparency applies to culture – the enacted values and daily lives of people. Can cultural systems be made visible and held responsible for what they do in the same way that the actions of political, economic, and military systems have become increasingly exposed and accountable? Can cultures be corrupt? What are the limits of cultural relativism? And how do we know that cultural transparency isn't just surveillance by another name?

In many respects cultural systems have already become transparent on a global scale. We know more about each other now than ever before. Even many of the world's poor have gained sufficient access to media and communications technology now to know what's going on and expect to be informed. Greater media coverage and advances in information and communications technology interact with unprecedented levels of transcultural contact to greatly expand the circulation of cultural information. Cultural visibility will increase significantly in the future as more and more of "us" see those "others," and as we are seen by them.

Reflexive Cultural Globalization

Today cultures are offered up for global consumption and tested against one another over the internet and through satellite television and open borders in brutal Darwinian fashion.
T. Friedman, *The Lexus and the Olive Tree*, p. 291

A key characteristic of cultural transparency is reflexivity – self-awareness. As people everywhere expand their peripheral vision and become exposed to more cultural otherness, even when they would prefer not to be, those individuals and groups also simultaneously take stock of their own everyday realities. This has always been the case, but the conditions of contemporary global communication – especially considering the increasingly symbolic nature of culture and the unprecedented abundance of cultural forms that are available – have led to a degree of transparency and interactivity that is changing the world. The core process at work here is *reflexive cultural globalization* wherein people constantly compare themselves and their ways of life to others.

We come to know ourselves and others through the increasingly transparent and interconnected interplay of cultural symbols and styles which articulate into the matrices of our living situations, causing us to collectively and individually interpret and respond to the interactions which result. Human consciousness and behavior cannot help but change as a consequence. As John B. Thompson writes:

> as our biographies are opened up by mediated experience . . . we find ourselves not only to be observers of distant others and events, but also to be involved with them in some way. We are released from the locales of our daily lives only to find ourselves thrown into a world of baffling complexity. We are called on to form a view about, to take a stand on, even to assume some responsibility for, issues and events which take place in distant parts of an increasingly inter-connected world. (Thompson 1995: 233)

Globalization doesn't just extend the many features of modernity; it stimulates profound personal and collective reflection on what modernity has wrought, who brings what to the party, and how globally dominant cultural traits mesh with local traditions and practices. As a consequence, globalization has created a crisis of culture in many parts of the world, instigating everything from repressive political actions to liberal reform movements and massive human migrations.

Symbolic cultural forms that circulate around the world often reduce much of what we know about each other to stereotypes, archetypes, ideal types, and extreme cases. Such cultural reductions may be unfair and misleading in some respects, but they nonetheless strongly guide popular perception and interpretation. Given the unprecedented quantity and complexity of images that everyone must try to manage today, the task of fairly making sense of others in the cultural hall of mirrors has become extremely challenging. Although judging cultures or individual members of cultural groups by stereotyped images may not always be fair to the groups or individuals being portrayed, people everywhere – even those with the most seemingly cosmopolitan outlook – make these kinds of judgments all the time. It seems natural to do so. Relying on generalized impressions of the appearance, values, and social practices of others serves as a time-honored strategy for survival that is grounded in human instinct and emotion (Stewart 2001).

The globalization of good and bad ideas

Just about every imaginable idea – from gender equality and wheelchair access to football hooliganism and child pornography – circulates today on a global scale. Every idea has cultural origins and meanings; some ideas are more widely shared and accepted than others. Reception, interpretation, and action taken by individuals and groups toward globally circulated ideas always reflect cultural differences and personal subjectivities. But certain fundamental principles – human rights, gender equality, cultural pluralism, social tolerance, constitutional liberalism, environmental responsibility, and political democracy – as well as more particular issues such as the fight against AIDS, malaria, and other devastating diseases, debt relief for impoverished countries, and the treaty on land mines, for example, are taking root in new ground. These are among the good ideas that circulate globally. Even the "worldwide movement against globalization" has found wide latitude (Giddens 2001). A list of the world's worst ideas that are also given great currency by globalization would be just as long. The robust production of global information results from a complementary set of factors. Increasingly complex interfaces and convergences among media technologies, the privatization of public media, the ambitious quest for economic profits, a lack of international regulation and control over media and information technology, and the deregulation of communications systems in many nations combine to spur the volume and intensity of all the tendencies circulating in globalization – good, bad, and otherwise.

Loving to hate America

People everywhere love, hate, and love to hate the United States of America. No doubt, the United States has become the foremost symbol of Western culture – an idealized, if resented, "other." One argument has it that America's liberal democracy, based on free market principles, is so superior to competing systems that it signals the final stage of mankind's ideological evolution – the "end of history" (Fukuyama 1992). In any case, there should be no doubt that because of its global visibility, power, and influence, the

United States serves as a universal reference point for all kinds of cultural comparisons.

Even though they may be admiring, or envious, of its success, many people around the world resent, even "hate," America. This feeling results in part from the widely perceived hypocritical and self-serving nature of American foreign policy and from the fact that the cultural players in today's globalized world do not compete with equal resources or opportunities across material and symbolic domains. America simply appears to have too much power and influence. As Gregg Zachary has written:

> From Moscow to Montreal, Kuala Lumpur to Kiev, Caracas to Capetown, many critics object to the Americanization of the world. To them, the American model consists of this: a preference for private profit over public good; winner-takes-all rules that reward the rich and penalize the poor, widening the gulf between the two; and the substitution of a generic pop culture – defined by English, Hollywood, the internet, and even American conceptions of bravery and beauty – for local alternatives. A haven for diversity at home, America abroad seems imperialistic, imposing a rigid culture on others. (Zachary 2000: 244)

People everywhere have been seduced by American popular culture; sometimes they resent the seduction, but keep coming back for more. American popular culture captures people's attention, stimulates their imagination, provokes their emotions, excites their senses, and makes some of them quite loathsome. Despite the ubiquity of American media and the appeal of its popular culture, however, the ideological and cultural consequences of the United States' hegemony ultimately do not always favor its own image or interests. While many people say they like the buzz of American pop culture and the utility of its consumer technology, others claim they don't like the spread of American ideas and customs (Pew Global Attitudes Project 2003).

Studies conducted by the Pew Research Center for the People and the Press and the British Broadcasting Corporation show that the global perception of the United States has been decreasing rapidly around the world since the turn of the century. Except for Japan, the Philippines, some African nations, and a handful of other countries, majorities or pluralities in 29 other countries in

Europe, Latin America, the Middle East, and Asia rail against the spread of American culture (Pew Global Attitudes Project 2002). The critical focus on the United States has sharpened greatly as American power has grown following the collapse of global communism, even among countries and cultures Americans typically consider to be their friends. An opinion poll of diverse nations conducted in 2003, titled "What the World Thinks of America," revealed that President George W. Bush was perceived in profoundly negative terms and that the United States is considered to be more dangerous to world peace and stability than the Al-Qaeda terrorist network. Nations surveyed were Australia, Brazil, Canada, France, Great Britain, Indonesia, Israel, Jordan, Russia, South Korea, and the United States (British Broadcasting Corporation 2003). Even teenagers from around the world hold increasingly negative attitudes toward America and Americans (DeFleur and DeFleur 2002). The negative perceptions are heightened by reactions to United States foreign policy – especially its support for Israel, political and military interventionism in the Middle East and elsewhere, disrespect for the United Nations, failure to cooperate with other nations on trade and environmental issues and treaties, and by George W. Bush's smirking expression, arrogant tone, and halting manner of speech when addressing the governments and peoples of the world.

Global anti-Americanism may be the most obvious example of how exposure to other cultures does *not* necessarily lead directly to greater tolerance, understanding, or appreciation. It often inspires just the opposite – retreat and lashing out – especially when cultural groups differ greatly in cultural values and power. But intercultural contact between groups can never be reduced to mean simply perceptions of the "other." One's own culture is always understood in relation to other groups as well; this is the highly subjective nature of cultural globalization. Every response to an exogenous cultural form is influenced by (even subconscious) perceptions of local conditions. The most dramatic, complex, and important example of how cultural transparency and reflexive cultural globalization interact today is the Muslim uprising against America and the West, a theme to which we now briefly return.

Open Society: The Guiding Principle for Cultural Development

> . . . the most important socioeconomic and cultural transformation over the past 150 years has been the transformation of relatively closed, exclusive, custom-based rural societies into relatively open, inclusive, innovation-oriented urban societies.
>
> World Bank, *World Development Report*, pp. 5–6

> All that is Islamic is good and that which is not must be avoided.
>
> 24-year-old Saudi Arabian man; in M. Yamani,
> *Changed Identities*, p. 127

In his influential books and lectures about globalization and the world economy, George Soros argues that the key to greater economic growth in developing nations and to peace and progress in general is the fostering of "open societies" (Soros 2002). Compared to closed societies that cling to tribal customs, open societies are universal (Soros 2002: 164). Open societies are based on three interacting principles: political democracy, a market economy, and the rule of law. They are characterized by innovation, creativity, knowledge flows, tolerance, dissent, risk taking, technological integration, and specialization. Open societies are "incubators of new values" (World Bank 2003: 7). Freedom is the core factor: "The spread of democracy, the integration of national economies, and revolutions in technology all point to greater human freedom and greater potential for improving people's lives. But in too many countries, freedom seems to be under even-greater threat" (UNDP 2002a: 2).[1]

Nearly all Islamic and Arab countries fail to meet the criteria of open societies. The economic and cultural conditions of the Middle East gravely reflect the problem. In the past two decades Arab per capita income growth has averaged 0.5 percent, second lowest in the world. More than half of Arab women are illiterate (UNDP 2002a). The region has the highest unemployment in the world (International Labour Organization 2006). Less than one percent of the Arab population uses the internet. The combined gross national product of the entire region is less than that of Spain (UNDP 2002b). Religious and government leaders refuse to permit polio vaccines and other modern health services. Speaking out against Islamic militants in his own country a few months after the 9/11 attack, President Pervez Musharraf of Pakistan lamented the lack of education and technology in Muslim countries and described their condition: "Today we are the poorest, the most illiterate, the most backward, the most unhealthy, the most unenlightened, the most deprived and the weakest of all the human race" (*The Times*, February 17, 2002).

Openness, tolerance, diversity, and pluralism are basic philosophical qualities of countries and cultures that have been able to modernize, globalize, and improve their standard of living (China being the outstanding exception). These characteristics simply do not exist in sufficient measure in the values and practices of most Islamic and Arabic countries to reap the potential economic and cultural benefits. Consequently, as the historian David Landes frankly describes it, the Middle East lacks an informed and capable workforce, rejects new techniques and ideas that come from "the enemy West," does not respect the gaining of knowledge in general, and gives women an inferior place. All these problems are "clearly related to attitudes cultivated in Islam and especially in the Islam of the Arab World" (Landes 1999: 410–11). But the nature of the exclusionary and hegemonic religious beliefs and practices of Islam must be understood in relation to at least two other mutually reinforcing, anti-modernist forces: (1) the enduring persistence of tribal belief systems and loyalties in Middle Eastern countries; and (2) the oppressive, autocratic nature of many political regimes which govern Islamic and Arab nation states – some of which, particularly Saudi Arabia, Egypt, Kuwait, and now Afghanistan and Iraq, have received significant economic, political, and military support from the United States and other Western nations for years.

Some observers – especially the late Edward Said (1997) – have greatly downplayed the role of Islam in explaining the descending spiral of Middle Eastern civilizations over the centuries, placing the blame instead on political structures in the region, the support given them by Western nations, and an underlying racism he believed discriminates against Middle Easterners of Arab or Muslim lineage. No doubt the way political boundaries were drawn in the Middle East after World War II, the influence of Western presence and foreign policy in the region since then, and the repressive behavior of authoritarian governments in many Arab Muslim states in recent years have contributed much to the lack of development. But such explanations don't sufficiently emphasize the dominant role of religion in regional culture. In fact, the kinds of arguments that are made by Arab apologists like Said can themselves be extremely misleading and counterproductive in this regard.[2] One cannot easily or sincerely explain away the influence of Islam, especially the cultural force of Sharia law, and the profound "religious basis of identity" (Lewis 2002: 102) in the failed development of Middle Eastern nation states.

Choosing to limit openness and retreat into Islamic religious orthodoxy and authority extends regional tendencies that have been functioning in the Middle East for centuries. As the West was exploring (and exploiting) the world in the fifteenth and sixteenth centuries and beyond, Islamic and Arab cultures, with some notable exceptions, stayed home and remained voluntarily isolated from the developing patterns of global trade and cultural interaction. According to Islamic religious dogma, the outside can only bring "evil." Capitalists, communists, Christians, Jews, Hindus, pagans, atheists, and others – any and all non-believers – are contaminated and simply not welcome: "As a rule of thumb, all non-Muslims . . . could be said to be *mushrikun* (those outside true Islam). They are polluted because they lie outside the group of believers" (Khuri 2001: 58). Whether referring to sporadic intercultural contact that took place centuries ago or to the latest geopolitical developments, many Muslim believers – not just the terrorists – think they have a duty to "remove the alien and pagan laws and customs imposed by foreign imperialists and native reforms, and restore the only true law, the all-embracing law of God" (Lewis 2002: 105). Even among Muslims living in Great Britain, more than 60 percent favor the introduction of Islamic Sharia law to settle disputes between followers of the faith living there (*Guardian* 2004).

Cultural exclusivity based on religious sanctimony and tribal tradition, anti-modernist governing structures at the national level, low levels of technological development, an historical paucity of independent media, the absence of public debate and discussion, a population explosion, widespread poverty, unemployment, and illiteracy have left Islamic and Arab countries unprepared for the challenges of globalization. But entry into the global systems of trade and exchange has also been problematic in the Middle East because it necessarily delivers what Islamic-based cultures there have been avoiding for centuries – outside influence of all kinds. The main reason for rejecting external influence is clear and predictable: "the lively exchange of goods and ideas implied in open diplomacy, trade, and communication threatens the integrity of their traditions and opens their members to competing religions, debilitating materialism, and moral corruption" (Almond, Appleby, and Sivan 2003: 132).

The Power of Transparency

In today's world there really is no place to hide. Contemporary mass media, the internet, and consumer communications technology make it much more difficult than before for political rulers and states to conceal their behavior from the global gaze or limit the ability of ordinary people to connect and communicate. It becomes common knowledge around the world now when national leaders deny journalists access to their territory, for instance, or when they ban or unfairly censor their citizens' contact with international media and the internet. China, Burma, Zimbabwe, Vietnam, North Korea, Saudi Arabia, Iran, and Sudan have all suffered this type of critical scrutiny recently. But it isn't just dictatorships and developing countries that feel the pressure of the global microscope. The world's most powerful institutions and persons have become vulnerable to popular surveillance too, precisely because their actions affect so many.

Chinese political leaders, for example, who had been accustomed to staying comfortably out of public view for centuries, discovered they had to be much more visible and accountable after the national telecommunications system they put in place raised viewer expectations beginning in the 1980s (Lull 1991). George W. Bush and Tony Blair felt the heat at home and around the world, especially after their attempts to justify the Iraq War were found to be based on faulty and misleading intelligence. The Roman Catholic Church has struggled to explain exposed sexual abuse by priests. Brazil's populist government was rocked by financial corruption caught on video tape at the same time as the up-and-coming political party in Mexico, the PRD, suffered from a bribery exchange that was dubbed the "video scandal," and lost the 2006 presidential election. Media and internet coverage of the riots in France in the past few years called attention to the economic and cultural plight of immigrants there. As television viewers around the world watched in disbelief as Hurricane Katrina ravaged the southern coast of the United States, CNN political analyst Bill Schneider pronounced that America appeared to be suffering "a total collapse of authority and government." The world watched corrupt American corporate CEOs Ken Lay, Jeffrey Skilling, Martha Stewart, Bernie Ebbers, and others march off to jail.[3]

Religion as cultural and political ideology – systems of ideas that express particular doctrinal beliefs and foster characteristic social practices – heretofore has not been subjected to such intensive scrutiny. Religious tolerance is such a strong value in Western secular cultures that it suppresses any criticism of religious thought and allows even less room for fault finding. George W. Bush quickly showed up at the large mosque along embassy row in Washington, DC, a few days after September 11, 2001, for instance, to announce that he believed Islam was not responsible for what happened. Bush referred to Islam as "a peaceful religion" (never explaining the basis of that interpretation) and said he believes the vast majority of Muslims around the world do not support terrorism.

That was not a completely informed or honest evaluation. As Salman Rushdie wrote in a *New York Times* opinion piece a few weeks after 9/11, "yes, this *is* about Islam." And not just about Islamic terrorists. Bernard Lewis points out that "most Muslims are not fundamentalists, and most fundamentalists are not terrorists, but most present-day terrorists are Muslims and proudly identify themselves as such" (Lewis 2003: 137). Edward Hotaling, the former Middle East Bureau Chief for CBS News who has written a compassionate and fair account of developments in the region, pointedly observes that "we labor under the illusion that Islam is a religion of peace just like other major religions and, thus defined, could have no relation to the war with the terrorists" (Hotaling

2003: 165). The "sword verse" from the Koran commands Muslims to "slay the polytheists wherever you find them, and confine them, and lie in wait for them at every place of ambush" (Sura 9:5). This passage is often cited by Islamists to justify acts of violence in the name of God. Such thinking was formalized in the official pronouncements of Iranian President Mahmoud Ahmadinejad for Israel to be "wiped off the map."

What the Islamic world, the United States, and everyone else must deal with today, however, is the subject of this chapter – the revelations of cultural transparency. The avalanche of books, newspaper and magazine articles, electronic journalism coverage, and internet postings devoted to Islam and the Arab world in recent years has brought to light the central tenets of Islamic religion and culture. The pressing question that arises in today's cultural landscape, therefore, is whether mainstream Islam – as it interacts with the complexities and contradictions of national, regional, and global political and cultural realities – can ultimately respond productively to the challenges that modernity and globalization will continue to pose.

Transparency or surveillance?

Transparency is based on the general principle that public access to as much information as possible is desirable. It's certainly more desirable than the opposite – hiding actions from public view – which has long been a strategy employed by persons and institutions that stand to suffer from exposure. When the media and internet focus their attention on the inner world of politics, business, and the military, powerful persons and institutions must become responsible for their actions to a degree they have never before experienced. Transparency produces a beneficial deterrent effect as well, discouraging immoral, unethical, and criminal activity before it happens. By facilitating transparency on a global scale, the mass media, internet, and personal communications technology help identify and discredit the lawbreakers, bullies, and moral violators of the world. Revealing cultural values and conduct on a global scale lays bare the real differences among us. It opens up the assumptions we live by to critical evaluation and discussion.

As we learn more about each other, we also learn more about ourselves and about our place in the world with others.

The question of privacy arises. At what point does probing daily life violate the rights of private citizens? Isn't there a "Big Brother" risk involved here? What about modern technology's role in the theory of the "Panopticon" – the all-seeing (pan-optic) prison surveillance system Michel Foucault used analogically to describe how those with power in society maintain absolute vigilance over members of a community who may not even suspect they are being watched? Foucault argued that since the sixteenth century, armies, schools, hospitals, and prisons in Western nations have used close observation and documentation to create "disciplinary societies" (Foucault 1977). Surveillance continues to be a fact of life today. It has expanded considerably. Some businesses, for example, monitor not only parking lots, lobbies, waiting rooms, and hallways with video cameras, but also individual employee work stations. Keeping track of workers' emails and web searches has become standard practice in many organizations. The Patriot Act and the government's monitoring of private phone conversations as part of the "war against terrorism" have become extremely sensitive privacy issues in the United States. The same kinds of troubling issues affect people everywhere in the world.

These are legitimate concerns. David Brin warned of this in *The Transparent Society*. But Brin also pointed out that the kinds of issues raised in this chapter are of a different order and scope. We must not confuse or conflate the effects of media and internet transparency, for instance, with the intrusions of government or corporate surveillance. They are different processes, serve different publics, and have different purposes. As John B. Thompson explains:

> Whereas the Panopticon renders many people visible to a few and enables power to be exercised over the many by subjecting them to a state of permanent visibility, the development of communication media provides a means by which many people can gather information about the few . . . thanks to the media, it is primarily those who exercise power, rather than those over whom power is exercised, who are subjected to a certain kind of visibility. (Thompson 1995: 134)

I have argued in this chapter that cultural systems should be subject to the same critical scrutiny that governments and other power brokers receive. Cultural ideas of all kinds have circulated around the world throughout history. The best ones catch on in many places, become indigenized, and contribute to cultural, economic, and political development. Today, many of the good ideas of globalization are taking root. Computers and digital media store unlimited quantities of images and texts, insuring that a ready stock of cultural information is always available. As part of the process, the world's political, economic, military, religious, and cultural elite must be able to stand up to the disinfecting sunlight of transparency and the discerning court of global public opinion. Acts of cultural intolerance, oppression, and abuse are becoming increasingly plain for everyone to see and repudiate.

Open and frank exchanges about cultural values and practices are discussions that *must* take place at the global level. Cultural transparency makes that possible. The very condition of being involutarily open to critical scrutiny is itself fast becoming a globalized value closely connected to the broader ecology of human rights.

Notes

1. Honorable Western values – especially the core ideas of freedom and democracy – have been undermined tremendously by the foreign policy and rhetoric of George W. Bush. As George Soros puts it, the American military intervention in the Middle East and the political rhetoric of President Bush has made freedom almost "a dirty word" (Soros 2004).

2. The analysis made by Edward Said in a pre-9/11 book about journalistic and academic interpretations of the Islamic world is particularly vitriolic and misleading (Said 1997). Granting that the Arab Islamic world is in a "dreadful state," Said offered no cogent explanation for the systemic problem other than to blame the policies of the United States and other powers and to accuse respected non-Muslim journalists and scholars of bias and a lack of professionalism when their views conflict with his own. In a rambling and self-pitying discussion, Said stooped to the level of truly vicious *ad hominem* attacks on numerous Western thinkers, especially Princeton professor

of Near Eastern Studies, Bernard Lewis, whose calm and reasonable account I draw upon throughout this book. We get the impression from Said that dozens of Western writers simply hate Arab Muslims and misrepresent Islam for no apparent reason. The only exceptions granted by Said are those Western scholars who are "pro-Palestinian, pro-Arab, pro-Muslim – who may or may not be right, but who are on what he sees as the right side. Motive trumps truth and fact" (Landes 1999: 417–18). The cumulative effect of Western observers, according to Said, is to make Islamic terrorism appear to be more "disproportionately fearsome" than he believed it really is (1997: xxxiv). The Arab Muslim writers he cites, on the other hand, are claimed to be uniformly careful, complex, and accurate.

Until recently, the same "respectful" critical distance given Islam was also given to Said, especially to his "Orientalist" argument. As Irshad Manji points out, however, while Said argued that the West "demonized [Muslims] as exotic freaks of the East, doesn't it speak volumes that the 'imperialist' West published, distributed, and promoted Edward Said's book?" (Manji 2003: 34), particularly in light of the fact that "outside" material is almost never translated or published in Islamic countries. Moreover, Western intellectuals have begun to realize that Said and his followers "have been succeeded by a new generation of politically correct scholars who will not dare to ask why it is that Arab countries seem stuck in a very different social and political milieu than the rest of the world . . . most Arab writers are more concerned with defending their national honor against the pronouncements of dead Orientalists than with trying to understand the predicament of the Arab world" (Zakaria 2003: 129).

3. Still, transparency lacks completeness and comprehensiveness. In politics and economics, only a fraction of the transgressions that occur – and the structural conditions that allow them to develop – are made public. The most powerful political and economic entities often find ways to avoid close scrutiny. Joseph Stiglitz (2002) points this out in his forceful critique of the role of the International Monetary Fund (IMF) in economic globalization. The IMF demands political and economic transparency from Third World countries as a condition for receiving financial support, according to Stiglitz, but "when the transparency spotlight was turned around to shine on the IMF itself, it was found wanting" (Stiglitz 2002: 229).

Chapter 7

The Open Spaces of Global Communication

Do contemporary advances in global communication serve mainly to strengthen and extend international power relations already in place, or do they offer realistic opportunities to transform those tendencies into a more humane and harmonious world? Can cultural barriers eventually be overcome through expanded, mediated human contact? How might the technological and cultural developments that are sweeping the world today bring about positive results by creating reflexivity and encouraging public dialogue on a global scale?

Any success that can be brought to fruition in the open spaces of global communication will depend on further expansion of a loosely structured, de facto global civil society that embraces innovation and introspection. This potentially transformative project develops in seven overlapping stages (Figure 7.1). In this chapter, I will describe the seven stages of the open spaces of global communication and explain how the idea progresses from one stage to the next – starting with a summary analysis of the characteristic conditions of the Communication Age and ending with a hopeful vision of its full potential.

Stage 1: Cultural Technology, Industry, Abundance

The astounding amount of information being produced and transmitted today, the rapid development of communications

1	Cultural technology, industry, abundance
2	Global visibility and transparency
3	Platforms for participation
4	Global consciousness and public opinion
5	Global wisdom
6	Institutional channels
7	Utopian potential

Figure 7.1 Stages of global communication

technology that facilitates worldwide transmission and connectivity, and the pervasive social interaction and cultural diffusion that result from these developments all combine to define the Communication Age and create robust possibilities for the future. The number and diversity of cultural forms available and the ease of access with which more and more people engage information and connect with others put the positive potential of contemporary global communication in motion. Information is power, Joseph Nye reminds us, "and today a much larger part of the world has access to that power" (Nye 2004: 105).

The sheer amount of information now being produced has enormous consequences in and of itself. Worldwide information production increased by an astounding 30 percent *each year* between 1999 and 2002, with the greatest growth showing up in telephone and email communication (Lyman and Varian 2003). The trend continues unabated. More than 25 years ago "the computer" was honored as *Time* magazine's "Person of the Year." At that time, 1982, "computer" and "connectivity" were not associated with each other in highly integrated ways. Ten years later, the synergy among computational functionality, information production, and human communication on a global scale had become clear. As Anthony Smith commented when the internet burst onto the world scene in the 1990s, information has become the "transforming, paradigmatic idea" of our time. Like DNA, Smith said, information functions as "the organizing principle of life itself" (A. Smith 1996: 66).

The metaphor of genetic influence is not overstated. The need to connect and communicate is hard-wired into human experience (Smith and Szathmáry 1999). People seek effective ways to communicate with others in order to manage environmental uncertainty to best advantage. The neural flexibility of the human brain (Clark 2003) resonates with the nature of communications technology to create the resources necessary to survive and develop by expediting what all people share – the need to interact with others. Among the technological advances associated with information technology that have contributed much to the process are:

- improved capacity, speed, and quality of communication technology (e.g. *wireless access, broadband, ultra wideband, video and audio streaming, global real time*);
- increased technical resolution and fidelity (e.g. *digitalization, high-definition video and audio, liquid crystal display monitors*);
- increased technological reach, access, storage, and user-friendliness (e.g. *miniaturization, portability, affordability, utilitarian design, modular convergence*).

However, we are mainly concerned with the larger issues that have opened up the spaces of global communication:

- a rapidly increasing number and variety of mass media outlets worldwide;
- extraordinary growth and diversification of the culture industries;
- industrial and consumer blending of information technology and the internet with hardware and content of the traditional media and culture industries;
- the rapid rise and adoption of personal communications technologies and the multiple levels of connectivity they facilitate;
- convergence between technological and non-technological aspects of everyday life; and
- an enormously expanded number and range of individuals and groups participating in cultural creation, production, distribution, and consumption.

The growth of communications and cultural technology provides new opportunities for a broad spectrum of interested parties. Many of the primary benefactors include the familiar players (Time Warner, Disney, Murdoch, Viacom, Bertelsmann, etc.) and a more recent assortment of powerful information technology and communications enterprises (e.g. Microsoft, Nokia, Comcast, Sony, Oracle). But profits from the production of contemporary communication and culture are not all paid in money, and the gains don't just accrue to the usual array of industrial forces. Beginning with the printing press, the telegraph, and the telephone, the development of communications technology has always challenged the authority of the prevailing centers of political, economic, and cultural power.

We've progressed from the age of "old media" through "new media" to "we media" (Gillmor 2004). By 2003 nearly half the adult users of the internet in the United States had employed the web to "publish their thoughts, respond to others, post pictures, share files, and otherwise contribute to the explosion of content online" (Gillmor 2004: 162). Blogging, podcasting, and voice-over internet protocol (VOIP) became popular forms of communication that avoid the usual corporate intermediaries. Empirical data from around the world provided by the United Nations makes it clear that, "especially in developing countries, most ordinary citizens have many more sources of information (both in quantity and diversity) to turn to than they did 10 years ago. And less of that information is subject to rigid state control" (UNDP 2002a: 6, 76). Popular access to basic information and cultural resources worldwide, facilitated by today's "technologies of diversity," brings about greater cultural self-determination for individuals everywhere (Cowen 2002: 126–7). All these tendencies point to what the United Nations' Development Programme calls the growth of "cultural liberty" (UNDP 2004).

Two important examples of how cultural liberty can grow in response to transnational media flows stand out from last century. People in Russia and throughout Eastern and Central Europe were motivated to act against their governments mainly because they had gained access to unofficial media channels and other informational resources, which exposed the profound cultural and political limits of the communist system. With transnational media and popular culture blanketing the world, "more people became more aware of other people at a distance, of different ideologies and sets of beliefs" (Rantanen 2005: 45). For example, "Soviet audiences watching films . . . learned that people in the West did not have to stand in long lines to purchase food, did not live in communal apartments, and owned their own cars. All this invalidated the negative views promulgated by Soviet media" (Nye 2004: 49). The political uprisings that resulted themselves became striking media content that was made globally visible, encouraging others to resist and eventually overthrow their state systems as well.

The People's Republic of China went through much the same process when, beginning in the early 1980s, the national telecommunications system was greatly expanded, terrestrial and satellite television programming from outside the country appeared, and a series of critical films made by young Chinese filmmakers were shown. Unofficial popular culture (including much pirated music, video, and film) became available to city residents and international tourism became more widespread. All these developments changed the popular consciousness in China and there has been no turning back (Lull 1991). The Chinese government still has to accommodate constant cultural change in order to maintain its political power.

Stage 2: Global Visibility and Transparency

When the United Nations oversaw the national elections being conducted in Afghanistan in 2004 it set up television monitors in outdoor locations throughout the country so people could see for themselves what was happening in the delicate and complex voting process. This approach – the "Witness Project" – was designed to defuse the rampant rumors and conspiracy theories that infect politics everywhere, but especially in the Middle East where democratic elections are so unfamiliar and little trusted.

In the 1980s rock musician and social activist Peter Gabriel formed WITNESS, an organization that exploits the power of global visibility and transparency to expose human rights abuses around the world (WITNESS 2005). By using video technology and the distributive power of the internet, WITNESS and its NGO partner groups in many countries have brought global attention to various struggles for the rights of indigenous peoples, the use of child soldiers in Africa, gender violence in Mexico, and environmental destruction that affects human communities everywhere, among many other issues. The organization's website says the group "empowers human rights defenders to use video to shine light on those most affected by human rights violations, and to transform personal stories of abuse into powerful tools of justice." In order to impact the global consciousness, WITNESS depends on mainstream mass media to circulate its work. WITNESS's partner video footage appears on mainstream media like CNN, BBC, ABC, CBS, and PBS among many other television outlets, and is presented in major film festivals around the world.

To routinely know much more than we've known before has become an expected, even natural, state of mind for people in many parts of the world. As former World Bank chief Joseph Stiglitz observed, "in successful democracies citizens regard transparency, openness, knowing what government is doing, as an essential part of government responsibility. Citizens regard these as *rights*, not favors, conferred by the government" (Stiglitz 2002: 51; italics his). Or, as David Brin argues, "In a transparent society, citizens . . . will refuse *not* to know" (Brin 1998: 270).

Stage 3: Platforms for Participation

In a classic essay that analyzes the role of television in democratic societies, Horace Newcomb and Paul Hirsch (1987) describe the visual medium as a "cultural forum" that encourages public expression and discussion of all kinds of topics and ideas, even the most controversial and unpopular ones. Of course that's not all that television and other electronic and digital media do. Commercial mass media have many other purposes and effects, not all of them life-enhancing by any means. But among its many roles and influences, television uniquely and powerfully performs as a platform that generates widespread public awareness, reflection, discussion, and debate of countless social, cultural, and political issues.

The ability of media and information technology to facilitate public discussion is also captured nicely by the idea of the "global commons" (Commission on Global Governance 1995). In Great Britain, the commons referred originally to centrally located tracts of land set aside in communities specifically to foster shared public communication − the issuance of political and cultural announcements and the conduct of informal debates. The American equivalent of the commons is the town square or the town hall meeting. Today's global commons "defines and is defined by the availability in media and cyberspace of spectrum or network space free of direct control by the forces of capital or the state" (Silverstone 2001: 14). The cultural forum and the global commons emphasize the roles of mass media, information technology, personal communication technology, and popular culture in the production of public discourse that transcends national borders and creates diverse and democratic participation in the global public sphere. A clear and striking example of this phenomenon is www.chattheplanet. com, a global chat room that facilitates robust discussion of international issues.

The decentralization of authority in global communication is perhaps best represented by the turn-of-the-century phenomenon of blogging. Blogs give rise to countless voices and opinions and serve as global outposts for fact checking. Any purported factual information disseminated by governments, religious groups, corporations, NGOs, media outlets, or other agencies or individuals immediately becomes subject to intense scrutiny and response from bloggers. When bloggers uncover errors or mistruths, their reports are picked up and further circulated by mainstream media thus insuring another level of discussion. In this way, blogs and diverse media function together as system-correcting mechanisms on a global scale.

The cultural forum and the global commons should not be thought of only in terms of news and politics, however. The entire range of media content − entertainment television, talk radio, contemporary literature, comedy, and popular music, for example

– raise themes and provide points of view that provoke widespread deliberations too. Pop culture stars play a crucial role in setting the critical agenda. To name but a few examples, think of Bono's efforts promoting Third World debt relief, U2's world tour advocating universal human rights, George Clooney's volunteer work in the Middle East and his Arab-friendly film *Syriana*, and Angelina Jolie's political activism in Sudan and Chad.

Considering how the cultural forum and the global commons tend to blend together, one metaphor has been used often to describe the hopeful quality of today's global communication: the "conversation." Kwame Appiah argues that transcultural conversations facilitated by technology are what we need "to live together as the global tribe we have become" (Appiah 2006: xiii). Technology journalist Dan Gillmor points out that instead of the customary "top-down, manufactured" production of information by institutional news media, we have entered the age of an "edge–center, infinitely complex conversation" that has created an "inherent messiness that will open communications in ways that benefit everyone" (Gillmor 2004: 46, 158, 67). And Thomas Friedman refers to "global conversations" about religion, terror, culture, and the future as part of the flat world phenomenon he believes defines life in the twenty-first century (Friedman 2003, 2005).

The complementarity and convergence of media and communications technology expand the power of the conversation, further unleashing the multi-channel potential to communicate. The flexibility of asynchronous communications like email and blogs make it possible for great numbers of people to participate. The social circulation of information, images, sounds, and opinion by mobile phone, email, web pages, message boards, blogs, and chat rooms allows diverse individuals and small groups to organize their initiatives and mount responses to global events on their own time schedule from anywhere (Lessig 2004). Open sourcing challenges the hegemony of established protocols and interests in business, politics, religion, and culture.

The populist potential of modern electronic and digital media isn't limited to the liberal democratic nations of the First World. When China rushed to develop its telecommunications system in the early 1980s, unpredictable, often negative reactions to the government's didactic information and dull entertainment programming were expressed by viewers. State authorities found that while they could effectively supervise production of most television programs, they could not control viewers' responses. Less than a decade after playing the lead role in the plan for national modernization, television and popular culture provoked a civil unrest that led to the standoff at Tiananmen Square in 1989 (Lull 1991). As information and communications technology have evolved and become more widely accessible since then, ordinary Chinese citizens now communicate and express themselves much more freely than before. Although personal comments on politics are not allowed in China, simple participation in online discussion boards, blogs, and podcasts has proven to be liberating: "the mere idea that you could publicly state your opinion about anything − the weather, local sports scene − felt like a bit of revolution" (C. Thompson 2006: 70–1). Today's cultural "freedom fighters" are "a half-billion mostly apolitical young Chinese, blogging and chatting about their dates, their favorite bands, video games − an entire generation that is growing up with public speech as a regular habit" (ibid.: 156). If the cultural forum and the global commons represent platforms for entering the open spaces of global communication, then public speech is the process those platforms enable and inspire.

An unprecedented "social infrastructure of communication" has also opened up a "world of Muslim opinion, discourse, talk, and teaching" that facilitates interaction within and among Islamic groups, including links between Islamic diasporas throughout the world and their homelands (Eickelman and Anderson 2003: x–xi). As we saw in earlier chapters, the new satellite television networks in the Middle East have been crucial in creating space for discussion. A new Arab public is emerging today because of Al-Jazeera's willingness to "put almost every issue − social, economic, cultural, political − under fierce public scrutiny" and the audience's enthusiasm for thinking about and discussing these topics (Lynch 2006a: 241). The Middle East Media Research Institute (MEMRI) translates media content from the Arab region into the major languages of the world and posts it on the web, creating additional opportunities for dialogue across language and cultural groups.

Stage 4: Global Consciousness and Public Opinion

The fourth stage of global communication refers to two interrelated phenomena: the increasing common awareness that develops when enormous numbers of people engage novel information and cultural forms, and the power of public opinion that emerges from that awareness.

People organize and evaluate their cultural vistas as situated individuals and members of various groups. They ponder their intercultural encounters in moments of conscious and subconscious reflection. They discuss new ideas with others. To borrow a term that grew from similar developments in the spread of media, culture, and politics in the 1960s, today's accelerated contact with information and cultural resources stimulates a global "consciousness raising" that promotes individual rights and a common humanity. We see early indications that such a process is taking place in the Middle East now too, mainly because of the increased presence of independent media and the internet. An annual opinion poll conducted in five Middle Eastern countries shows that people in Arab Muslim countries are beginning to believe that their governments should act in the name of "all citizens, not just Arabs or Muslims," and that women should have the right to work outside the home (Telhami 2006).

Worldwide "interpretive aggregates" also develop from the massive exposure. These impromptu groups are composed of globally dispersed individuals who don't know each other personally but interpret known-in-common themes similarly. They are not (warm) communities or even (cold) networks. Interpretive aggregates are ad hoc issue-by-issue coteries of widely scattered individuals whose opinions on controversial matters of common interest happen to coincide. Global consciousness raising and the forming of interpretive aggregates reflect two potent, interconnected consequences of media globalization – the global mass audience and global public opinion.

The notion of the mass audience has a long history in traditional critical theory. The mass audience, according to the classical Marxist view, is a media–manipulated artifact of the "mass society."

Human beings are considered to be isolated, powerless, alienated persons who have no choice but to depend on the media for information, entertainment, and companionship. They become dominated by the mass media and other impersonal institutions that surround them. This view doesn't make sense today, if it ever really did. Large, anonymous audiences should not be equated with passive audiences (Webster and Phalen 1997: 116). To the contrary, the very size of the global audience empowers the persons who form it in ways they could not achieve as individuals acting alone or as members of small groups. The collective awareness and opinion of the global audience greatly influences political decisions and cultural trends. Global public opinion – researched, interpreted, packaged, and circulated worldwide by commercial polling companies, international news agencies, the culture industries, and the internet – grows in direct relation to the access people have to information.

Aggregated responses to world developments become part of the developments themselves and subsequently modify the discourses that are produced about them. World opinion anticipating and responding to the United States' invasion of Iraq, for instance, reinforced and spread resistance to the military assault and occupation. Strong anti-war sentiment that emerged later in the United States was bolstered by the results of global opinion polls that showed President Bush and his policies had become extremely unpopular abroad and at home. The change in public opinion led to calls by prominent politicians from both parties for bringing the troops home. Israel and the United States felt the crush of world opinion as people watched the devastation of Lebanon during the 2006 conflict, a turn of events that helped end major hostilities. Tremendous external pressure has also been brought to bear on Israel to end its occupation of the Palestinian territories, and for China to withdraw from Tibet. Global pressure about human rights ended apartheid in South Africa. World public opinion forced the Mexican government to stop harassing its indigenous population in Chiapas. The government of Myanmar has had to defend itself against world opinion in the case of dissident Aung San Suu Kyi. Global opinion even quickly condemned American TV evangelist Pat Robertson's call for the assassination of Venezuelan president Hugo Chavez in 2005, forcing him to backtrack and apologize publicly. World public opinion uniquely shapes major decisions and then further interprets the outcomes of events in a back-and-forth process of monitoring and display.[1]

Stage 5: Global Wisdom

In an interview with CNN's Larry King in the aftermath of the terrorist attacks on the World Trade Center and Pentagon in 2001, Queen Rania al-Abdullah of Jordan offered an important perspective on the tragedy. She said that the shock of the terrorist assault has the potential to produce a global "moral consciousness." Precisely because it took place in the age of global electronic and digital media, September 11 was first and foremost a symbolic event with tremendous emotional consequences. No other incident in world history compares with its multimediated, intertextual reach and impact. Has anyone anywhere not seen at least one visual representation of 9/11?

What Queen Rania was suggesting when she spoke of a worldwide moral consciousness has to do with what has occurred discursively *since* the Twin Towers fell and *after* the immediate circulation of television images, internet visuals, still photographs, reports, and commentaries. Her great hope – which has already begun to play out on the world stage – is that the terrorist strikes against modernity, secularism, America, and the West have stimulated a profound global process of soul-searching. Because people come to such introspection with widely varying motivations and goals, any existential journey to a shared moral consciousness will never end. But the process itself inspires reflection across cultural boundaries. That imperfect undertaking can promote greater global wisdom. Such cultural introspection has been made *possible* by modern communications media, technology, and industry, but it has been made *necessary* by contemporary political and cultural history. The shared base of commonly held information that is growing so rapidly around the world today begs for ethical interpretation.

No meaningful introspection or elevating of moral consciousness can evolve without the global force of mass media, the culture industries, and the internet. The very program on which Queen Rania appeared, CNN's *Larry King Live*, attracts middle-class viewers in more than 200 countries. Newsmakers everywhere eagerly accept invitations to appear on CNN and other high-profile television networks. The mix can be impressive. One edition of *Larry King Live*, for instance, featured Pakistan President Pervez Musharraf, former Soviet Premier Mikhail Gorbachev, Prince Abdullah Ben Abdul Aziz of Saudi Arabia, *Washington Post* editor and journalist Bob Woodward, and various representatives from Al-Jazeera – all connected by satellite from around the world – discussing the consequences of global terrorism.

In their form, media discussions about the moral issues of the day do not resemble anything close to pure participatory democracy, rhetorical or political, not even among the invited participants. Guests appearing on *Larry King Live*, even when the program is carried by CNN International, must speak English. CNN International appeals mainly to global middle-class residents, tourists, and business travelers. CNN, BBC International, and other international broadcasters transmit by satellite and cable, whose subscription costs lie beyond the economic grasp of the vast majority of the world's population. Al-Jazeera, Abudabi, Al-Arabiya, and other Arab television networks likewise use satellite technology to reach their middle-class viewers in the Middle East and around the world.

The very fact that the necessary elements of a global conversation have materialized at all, however, is unprecedented and positive. And while the international English-speaking middle class may be the social group best able to take advantage of global media and information technology, it's also true that people who fall into this category wield disproportionate influence over political and cultural developments directly and by the effect of their opinions. Moreover, while subscriptions to cable and satellite television and the internet may primarily be the privilege of the global middle class, many of the same images and discussions circulating about key news stories, issues, and controversies also appear on widely available terrestrial radio and television stations in every language. Of course, the content of all mass media – particularly major news stories – also circulates rapidly through unmediated networks of social groups representing every socioeconomic level and cultural orientation. It is the cumulative weight and significance of all these aspects of media and cultural globalization taken together that carry such great significance.

At the heart of the process lies not only elevated awareness of the events and issues that define world history, but also *awareness of that awareness* and of its consequences for moral decision making. People everywhere know that they know more than they ever knew before. They also know that others share the same basic information and that these others know that the information they possess is widely held. These interconnected realizations combine to influence what people do with shared information and how they feel about it. The very fact that people everywhere can ponder, reason, and emote over key world events together, to an increasing extent unrestricted by the limits of time and space, has become a powerful influence on the global imaginary in general and on perceptions of individual events in particular.

Intercultural dialogues that are created through global communication have the capacity to evolve into a loosely convergent global wisdom – an intangible but forceful development that can shape moral reasoning in an enlightened way and positively influence the political decisions that result. If this scenario plays out successfully on the world stage, then David Brin may be right when he says:

> civility just might make a comeback, after all. But not as something exhorted, or enforced from on high. Rather, it may return as a byproduct as we all learn to live in this new "commons," a near-future society where wrath seldom becomes habitual, because people who lash out soon learn that it simply does not pay. (Brin 1998: 169)

Stage 6: Institutional Channels

Authors of the United Nations' *Human Development Report* (UNDP 2002a) concluded that "a civic forum, giving voice to different parts of society and enabling debate from all viewpoints" is absolutely necessary for "deepening democracy in a fragmented world"

(p. 75). The United Nations document primarily addresses the plight of developing nations. Essential to making human progress in those countries, according to the international experts who wrote the report, are further development and diffusion of communications technology, the expansion of media channels, and the growth of effective civil societies.

Throughout this book I have emphasized the strong impact of market-driven channels of influence and personal initiative more than official channels and government. But the United Nations, its ancillary organizations, and other international bodies continue to play decisive roles in development of the human potential through communication too. The UN charter formally mandates that the organization function as "an instrument at the service of humankind, a mechanism which links us all in our efforts to build a better world," in part by encouraging open and equitable communication within and among nation states (United Nations 1999: 2).

In order to do this, the UN has constituted an Information and Communications Technologies (ICT) Task Force to "bridge the global divide, foster digital opportunity, and thus firmly put ICT at the service of development for all" (United Nations Information and Communication Technology Task Force 2005). The International Telecommunications Union, another UN organization, set out a Declaration of Principles and Plan of Action at the first World Summit on the Information Society held in Geneva in 2003 and followed it up with a meeting in Tunis two years later where the recommendations were put into practice (International Telecommunications Union 2005). The idea of the internet as a "global resource" requiring fair and responsible growth and management was passionately and repeatedly stressed. About the same time – late 2005 – the United Nations Educational, Scientific, and Cultural Organization (UNESCO) overwhelmingly passed a resolution stemming from its Universal Declaration of Cultural Diversity to "protect and promote the diversity of cultural expressions" and "to create the conditions for cultures to flourish and to freely interact in a mutually beneficial manner" (United Nations Educational, Scientific, and Cultural Organization 2005).

The United Nations General Assembly, Security Council, and associated organizations like UNESCO are not the only institutional channels through which essential transnational and transcultural negotiations take place. The World Economic Forum (WEF), incorporated as a non-profit foundation in Switzerland with UN endorsement (and much maligned by many anti-globalization forces), functions as a "global knowledge hub" that advocates "entrepreneurship in the global public interest." As a top priority responding to the current global crisis, religious, business, and political leaders of the WEF created the "Council of 100" at their 2004 meeting in Davos as an attempt to bridge the rift between the Islamic world and the West. Representatives from many developing countries have created the World Social Forum – where activists and agents from non-governmental organizations discuss alternative globalization policies and practices. And the independent Commission on Global Governance met in 1995 to stress the need for shared values, a global civic ethic, and enlightened leadership to help create a "global neighborhood."

Building on initiatives like these, David Held and his colleagues (Held et al. 1999) describe a visionary "global civil society," a proposal Held further develops in subsequent writing (Held 2004). By enacting international policies in economics, politics, and law that reliably reflect the ideals of a global social democracy, Held believes a "new global covenant" can emerge to promote greater social solidarity and justice worldwide (Held 2004). Held maintains that "the conditions facilitating transnational cooperation between peoples, given the global infrastructures of communication and increasing awareness of many common interests, have never been so propitious" (Held et al. 1999: 5).

As the material and symbolic conditions of life have changed over the years, so too has the notion of a civil society. Just thinking of civil society as a global phenomenon represents a conceptual migration away from its traditional and more parochial meaning toward what Held calls an "internationalism relevant to our global age" (Held 2004: 178). But beyond the generally positive connotations the term inspires, exactly what constitutes a civil society and how it should function have never been widely agreed upon. The civil society can be considered part of the state apparatus or separate from it. It may be connected to the market or be excluded from it. In secular nations, civil society generally refers to the proactive involvement of citizens in their communities through voluntary associations, foundations, and religious organizations; in theocratic societies the civil society is almost always equated with religious ideals and practices.

By any definition, civil society develops through willing contributions made by people to nurture the healthy growth of their communities. The civil society originates and matures in a cultural space that commutes between personal independence and social interdependence. As modern societies develop, individuals engage with others to pursue their private interests. For those societies to advance, however, the pursuit of private interests must be counterbalanced by active commitment to social responsibility and community. So while many individuals in the modern world acquire their identities by declaring their relative independence from others, they should also manifest "a sense of shared interests in which individuals recognize both the duty they have to support themselves and their duties toward one another" (Edgar and Sedgwick 1999: 63).

Stage 7: Utopian Potential

On a warm summer day in 2005 many of the world's most famous pop musicians staged the Live 8 benefit concert calling for debt relief and the eradication of AIDS and poverty in Africa. According to the organizers, Live 8 was viewable by 85 percent of the world's population. The concert originated in Europe and the United States and was transmitted in real time around the world via satellite television and the internet with an estimated audience of more than two billion viewers. Text message lotteries determined who got tickets to the live performances. Donations to the cause were accepted by mobile phone and the internet. DVDs, CDs, and audio and video downloads of the event are still being sold and Pink Floyd fans continue to buzz about the group's brief reunion. Live 8 – a true twenty-first-century communications event – was the most successful international pop music happening in history. The global spectacle facilitated an extraordinary outpouring of financial contributions and clearly influenced the political agenda at the G8 world economic summit that was held in northern Scotland the following week.

The G8 summit of 2005 was dramatically influenced by another global event that originated that summer in Great Britain: the bombing of the London transport system by Islamist terrorists five days after the concert ended and just before the G8 meeting began. The juxtaposition of these highly symbolic events vividly illustrates both the utopian potential made possible by the open spaces of global communication and their enigmatic vulnerabilities.

Making genuine progress toward a more humane global coexistence requires that imbalances and injustices in international economic and political relations be rectified (Held 2004). Just as vital to human development, though, is the need for improvement in global *cultural* relations, a less discernable project that cannot be reduced to military might, politics, or economics and is far less amenable to political negotiations and policy mandates. In the search for whatever common bonds of humanity we might call upon to bring us together more and achieve greater social justice, a broad commitment to promoting greater cultural understanding will be essential. The pen ultimately may not be stronger than the sword when push comes to shove in geopolitical struggles, but cultural transparency, expanded awareness, global public opinion, and the counter-hegemonic force of symbolic power in general have become influences that no nation, religion, culture, or high-profile leader today, no matter how dominant or confident, can ignore.

A cultural literacy fitting for the Communication Age requires that people sincerely question the limits of their traditions and political positions, respect cultural differences, accept diversity, and continue to develop multiple and complementary personal identities (UNDP 2004: 88). Global citizens everywhere have much to learn about recognizing and relativizing their cultural biases and about harnessing the counterproductive, sometimes devastating, tendencies and consequences those biases can bring. The evolving presence of global discourses and the capability of enhanced communication tools make cultural introspection, discussion, and dialogue technically and emotionally feasible. Individual initiative and the desire for a more cosmopolitan consciousness will be key. As Terhi Rantanen argues, while "the ideal of united nations is not realistic, the ideal of individuals united beyond nation states is emerging" (Rantanen 2005: 158).

Religious fundamentalists, nationalists, and unabashed advocates of the "free market" all promote a particular kind of unity that serves their particular interests. Those projects, as I hope to demonstrate in the following chapter, are no longer viable. The open spaces of global communication promise not unity, but opportunity for meaningful dialogue and nurturance of the global public sphere. Cultural negotiations that global media inspire will do much to determine the "moral future of civilization" by influencing how the world can be productively understood by its citizens (Silverstone 2006). The challenge that lies ahead is formidable, but the opportunity for meaningful change is real. As Dan Gillmor observes: "we tend to be bound by our past, even when we can imagine the future. Yet sometimes we are transformed, and media can be at the center of how we see these changes" (Gillmor 2004: 236). He might have added, "and how we make the changes come about." No doubt, the lives of global citizens everywhere have been dramatically impacted by the sheer amount of information that fills the open spaces of global communication. To fulfill the potential for cultural change, however, we'll have to frankly address the barriers that stand in the way.

Note

1. Although global public opinion often develops in unmanaged ways to challenge the influence wielded by the world's political-economic power holders, purposeful attempts are also made by the powerful to shape global opinion for strategic reasons. Aid given by the United States to the victims of the tsunami disaster in Indonesia in 2004, for example, became an opportunity to show compassion and generosity. The fact that so many aid recipients were Muslim was promoted by American foreign policy makers to demonstrate the claim that the country harbors no religious prejudice against Islam. Promoting this kind of influence is a completely reasonable thing to do. Joseph Nye argues that the United States and other Western nations should in fact do much more of this in order to cultivate favorable global public opinion by using soft power – "the ability to shape the preferences of others . . . the ability to attract [others to culture and political ideals]" rather than depending on sheer economic and military might to achieve their goals (Nye 2004: 5–6, x).

It's not easy to assess the success or failure of attempts to manufacture agreeable public opinion. Many have argued, for example, that the Cold War was won by the attractive force of Western symbolic forms like music and movies and a vision of personal freedom. But people living in Europe's communist states already had much in common ethnically and culturally with the outsiders who were trying to influence them and were vulnerable because of the lack of religious ideology in the system. By comparison, American officials who design and implement the Middle East propaganda strategy say that the Cold war conducted against a "godless enemy" in the twentieth century was much easier to win than the one being waged now against cultures that are grounded in an all-encompassing belief in god.

Chapter 8

Fundamentalism and Cosmopolitanism

(Athens) Revealed at the core of a floating landscape was a male figure crouching on top of a perfect white cube – a symbol of the Earth. The man stood and began walking, the cube twisting and rotating beneath his feet representing man's evolutionary journey towards becoming a logical, spiritual being, searching for knowledge. The galaxy of floating rocks surrounding the cube then rose into the air as the faces of the rock fragments were transformed through video into images of human faces and bodies – a celebration of the beauty and diversity of humanity. Finally, the rock fragments lowered and came to rest in the water to represent the Greek Islands. Two lovers ran into the water, throwing off their clothes to play and swim in the sea, at which point Eros, the god of love, emerged from the water, flew above the lovers and out toward the edge of the scene to greet the next arrivals into the stadium. (www.yenra.com August 14, 2004)

Returning to its place of origin, the spectacular Opening Ceremony at the Athens Summer Olympics celebrated the potential of the universal human mind and body to develop and unite through the quadrennial ritual of international sporting competition. Emanating from the world's cradle of Western civilization and taking place under threat of terrorist assault, the opening ceremony represented much more than athletic games. The striking images extolled the achievements of scientific knowledge that have evolved through the fundamental principles of rational thought – the very basis of the Enlightenment and the foundation for much of modern Western culture. The image of the spirited lovers playing in the sea made it clear that the body must also be free – responsibly so, of course – for women and men to express themselves and approach their potential as human beings.

Notwithstanding its disruptions and imperfections – world wars, terrorist attacks, failed drug tests, judging scandals – the Olympic Games has long served as the world's most visible living symbol of hope for international and intercultural understanding, appreciation, and cooperation. By convening a wide range of cultures under comprehensive rules that protect the rights of each participant, the Olympic Games represents the promise of tolerance and peace among the world's diverse peoples.

Can the democratic and humanistic principles that characterize the Olympic Games extend beyond sports? Will the open spaces of global communication help create conditions for the cultural liberty that the United Nations considers so vital to human development? What are the chances that our conflicted world will ever evolve into the cosmopolitan society Anthony Giddens described in his pre-9/11 assessment of globalization's influence (Giddens 2000)? What obstacles stand in the way?

As the title of Giddens' book – *Runaway World* – and recent history plainly suggest, increased global connectedness among the world's populations guarantees no positive outcomes. Postmodernity and globalization provoke widespread anxiety. The actions of superpowers and extremist groups destabilize and threaten everyone. Destructive animosities and conflicts that inhabit centuries-long ethnic struggles have sharpened in recent years. But it is the deeper, more structural problem of religious fundamentalism – "patterns of religious militancy by which self-styled 'true believers' attempt to arrest the erosion of religious identity, fortify the borders of the religious community, and create viable alternatives to secular institutions and behaviors" (Almond, Appleby, and Sivan 2003: 17) – that impedes human development in the most substantial and disturbing way. As E. O. Wilson describes it, "there is something deep in religious belief that amplifies societal conflict . . . Our gods, the true believer asserts, stand against your false idols, our spiritual purity against your corruption, our divinely sanctioned knowledge against your errancy" (Wilson 2006: 1483).

How did things get that way? As Charles Darwin realized when he wrote *The Descent of Man*, the social organization of religious thought – indeed, even the most primal belief in the existence of a "universal Creator" – did not "arrive in the mind of man until he had been elevated by long-continued culture" (Darwin 1871/1998: 636). By creating myths of an omniscient supernatural force, an "all seeing Deity" in Darwin's words, many cultural groups found powerful ways to codify moral values and enforce standards for social behavior. The "moral sense" and "conscience" of the human being does not originate with religion. They began with "social instincts, largely guided by the approbation of our fellow men, rules by reason, self interest, and [only] in later times by religious feelings . . . confirmed by instruction and habit" (ibid.: 137). Religion became naturalized through many years of routine cultural practice. It offers structure, order, and stability while permeating and indoctrinating cultural groups. Religious prophets become tribal leaders to whom "abject submission is looked [upon] as a sacred virtue" (ibid.: 122). And "because most religions offer no valid mechanism by which their core beliefs can be tested and revised, each new generation of believers is condemned to inherit the superstitions and tribal hatreds of its predecessors" (Harris 2005: 31).

How religion or any cultural tradition or trait transmits from one generation to the next and spreads so profusely is difficult to explain. Richard Dawkins identifies the basic unit of cultural propagation, including religion, as the "meme." Memes are replicators that allow advantageous cultural traits to evolve: "Just as genes propagate themselves in the gene pool by leaping from body to body via sperms or eggs, so memes propagate themselves in the meme pool by leaping from brain to brain via a process which, in the broad sense, can be called imitation" (Dawkins 1989: 192). Memes for "blind faith" (or the "god meme") propagate "by spoken and written word, aided by great music and great art" and by their "survival value" and "psychological appeal" since religion "provides a superficially plausible answer to deep and troubling questions about existence" (ibid.: 193). Over time, our ancestors became traumatized by religion. The fear of God, and especially of going to Hell, transmits like the fear of snakes from one generation to the next through processes of psychological adaptation.

Religion is not the only basis for development of fundamentalist thought and no single group holds a monopoly on religious fundamentalism. But religious fundamentalism plays a determining role in a great many global deliberations and developments. Distinguishing ideology from religion – a clever political expediency – is inaccurate and misleading. Ideology is a "body of ideas reflecting the social needs and aspirations of an individual, group, class, or culture" (*American Heritage Dictionary*). It is a system of ideas expressed in communication (Lull 2000). Religions are particular "integrated systems of the expression of man's belief in and reverence for a superhuman power recognized as the creator and governor of the universe" (*American Heritage Dictionary*). Religious ideology interacts with, helps shape, and even defines some cultural groups by furnishing shared values, assumptions, rules, and social practices that promote personal and collective identity, security, and belonging.

The Passion of the Religious Culture

Faith is saying, "I will ignore my God-given gifts for discerning reality and instead throw my lot in with blind belief in something that was forced into my head before I could even think." Isn't that how we get adults in this world who fight wars based on which contrived fairytale they were brought up on – the magic apple and talking bush or the flying horse and circling the black rock?

B. Maher, *When You Ride Alone, You Ride with bin Laden*, p. 53

Despite massive destruction wrought in New York, Bali, Madrid, Beslan, London, New Delhi, and other parts of the world in the past few years, the greatest obstacles to long-term peace and prosperity in today's fast globalizing world are not religious terrorists. The more significant and perplexing barriers develop from the very existence of religious ideologies and cultural practices that disrespect other faiths and discredit other ways of life. This is the "one true God, chosen people" problem that defines and animates the major monotheistic religions – Judaism, Christianity, and Islam. The attitude is one of inestimable arrogance. As Khaled Abou El Fadl suggests, "Perhaps all firmly held systems of belief, especially those founded on religious conviction, are in some ways supremacist: believers are understood to have some special virtue that distinguishes them from adherents of other faiths . . . [yet the fundamentalists] do not merely seek self-empowerment but aggressively seek to disempower, dominate, or destroy others" (El Fadl 2002: 5). Those "others" – *goyim*, pagan, infidel – appear prominently in the rhetoric and practices of all three monotheistic faiths as impure, threatening, and in desperate need of religious conversion, control, or elimination (Peters 2003).

While most believers from the major religious groups would likely not describe themselves as fundamentalist, radical fundamentalism is clearly on the rise and fundamentalist-inspired thinking increasingly infects the religious mainstream of each group. Considering each other to be godless barbarians, Christians and Muslims repeatedly committed monstrous acts of violence against each other – merciless massacres, beheadings, even cannibalism – from the eleventh to the thirteenth centuries. Ridley Scott's film *Kingdom of Heaven* spectacularly reveals how epic battles over religious ownership of Jerusalem during the period of the Crusades resembled a terrible game of "king of the mountain" played by vicious men. Violently attacking each other because "God wills it," each side claimed to "speak the truth" and vilified the other as an "enemy of God." This happened even though Jews, Christians, and Muslims all claim to worship the same God and base key assumptions of their belief systems on interpretations of their common ancestor Abraham and the creation myths of the Old Testament.[1]

The legends and myths that emerged from the Middle Ages – the great warriors, victories, losses, causes, and struggles for salvation – were indelibly inscribed into the consciousness of Christian and Muslim believers. The chaotic social and cultural conditions that prevailed in Europe and the Arab world at the same time encouraged extreme dependency on religious ideology and institutions to provide stability and cultural identity for Christians and Muslims. That medieval mentality has never fully subsided. It combines with and reinforces creationist stories and other religious and cultural folklore to intensify the antagonisms we see today.

Religious fundamentalists seek a world free of complexity where surrender to God and an unswerving belief in the dogmas presented in the holy books are not questioned. Noting similarities between neofundamentalist Muslims in Europe and fundamentalist Christians in America, Olivier Roy describes how religion-based cultural ideologies "become a sort of neo-ethnicity . . . encompassing all aspects of the believer's life" where "faith is the fault line between the good people and the wicked" (Roy 2004: 332, 329).

Any critique of religious fundamentalism, however, should not be reduced to differences between Christians and Muslims or clashes within the groups (e.g. Catholics against Protestants, Sunni fighting Shia). Social hierarchical and gender discrimination of Hindu fundamentalism has long corrupted Indian culture and politics and continues to stoke conflict with Muslims in South Asia. The ideology of the first monotheistic religion, Judaism, "remains a lightning rod for intolerance to this day" (Harris 2005: 93). Orthodox Jews see themselves as "irretrievably different" from non-Jews and are as much at odds with the "civilizing insights of modernity as any other religion" (ibid.: 94).The Jewish identity as "God's chosen people" surfaces today in forms such as filmmaker Stephen Spielberg's charity organization, "The Righteous Persons Foundation." While Jews themselves have certainly suffered from ethnic intolerance, the many fundamentalists among them must also be held accountable for their own noxious mixture of religious self-righteousness, bigotry, and discrimination. As Stuart Sims argues in *Fundamentalist World*, "the whole notion of a Jewish State involves a fundamentalist mindset, since it's a return of a people to the territory where their traditional belief system originated and flourished in its purest state" (Sim 2005: 141).

The arrogance and violence of Israeli state policy has long brought widespread condemnation, except in the United States where political leaders have managed to convince most Americans that support for Israel serves their national interests. The massive Israeli lobby in Washington extracts an exorbitant amount of American money and technical resources for Jewish causes in Israel that manifest little, if any, real benefit to the United States (Mearsheimer and Walt 2006). The alliance between America and Israel also conveniently feeds the belief held by fundamentalist Christians that Jews must survive today so they can play their part in what is promised in the New Testament – the last battle between "good and evil" where Jews must convert to Christianity or perish. When Israeli and Hezbollah military forces clashed in Lebanon in 2006, many evangelicals interpreted the destruction of human life there, together with the chaos that was raging in Iraq, Afghanistan, and the Palestinian Territories, as sure signs that the fiery "End Times" were approaching. TV evangelist Pat Robertson even flew to Jerusalem to meet with Israeli Prime Minister Ehud Ohmert during the war with Hezbollah to cheer the Jewish forces on. Palestinians, of course, suffer in every way from Israeli policies, including the claim that Jerusalem – so long contested between Christians and Muslims – rightly belongs to Jews. Religious orthodoxy and right-wing extremism in Israel have increased to such levels in recent years that they undermine Israel's own interests as well (Cramer 2004).

Fundamentalist America

> Freedom and liberty are not America's gift to the world; they are the Almighty's gift to mankind . . . May God bless you all.
> President George W. Bush, Kennesaw, Georgia, February 20, 2003

It became increasingly obvious as his time in office wore on that a contrived moral code and missionary foreign policy inspired by Christian fundamentalism formed the core of the George W. Bush doctrine – an ideology that also represents the values and beliefs of many Americans. It didn't happen spontaneously. The influence of the Christian right grew throughout the last decades of the twentieth century. But when President Bush took office in 2000, the well-organized Project for the New American Century, an almost exclusively male, neoconservative political action group dedicated to the proposition that American leadership based on "military strength" and "moral principle" is "good for America and good for the world," began to significantly impact foreign policy and defense (Project for the New American Century 2006). Unabashed promotion of American manifest destiny was advocated by the president's closest advisors – Dick Cheney, Karl Rove, Paul Wolfowitz, and others – who further injected right-wing ideology and religious beliefs into national political leadership and decision making. Fundamentalist religious leaders themselves also had the ear of the President and ruling party of the world's most powerful nation.

However narrowly, the American public voted George W. Bush into office in 2000 partly in response to the sex scandal that had rocked the moral authority of the Clinton administration. The Christian right organized to support Bush, a sinner who had come home to God and now was thought to represent their interests. Who are these fundamentalist-thinking Americans? Some 84 percent of Americans identify themselves as Christians and of that number nearly 40 percent call themselves "evangelical" or "born again" (ABC News 2003). Their influence is not just a matter of reasoned and respectful differences of opinion with non-Christians about objective reality. Nearly 80 percent of American Christians believe in the virgin birth and two-thirds think the Christmas story, including the presence of angels and the guiding star of Bethlehem, is historically accurate (*Newsweek* 2004: 51). Only a small minority of Americans believe in evolution and nearly two-thirds say creationism should be taught in school. Some 42 percent believe that all "living things have existed in their present form since the beginning of time" (Pew Forum on Religion and Public Life 2005; Pew Research Center for People and the Press 2005). Many American teenagers continue along the same path. Three-fourths of American teens say they are religious, follow their parents' religious affiliations, and appear to be more tied to mainstream cultural values than previous generations (C. Smith 2005).

Fundamentalist Christians believe that following Christ is the only way to "salvation" (Parker 2004). Evangelical Christians in America – those fundamentalists who especially stress the importance of personal salvation – were once considered a fringe presence even within the Republican Party. But during the Bush presidency, evangelicals expanded their influence on domestic and foreign policy and moved closer and closer to the mainstream of the party, for which they vote overwhelmingly. They consider safety and security at home – including military strength, controlling weapons of mass destruction, and fighting terrorism – more important than acts of altruism, such as international relief efforts, aid for improving living standards in developing countries, protection of religious freedom in foreign countries (Greenberg 2004). Most evangelicals strongly believe that the world will end in the battle at Armageddon (Pew Forum on Religion and Public Life

2004). Like their Jewish and Muslim counterparts, fundamentalist Christians steadfastly oppose rights for homosexuals and same-sex couples (Parker 2004).

George W. Bush used his wide base of support among evangelical Christians to parlay widespread fears about terrorism into a good versus evil debate, a politics of fear, and a rampageous military-political strategy that appealed to many American citizens who were, and still are, reeling from 9/11. The force of Bush's war presidency and the basic indifference and hostility he displayed toward disapproving world opinion was driven by a sense of moral duty he said his "higher Father" had invested in him (Woodward 2004). Bush's certainty that "God is on his side" and the growing "global imperative of political and religious evangelism" that he and his religious compatriots promote has led even some conservative observers to warn that, just like previous imperial powers pretending to operate with divine authority, American status and influence in the world is already in decline (Phillips 2006).

President Bush was held accountable for his beliefs and policies by the American public in 2004 when citizens exercised the most basic and meaningful democratic right in which they can engage – the popular vote. The result of that election sent shock and sadness around the world, including throughout much of the United States. Religion appeared to many observers to have been the key factor in the election result. Although most Americans who favored Bush would not likely describe their support for him as based solely or mainly on religious conviction, the dominant reason people gave for voting for him was "moral values," clearly referring to his perceived personal character and commitment to a Christian-based, neoconservative ideology.

Hardcore fundamentalist Christian activism spreads influence outside the inner circles of politics too. Numerous watchdog groups monitor the mass media and culture industries and search for "moral violations" they can report to government authorities. The network television series *The Book of Daniel*, which many Christians believed mocked their faith, was cancelled in 2006, for instance, under pressure from the fundamentalist organization Focus on the Family, which had organized a massive letter-writing campaign. Mormons mobilized efforts to try to get the HBO series *Big Love*, a program about polygamous families, taken off the air. Movies that portray religious themes are especially likely to raise the ire of the faithful. Many Christians regarded *The Last Temptation of Christ* (1988) as blasphemous and boycotted the film. Reaction by Christian believers to release of the box office hit *The Da Vinci Code*, marketed as an "accurate fictional" story that questions the validity of Jesus' innocence and the origins of the Bible, was predictably extreme. But not as extreme as it would have been in centuries past. As Rev. Gregory L. Foley of Our Lady of the Most Holy Rosary Church in San José, California, told the *San José Mercury News* upon release of *The Da Vinci Code*, "In days of old, the author and filmmakers would have been hunted down and given one last chance to make a confession before being burned at the stake as heretics." Fundamentalist Christian cultural crusading isn't just defensive in nature. Televangelists blanket terrestrial and cable television, radio, the internet, the publishing industry, and their cavernous churches with fiery messages from God, schemes for salvation, and requests for money.[2]

In *Fundamentalist World*, Stuart Sim laments the fact "that religion can continue to be such a potent factor in our [Western] lives, after nearly three centuries of Enlightenment thought" (Sim 2005: 219). The future of religion's influence in contemporary Western culture is not clear, however. Empirical data show that while "evangelicalism is growing in the USA . . . secularism is also on the rise" (Dennett 2006: 319). And while the West is often described as Christian, that characterization misleads in several respects. Religious freedom and the right to express non-religious views are political guarantees in modern Western cultures. These freedoms have helped draw immigrants of all religious persuasions to North America and Europe for centuries. Western societies have become a polyglot of religious and non-religious thought. Moreover, despite the sizeable number of evangelicals in America, Christianity has weakened in many respects throughout the West, especially in Europe. When Pope Benedict XVI assumed his post in 2005 he complained that "there is no longer evidence of a need for God, even less for Christ" in the West. Attendance of church services in Europe has dropped off greatly through the years. Gay marriage has been legally accepted in Canada, Belgium, Holland,

Spain, and in some states in the United States. Overall in America, however, religious tradition persists and has become more visible. The idea that "religion is very important" remains a cultural fact in the United States (World Values Survey 2005).

The active passivity of Islam

> *Islamic fundamentalism is a universalism – it believes that its tenets speak to all of humanity. Among fundamentalisms it is the most significant variety in the world.*
>
> B. Tibi, *The Challenge of Fundamentalism*, p. 36

The passion of the religious culture runs deepest in the Islamic world. While radical Islamists express the most visible resistance to the sharp edges of modernity and globalization, their rhetoric and the symbolic force of their actions represent the essence of a cultural view that long pre-dates the current wave of violence. It's a general attitude that is tacitly accepted by millions more. In fact, the most consequential obstacle to lasting global peace and cultural progress in the Muslim world, according to Irshad Manji, is not the terrorists or the radical fringe. It is the "paralyzing sickliness of the entire religion – the untouchability of *mainstream* Islam" (Manji 2003: 49; italics mine).

Religious conviction with minimal reflection and little or no sense of true universal humanity creates a deadly dangerous world-view. It happens even at an unconscious level. As Manji points out, "Most of us Muslims aren't Muslims because we think about it, but rather because we're born that way. It's 'who we are'" (Manji 2003: 16). That's why it's fair to say that mainstream Islam, not the radical or violent minority, has become the dominant "culture of complicity" (ibid.: 63), and that it is reasonable to conclude that "the number of passive Muslim supporters of terrorism is far greater than Westerners want to contemplate" (Hotaling 2003: 165). Fanatical groups are only "extreme manifestations of more prevalent intellectual theological currents in modern Islam" (El Fadl 2002: 7–8).

Asserting the claim that (our) God alone embodies absolute truth has been a characteristic of all monotheistic religions over the centuries. But the infallibility conceit persists more in Islam than in Christianity and most other faiths, is thought to be backed up by a command from Muhammad to eliminate all rivals, and is woefully out of step with progressive trends in modernity, including the way other monotheistic faiths have become more integrated into secular global realities (Cook 2000: 33). It wasn't terrorists who outlawed the practice of religions other than Islam, punishable by imprisonment and even death, as an Islamic principle. Polytheism (*shirk*), the worship of any God other than the "one true God," has represented the ultimate wrong in Islam throughout the religion's history. Apostasy – the personal abandonment of the faith – is subject to punishment of death in Islamic law. Apostasy was considered a capital offense in early Judaism and Christianity too, but "of the Abrahamic faiths Islam stands alone in its inability to renounce this barbaric doctrine convincingly" (Dennett 2006: 289).

The word Islam means to "submit" or "surrender" to God's will. A Muslim is "one who surrenders." Although submission or surrender to higher religious authority is by no means peculiar to Muslims, unique and compelling factors stand out when considering the special case of Islamic fundamentalism. First is the sheer number of Muslims worldwide, estimated to range between one and two billion people. That number will continue to grow absolutely and in proportion to other religious groups, mainly because of the birth rate in Muslim countries. Second is the degree of submission to God expected of Islamic faithful compared to other groups whose fundamentalism has been tempered by secular authority and political history. There is no expression in Arabic for "Muslim moderate," explained Khaled Abou El Fadl to the World Affairs Council in San Francisco, "only for 'extremist' or 'Muslim'" (El Fadl 2005).

The underlying structure of the faith and predominant vision of the future rest upon one undeniable fact: world history for the past 1,000 years threatens what is clearly promised in the Koran – world domination by Islam. Western global supremacy today interferes with Muslims' own imperialistic and hegemonic ambitions. Consequently, Western influence represented by modernization, globalization, and the presence of non-Islamic religions in the Middle East can be considered evil forces that interfere with God's plan. Islamic scholar Bassam Tibi characterizes this condition as a "clash between two universalisms – one secular, one divine – each claiming global validity" (Tibi 2002: 61).

The only possible escape from the hopelessness into which so many Middle Eastern Muslims are born is to respond productively to the findings, implications, and recommendations of the United Nations' Arab Human Development Reports (UNDP 2002b, 2003b). Unfortunately, the tendency to keep grinding away on centuries-old disputes, especially the classic religious wars, contributes to interminable acts of revenge and lack of economic, cultural, and political development. These historical resentments interact with more recent cultural losses and humiliations including early Western colonialism, Soviet expansionism, the Palestine–Israel conflict, and the presence of outsiders on Muslim sacred ground.

Other Fundamentalisms

The term "fundamentalist" first arose in the early twentieth century in the United States as an expression that referred to Protestants who believed they were interpreting the Bible literally. Fundamentalism has most often been associated with radical Islam and evangelical Christianity in recent years. While religion has become the most visible and threatening surface of the fundamentalisms appearing on the world stage today, it is not the only one. Fundamentalism in general implies ideological and cultural extremism – "an assertion of formulaic truth without regard to consequences" (Giddens 1994: 100). Authoritarian arrogance attached to dogma breeds the requisite conditions. As Stuart Sim points out, "not every fundamentalist is a terrorist, but every fundamentalist is a dogmatist, and that is enough for the rest of us to worry; especially when dogmatism generates a desire to suppress all other viewpoints" (Sim 2005: 15). Fundamentalism, therefore, refers to the *enduring, active advocacy of any entity that claims to be a fully determining authority or ultimate truth on matters of basic social, cultural, or political importance*. From this perspective, extreme advocates of the nation and the market can also be considered fundamentalists.

Nationalism as it is exercised in the world's more developed countries has been "the most successful ideology around the world for the last two centuries" (Rantanen 2005: 82). Strong devotion to protecting and promoting the interests of the nation state, of course, do not have to imply extremism. The nation state can provide unmatched social guarantees for its citizens and safe haven for refugees from other lands.

Nationalism assumes radical contours when a significant percentage of the state's inhabitants respond intemperately to what they consider present or imminent threats. Nationalists defend their territory against outsiders who might endanger the integrity or viability of the political and cultural system. Under these circumstances, loyalty and unity of purpose are expected of citizens (Edgar and Sedgwick 1999: 254). American nationalism has become considerably more prominent since the terrorist attacks of 2001, for example. Russian nationalism arose in response to economic instability and ethnic unrest after the fall of communism. The current leftist turn in Latin American politics has its roots in nationalism. The most notable case of nationalism in the West may be reaction by Europeans to the immigration of Muslims over the past half century, a complex process that has been difficult to manage agreeably because of Europe's pressing economic needs in an era of declining native populations and the ease of movement made possible by Europe's relatively open borders. Citizens of many European nations, already uncomfortable with the cultural ambivalences that go along with joining the European Union, believe their successful secular nations and cultures are under attack by outsiders who prefer not to assimilate. Reactions range from extremist political movements headed by Jorg Heider in Austria and Jean-Marie Le Pen in France, for instance, to the more nuanced position that was espoused by Pim Fortuyn in Holland, until an assassin's bullet took his voice out of the mix.

Nationalist and religious fundamentalisms do not exclude each other. To the contrary, they often resonate with and strongly reinforce each other, sometimes with considerable hard-power resources at their leaders' disposal. Israel's military prowess in the Middle East may be the most striking example. Fundamentalist ideology is woven directly into the fabric of cultural values, institutions, and routines. For instance, the United States Marine Corps – considered to be the elite fighting unit of the American military – has as its identifying slogan, "God, Country, and Corps." It is just this combination of strong religious belief and nationalism that the thinkers of the Enlightenment set out to change in eighteenth-century Europe.

Market fundamentalism

The prospects for a more peaceful and prosperous world do not turn entirely on questions of ideology and culture, and the fundamentalist mindset is not limited to religious or nationalist projects and loyalties. "Market fundamentalism," a term coined by George Soros (1998, 2002), describes the dangerous belief that the self-regulating mechanisms of economic markets should be left untouched in order to insure maximum allocation of material and financial resources. Like the extremist views that underlie and characterize the other fundamentalisms, however, market fundamentalism cannot deliver what the world needs to grow more safely and harmoniously. America's generic prescription for economic growth in developing countries administered at the end of the last century – the "Washington consensus" strategy of dramatically lowering trade barriers and radically deregulating markets – didn't always work. It often backfired disastrously. The collapse of Argentina's banking and investment system in the 1990s may be the most well-known example of the failure of this particular brand of market fundamentalism.

Even in strict economic terms, positive market outcomes can never be guaranteed. Moreover, markets "are not capable, on their own, of taking care of collective needs" such as law and order and the very economic regulation that is required to bring about greater social justice and a fairer distribution of public goods within and between nation states (Soros 2002: 6). Even the much-criticized World Bank recognizes that "prosperity and well being, like peace, are indivisible and must be shared if they are to be maintained" (World Bank 2003: 191). Joseph Stiglitz, the World Bank's former chief economist, strongly denounced the way economic and cultural globalizations have been managed. Economic fairness and sustainability, Stiglitz argues, must be institutionalized and practiced globally. He says a more human face must be put on economic globalization by respecting and protecting diverse cultural values and identities. Favorable conditions for economic growth, according to Stiglitz, won't develop by just "replacing the old dictatorships of national elites with new dictatorships of international finance" (Stiglitz 2002: 247). Poorer nations need internal development to reach their economic potential, each according to its own particular circumstances, and rich nations must help (Stiglitz and Charlton 2006).

On the other hand, to describe the aggressive role of the market as producing nothing more than social and economic "tyranny" (Bourdieu 1998), or to categorically condemn economic globalization as inherently and irreversibly flawed, grossly misrepresents what's happening and threatens to impede progress for those who suffer most. Economic development for everyone today depends on successful participation in fair international trade, particularly for those economies and cultures that lag behind the global standard (Norberg 2003). An economic model based on "free competition on a global scale has liberated inventive and entrepreneurial talents and accelerated technological innovations" for nations across the developmental spectrum in the past (Soros 2002: 4; Zakaria 2003), and promises the same today. As Francis Fukuyama argues, while all people may not want to live in liberal democracies, most desire to live in a modern and prosperous society (Fukuyama 2006). Robust participation in cross-cultural interactions of all kinds is required to reach that goal. The market also functions in positive ways for individual consumers by producing and circulating the resources that ordinary people need to do their cultural work.

Among the most pressing challenges the world faces in the immediate future is finding a system of global regulation and governance that strikes the proper balance between economic freedom and social justice. Global economic and cultural activity requires closer monitoring and better regulation. To that end, the principles of the United Nations' Global Compact must be respected and expanded to encourage more transparent, accountable, and democratic participation in global economic and political affairs by all nations (Held 2004).

The Democratic Secular Imperative

Fundamentalist religious, national, and market forces all militate against the cosmopolitan promise of the Communication Age. None of these fundamentalisms will ever be eliminated, but they can be marginalized gradually through cultural transparency, more effective global governance, and the spread of democratic secularism. Religious intolerance under any scenario will continue to be the most enduring impediment to human development.

Freedom *from* religion is just as important as freedom *of* religion and must be defended with equal intensity. Both freedoms are central to Western cultures and have been largely responsible for their success. The triumphant struggle for freedom from religious persecution and intolerance led to the creation of democratic secular societies, which have become the most stable and prosperous of nations, and whose foundations are protected vigorously by their citizens. As the British philosopher A. C. Grayling reminded attendees of the World Economic Forum in 2004, "Western secularism and representative democracy were hard won, over centuries, and reside at the core of Euro-American identity. They are amenable to discussion but not compromise" (The Davos Report 2004: 7).

Secularism refers broadly to the process in which religious thinking, practice, and institutions lose social significance (B. Wilson 1966). Secular influence never completely replaces religion in any society; it relativizes it ideologically and decreases its civil authority. Secular societies grant non-religious codes and practices legal standing over religious considerations or laws. Grayling argues that in its ideal form, "secularism is a very neutral thesis that simply states that all religions and the state . . . should be kept distinct from one another so that different religions can flourish and survive without any one of them being privileged above the others." This means that, "the public domain in the state can be a neutral one where everyone meets as equals." Secularism, he says, is "nonreligious, not anti-religious" (The Davos Report 2004: 14). That the civil contract supersedes religious authority remains the central proposition that holds secular societies together and contributes so much to their well-being.

The contrast between secularism and religion actually forms a false opposition that grants religion undeserved moral authority. The moral principles of humankind don't *originate* with, but are *reflected* in the major religions. Human beings created religions in various cultural contexts in part to formalize "natural laws of morality," which are "knowable by human beings through their powers of reason" (Dolhenty 2005). Basic moral principles (e.g. "do good, avoid evil," "people are responsible for their actions") are survival strategies and moral development is an evolutionary process. Man invented gods to rationally comprehend the universe. As Charles Darwin surmised, "As soon as the important faculties of the imagination, wonder, and curiosity, together with some power of reasoning, had become partially developed, man would naturally crave to understand what was passing around him, and would have vaguely speculated on his own existence" (Darwin 1871/1998: 97). The creation myths were early stabs at scientific explanation: "fabricating them was the best early scribes could do to explain the universe and human existence" (E. O. Wilson 2006: 1483). Certain cultural products of these evolutionary processes – particular faiths and religions – have proven to be such attractive ideas for people over the millennia that they could never be discarded completely in any society, including communist states where religious practice is illegal. No respectable scholar, including Charles Darwin, denies that religion has served the West by helping to spread a firm moral foundation upon which comparatively fair and productive societies have developed.

Secularism ultimately succeeds where religious authority fails because it privileges science, reason, and tolerance over emotion, superstition, and dogma as the basis of society. Science and reason give people "better materials with which to think about the world" (Appiah 2006: 42). Consequently, democratic secular societies generally welcome most forms of outside cultural influence. Because secularism inspires tolerance, diversity, equality, and freedom, it creates superior opportunities for personal and collective development. The strong strain of European secularism, for instance, supports global climate control, the supremacy of international courts of law, human rights treaties, peacekeeping, foreign aid, and the general use of multilateral institutions and cooperation to solve global problems (Nye 2004: 82). Furthermore, history has shown

that democratic secularism and "Western values [in general] . . . a
not just a current fad, but integral components the human race is
likely to live in for some time to come" (Cook 2000: 41).

A confrontation between fundamentalist intolerance and cosmopolitan open-mindedness has become the global spectacle of the
early twenty-first century. Can secular constraints effectively limit
the harm caused by religious oppression? What kinds of religious
identities and sensitivities can we expect to emerge from the traditional ones? Ultimately, "how far and to what extent [does]
Islam – and, of course, parts of the resurgent fundamentalist West,
especially the religious right in the United States – [have] the
capacity to confront [their] own ideologies, double standards, and
limitations" (Held 2004: 177).

Some hopeful signs have appeared. Findings from the World
Values Survey "show that people in Muslim countries have as
much support for democratic values as do people in non-Muslim
countries" (UNDP 2004: 5). The influence of Islam in Turkey,
for example, has been significantly counterbalanced by development of a secular government, a functioning civil society, a growing
economy, and a relatively cosmopolitan outlook that includes a
strong desire by many Turks to become part of the European
Union. Called by one veteran observer, "the most powerful symbol
of modern Islam in the world today," Turkey's presiding Justice
and Development Party "has shown devotion to Islam is entirely
compatible with liberalism, pluralism, and democracy," where
dissent has become an accepted principle (Zakaria 2004b: 39).

While people in most Muslim countries favor political democracy in the abstract, they resist advancing the measures that are
needed for *cultural* development – gender equality, freedom of
expression, and social tolerance (Inglehart and Norris 2003; World
Values Survey 2006). A troubling paradox thus exists in the
sequence of national development in the Islamic world. Economic
development frees societies to make cultural changes. But economic development cannot materialize without an educated workforce that benefits from professional expertise, skilled labor, the
public presence of women, and an honest appreciation for social
and cultural diversity in general. Traditional religious values and
practices make that combination of cultural developments difficult
to achieve.

ople resist change for religious reasons is understandable,
nal, in a detraditionalizing world (Giddens 2000: 15–16).
tic political, religious, and cultural reform has arrived at
:imes, in various ways, at various places throughout the
modern history. Considering the pressing question of
.t should come as no surprise that the most thoughtful discussions and persuasive proposals for the massive project of reformation and modernization today come from Muslim intellectuals
living in, and influenced by, the cultural realities of the West
where lived realities make the advantages of cultural change most
clear (e.g. El Fadl 2002; Manji 2003; Ramadan 2004; Rauf 2004;
Tibi 2002).

One Moral Universe?

Jean Charles de Menezes, a young Brazilian citizen working in
London, was shot to death by police a few days after the terrorist
attack in 2005 sent the city into a panic. Thinking de Menezes
may have been attempting to carry out a similar attack, police
chased him onto a subway car and gunned him down. It became
clear shortly afterward that killing the young man had been a
tragic mistake – de Menezes was not a terrorist. Police authorities
and Prime Minister Tony Blair expressed sorrow and regret but
warned that such misfortunes can occur in a world made unstable
by terrorists.

People around the world were saddened by de Menezes' widely
publicized death and some were outraged. The Brazilian government and many of its people demanded explanations, apologies,
and reparations from the British. Brazil's foreign minister in
London complained that even under the pressure of terrorism,
"human rights must be protected." News media, the internet, and
mobile phones were the primary forms for reporting and organizing the global response to the shooting.

There is great irony and an important point to be made about
the outcry for justice in the de Menezes case that bears directly
on issues being discussed in this chapter. Those who criticized the
actions of the London police and demanded legal retribution were

2nd floor, Left: 730 - 999 →

2nd Floor, Right: 600 - 729 ←

2nd Floor: Oversize Books

1st Floor: 000 - 599 / General Reference / Fiction

Shelfmark: ☐☐☐ . ☐☐☐☐☐ ☐☐☐

Title:

Shelfmark: ☐☐☐ . ☐☐☐☐ ☐☐☐

Title:

Shelfmark: ☐☐☐ . ☐☐☐☐ ☐☐☐

Title: Athens Log in:

ce of health culture.

Please use this slip to note down the books
you have found on the catalogue

*Shelfmarks consist of a number plus the three first letters of the
author's name - e.g. 791.4301 BAZ*

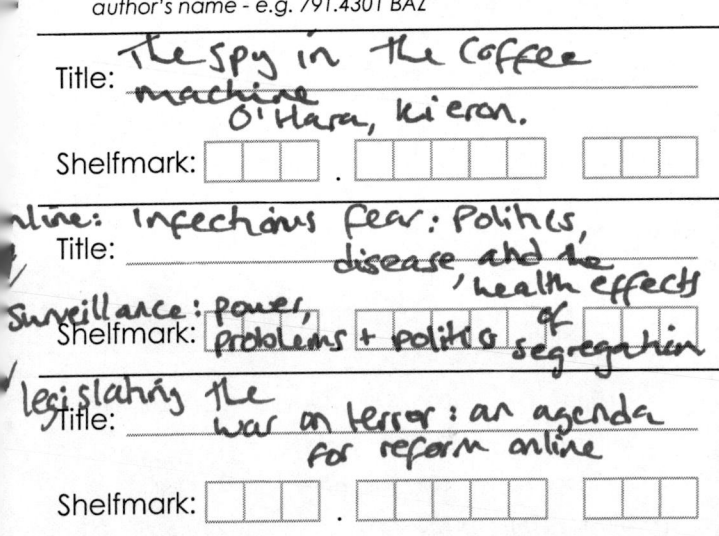

Title: The Spy in the Coffee
machine

O'Hara, Kieron.

Shelfmark: ☐☐ . ☐☐☐☐ ☐☐☐

line: Infectious fear: Politics,
Title:
disease and the
health effects
Surveillance: power,
Shelfmark: problems + politics of
segregation

legislating the
Title: war on terror: an agenda
for reform online

Shelfmark: ☐☐☐ . ☐☐☐☐ ☐☐☐

calling upon an idealized, completely fair standard of justice to settle the case. It was assumed that some universal sense of legal culpability should prevail, and that the rights of individual persons, even outside their native lands, must be protected. By dramatic contrast, delivering truly fair legal or social justice rarely occurs in Brazil, where the police tend to be particularly brutal and the courts corrupt. And no one cites Brazil for its excellence in protecting the rights of individual human beings under any circumstances, unless the individual is rich or otherwise well connected.

The call for an idealized, universal standard of justice in the wake of the death of the young Brazilian has far-reaching implications for the global imaginary. Bassam Tibi – the Muslim intellectual born in Syria who now directs an academic research center in Europe, and whose work I reference throughout this book – proposes that world peace and understanding depend on "ethical convergence" that takes the form of "cross-cultural consent to a secular international morality" (Tibi 2002: 182, 113). He argues for active cultivation of a "universal moral code" based on two unassailable principles of our common humanity – individual human rights and social democracy.

The United Nations endorses "universal human rights" and the Commission on Global Governance (1995) advocates a core set of "universal values" that specify everyone's rights and responsibilities in a global democracy. David Held calls for a set of "universal ethical codes" and "common values" that promote "the common heritage of humankind [and] lay the ground for a new conception of internationalism" (Held 2004: 17, 162). Joseph Nye describes how further adoption of "prevailing global norms" including liberalism, pluralism, and autonomy can reduce international tensions (Nye 2004: 31–2). And Kwame Appiah speaks of "core moral ideas" that can help bring about a global cosmopolitan consciousness (Appiah 2006: 162–3).

These overlapping concepts – ethical convergence, a universal moral code, universal human rights, universal values, universal ethical codes, common values, prevailing global norms, core moral ideas – all presuppose acceptance and protection of the individual person as the fundamental social category. That idea finally must be supported by every religious and cultural group, according to Shirin Ebadi, the Iranian lawyer and human rights activist who won the Nobel Peace Prize in 2003: "The Universal Declaration of Human Rights is needed universally, and is applicable to both East and West. It is compatible with every faith and religion. Failing to respect our human rights only undermines our humanity" (Ebadi 2005). To that end, the Universal Human Rights declaration continues to provide a realistic, solid structure around which some semblance of a global civil society can be developed. To accept the provisions of any universal moral code, however, means that, "individuals will have to shed their rigid identities if they are to become part of diverse societies and uphold cosmopolitan values of tolerance of and respect for universal human rights" (UNDP 2004: 12).

The essential question, therefore, always becomes *whose* human rights ultimately shall be protected in the modern world – those of the individual person or those of the (imagined) collective? In Western cultures the principle of individual human rights has been firmly established through political and legal channels and is widely believed to function to everyone's benefit. In Muslim societies, however, the collective is paramount and "each person is considered to be but an appendage" (Tibi 2002: 24). Individual rights are thought to be anti-Islamic. Discursively and pragmatically, the idea of "Islam" exists as a sacred unity.[3] Religious authorities create and perpetuate their hegemony around that ostensibly unchallengeable ideology. Political regimes that rule the Muslim world exploit the sacred collectivity for their purposes while vying with religious authority for social control. Saudi Arabia has refused to sign the United Nations' Declaration of Human Rights, for instance, precisely because the document focuses on the rights of individual persons, a perspective the government claims does not acceptably meet religious or political criteria. If a universal moral code is to stand any chance of success, according to Tibi, it must be based on rationality and free individual persons, not on an aggregate of conforming souls who are duty-bound to a collectivity: "there can be no compromise on the validity of individual human rights in international relations – despite all the cultural and civilizational differences" (Tibi 2002: 193, 91).

A "modest cosmopolitan" alternative

> We probably have to become cosmopolitans without the prospect of a
> cosmopolis.
>
> J. Tomlinson, *Globalization and Culture*, p. 199

As British cultural theorist John Tomlinson puts it, a cosmopolitan
person "delights in [cultural] difference" (Tomlinson 1999: 186).
He or she acts simultaneously as a cultural universalist (embracing
sameness across cultural groups) and a pluralist (appreciating cultural differences). This balancing act requires reflexive awareness
wherein individual persons must be "open to questioning their
own cultural assumptions" (Tomlinson 1999: 194), be sincerely
respectful of others, and be willing to adapt and change. The
cosmopolitan lives with ambiguity, some discomfort, and multiple
identities: "Being a 'citizen of the world' means having a cultural
disposition which is not limited to the concerns of the immediate
locality, but which recognizes global belonging, involvement, and
responsibility, and can integrate these broader concerns into everyday life practices" (ibid.: 185). Citizens of the world certainly don't
have to abandon their religious beliefs (and most never would),
but they must willingly take their place in the pluralistic world
with others. They need not become complete and dedicated cosmopolitan persons, but they must develop cosmopolitan qualities
and a more diversified and complex cosmopolitan identity
(Rantanen 2005: 124).

Tomlinson argues for a "modest cosmopolitanism" that he
believes is "plausibly within our grasp" (Tomlinson 1999: 207).
Given the firmness with which cultural and religious anchor points
tend to be defended, however, asymmetrical cosmopolitanism may
be all that can be hoped for in the short term. Even before the
wave of terrorism at the beginning of the century stunned the
Western world, Tomlinson worried that the "global sense of moral
involvement demanded of the cosmopolitan" and the practical
potential for worldwide cultural development will be extremely
elusive. He warned "of an increasingly crowded social and cultural space; of the violent clash of cultures and ideologies and the
building of high fences – the retreat into various entrenched . . .
'localist' fundamentalisms" (ibid.: 182).

Inside those high fences – literally and figuratively – is where we find ourselves now. We should not be surprised. Cultural groups and the societies they created were formed originally by individuals to increase their chances for survival. Defending culture becomes a social instinct and an inherited tendency within particular communities and, as Charles Darwin noted, and all too often we see that the other side of the coin, positive "social virtues . . . are practiced almost exclusively in relation to men of the same tribe" (Darwin 1871/1998: 120). The challenge before us now, in the words of Kwame Appiah, is "to take minds and hearts formed over the long millennia of living in local troops and equip them with ideas and institutions that will allow us to live together as the global tribe we have become" (Appiah 2006: xiii). He asks: how might we find ways to encourage the diverse peoples of the world to "abjure all local allegiances and partialities" and take greater personal and collective responsibility for "this vast abstraction, humanity?" (ibid.: xvi). The concluding chapter will address that question.

Notes

1. For a particularly well-researched and interpreted account of the "competition among the siblings called Jews, Christians, and Muslims," see F. E. Peters, *The Monotheists* (2003).
2. In researching Christian fundamentalism for this book, I was struck by one particularly creative request for financial donations made by Pastor Kenny Foreman of the Cathedral of Faith evangelical church in San José, California: "You can give without loving, *but you cannot love without giving!*"
3. Of course, tremendous diversity and internal conflict exist within Islam (Nasr 2006). The division between Shiites and Sunnis – so evident now in Iraq and historically between Iraq and Iran – dates back to Muhammad's death more than a thousand years ago. Blowing up each other's mosques is the basic strategy of the warring sectarian militias in Iraq. Sunni mosques are not allowed in Tehran, the city of 14 million in Shia-dominated Iran (Ebadi 2006). Scores of other subdivisions populate the Muslim world too, but "Islam" is routinely invoked as a holy unity to be defended against outsiders.

Chapter 9

Communicating the Future

Belief is the wound that knowledge heals.

U. Le Guin, *The Telling*[1]

Never before in history have so many disparate cultures suddenly become so aware of each other. Cultural belief systems and ways of living develop over long periods of time and resist change. People seek, avoid, perceive, and retain ideas, information, and experiences that accord with the assumptions and routines of their cultural socialization. Given all this, an unprecedented degree of openness and flexibility will be demanded of individuals and societies as we negotiate our shared futures. Is that a realistic expectation?

What I advocate in this book responds to the pressing need for communication-based "dialogic democracy" on a global scale that embraces reciprocal "active trust" across cultural groups and a sincere "recognition of the authenticity of the other, whose views and ideas one is prepared to listen to and debate" (Giddens 1994: 106). The transformative capacity of culture ultimately makes it possible for this happen. It will not, indeed cannot, come about quickly or smoothly. The encouraging trends described in this book confront substantial resistance from the entrenched fundamentalisms discussed in the previous chapter, and from other formidable countervailing influences. Chief among them are:

- the sheer scope of the global information landscape that creates a sense of shock, helplessness, uncertainty, suspicion, and distrust for some;

- censorship by state authorities in various nations that limits the flow and reception of ideas and information;
- corporate influence over the production of media content;
- contamination of global communication by the spread of political and religious propaganda and disinformation;
- the sensationalist tendencies of media, the culture industries, and contributors to web content;
- the digital divide between and within nations and cultural groups, and the underlying economic and educational gaps that influence differential access to and use of communications technology;
- lack of literacy skills, not only among persons in developing countries;[2]
- excessive self-centeredness emerging from the combination of increased societal individualism, more diverse media content and cultural offerings, and the personalizing features of information and communications technology.

As we come to the end of the labyrinthine journey that's been undertaken in these pages, I want to emphasize the crucial importance of tolerance and intolerance as they impact all future cultural developments, and conclude by explaining why I believe the very nature of human communication offers the single greatest hope for what lies ahead.

The Paradox of Tolerance

> *Unlimited tolerance must lead to the disappearance of tolerance. If we extend unlimited tolerance even to those who are intolerant, if we are not prepared to defend a tolerant society against the onslaught of the intolerant, then the tolerant will be destroyed, and tolerance with them . . . We should therefore claim, in the name of tolerance, the right not to tolerate the intolerant.*
> K. Popper, *The Open Society and Its Enemies*, p. 265

This is what the philosopher Karl Popper called the paradox of tolerance. He argued that "any movement preaching intolerance places itself outside the law, and we should consider any incitement to intolerance and persecution as criminal" (Popper 1945: 265).

Popper was condemning the most damaging of human tendencies. Intolerance implies not just a lack of tolerance; agents of intolerance actively advocate narrow-mindedness, dogmatism, and bigotry. Today, fundamentalist intolerance of any kind can no longer be tolerated by the world community. Refusing to tolerate intolerance must become a global priority.

Now, as in Popper's day, the antidote for intolerance is the robust circulation of information and an open exchange of ideas. Fortunately, the technological and industrial resources that make this possible today are a thousand times more developed than they were when Popper wrote. The mass media, the culture industries, and the internet act as a global echo chamber, saturating the world with information that keeps moving through direct and mediated social networks. The massive effect this process has on the consciousness of people everywhere is monumental. One certain consequence is that differences among cultural groups will continue to intensify, even to the point of violent confrontation. More information and greater cultural transparency will provoke "a rough transition before [their] advantages crystallize around us" (Brin 1998: 329).

Researchers at the University of Michigan conduct ongoing surveys of the cultural values that are held by people in countries representing 85 percent of the world's population (World Values Survey 2006). In that research, a culture's level of tolerance has been found to be the main criterion that distinguishes one group from another.[3] Not surprisingly, "secular-rational" societies are more tolerant than "traditional-survivalist" societies. The overarching cultural quality that correlates most closely with secularist-rational groups is a combination of traits the researchers label "self-expression." Self-expression is composed of high levels of social tolerance, gender equality, freedom of speech, and interpersonal trust.[4]

Conversely, societies that are characterized by "survival" values – where the role of religion, deference to authority, conservative social attitudes, and high levels of national pride are stressed – have become the world's comparatively poor "societies of scarcity" (World Values Survey 2006; Inglehart 2006, personal correspondence). These societies lack cultural options, diverse narratives, and economic development. Does that mean that the traditional Muslim nations of the Middle East – which number among the most extreme societies of scarcity – will be forever locked in relative poverty? Will they ever develop the cultural progress and economic capital that the core values of self-expression make possible? Can the hold on culture that is exercised by religious fundamentalism ever be broken?

Two scholars who study the role of media and information technology in the Muslim world, Dale Eickelman and Jon Anderson, make a key distinction. They argue that in Islamic countries the liberating force of human agency – the culture-on-demand tendencies that have been discussed throughout this book – actualizes most often at the individual level while "amplified extremist voices" dominate public space at the institutional or cultural level. Given the dominance of collective identity over individual autonomy in the Middle East, the authors conclude that, "there are no guarantees [that] liberal expectations long attached to enhanced flows of communication and information" will bear fruit in the region (Eickelman and Anderson 2003: xiii–xiv).

Of course there can be no guarantees. None of the multifarious, often contradictory, social and cultural tendencies evident throughout the world today will disappear; they will transmogrify into other unforeseen uncertainties, threats, and opportunities. Given this complex reality, what options exist for bringing about meaningful, positive cultural change?

The Dalai Lama, Archbishop Desmond Tutu, Shirin Ebadi, and Bishop Carlos Belo of East Timor took out a full-page advertisement in *The New York Times* in late 2005 to print the full text of the United Nations' Universal Declaration of Human Rights. Claiming that, "all people are brothers and sisters on the face of the Earth," the renowned religious leaders proposed that the cornerstone UN document should be considered "the common standard of achievement for the followers of all religions or none." The same leaders convened an inter-faith congress on "World Religions After September 11th" in Montreal the following year.

The motives and initiatives put forward by these peace-loving individuals were clearly sincere. Their call for global consensus on the Universal Declaration of Human Rights was a wise and bold recommendation. Media attention that was given to the cause increased global awareness and reflection. Indeed, any effort to encourage dialogue among groups that are fundamentally opposed to each other is welcome. But one glaring difficulty with the interfaith solution stands out: while religious leaders have shown they can interact respectfully with each other when the occasion calls for it, at core the doctrinal differences that separate them remain deeply problematic. Allegiance to the belief systems that comprise the major religions in many ways have "immunized them against the power of conversation" (Harris 2005: 45).

It is the "conversation," of course, that Kwame Appiah and many others have argued we must, and can, have. Inspired by historical precedents set into motion by the Enlightenment, French Revolution, League of Nations, and the Universal Declaration of Human Rights, Appiah sees positive potential for real collaborative development across cultural groups. Utilizing the communications resources available today, Appiah urges that people engage each other with a true humanitarian spirit across cultural borders. Gradually, Appiah says, disparate groups will develop "new ways of seeing things" that can help them reduce their points of conflict (Appiah 2006: 73).

The Great Chain of Communication

If culturally diverse people will ever be able to cooperate more productively on a global scale than they do now, that development won't be caused by the grace of God or the comforting speculations of compassionate philosophers. It will emerge as the fragile product of an enduring and tumultuous struggle for survival. The success of the struggle in the long run will be determined by the same processes that have gotten human beings this far – communication. *Homo sapiens* became the most advanced species on Earth because they found increasingly sophisticated ways to exchange signs and use their communication skills to cooperate in the present and plan for the future. The evolutionary trajectory is long and the evidence is compelling.

When our human ancestors began to walk upright more than three million years ago, their hands were set free to do other work. That led to the development of rudimentary technologies and the skills required to produce them. Early humans crafted simple instruments and weapons to forage, hunt, prepare food, and defend themselves. But by the time the first modern humans appeared 50,000–60,000 years ago, their tool kits contained much more than indigenous utensils and weaponry. Through multiple stages of adaptive evolution, communication became the social process that separated *Homo sapiens* from other primates. Fundamental survival skills began to include verbal utterances, non-verbal signaling, drawing, writing, and other forms of representation and expression (Johanson, Edgar, and Brill 2006). Spoken language developed after countless generations of genetic mutation gave humans a larynx and the increasingly flexible use of the mouth and tongue. These physical modifications – together with expanded brain size and corresponding increased cognitive ability – made it possible for complex forms of communication to gradually evolve. The imagination grew as the physical and cognitive abilities developed, giving humans greater mental agility for envisioning how to compete and survive. Creative thinking, innovation, and oral and written interaction became essential human characteristics. As language developed, it opened the mind to new ideas, extending the range of what could be imagined. Expressive art such as decorated tools, beads, ivory carvings of humans and animals, clay figurines, musical instruments, and cave paintings became taken-for-granted elements of daily life (Leakey and Lewin 1993).

The development of elaborate modes and codes of human communication produced differentiated forms of social interaction, the birth of communities, and the eventual creation of distinct language groups and cultures. These steps forward were made possible by one of biology's most basic principles – diversification of structure. Human beings, like other biological species, mutated into communities of descent. Today, we call these human communities of descent, "cultures." Cultural groups have always competed with and defended themselves against threats from nature, including other cultural groups. And therein remains our most profound challenge. Aggressive, destructive behavior also forms a basic part of human evolution.

People tend to stay loyal to their cultural groups even when it appears perfectly logical to others, inside and outside the group, that "almost everyone would be better off if they ceased to identify with subgroups – Muslim, Serb, or Croat; Tutsi or Hutu; Jew or Arab; Protestant or Catholic – and worked together for the common good" (Smith and Szathmáry 1999: 147). Why is this so? As John Maynard Smith and Eörs Szathmáry argue, much of the influence results from the persuasive power of two communication forms: myth and ritual.

Consider how religious assumptions and loyalties are formed and maintained. The belief systems and socializing practices of all three major religions are reinforced time and again through the propagation of historical narratives and the performance of carefully orchestrated rituals including pilgrimages, religious services, speeches and sermons, group prayers, group singing, and holiday celebrations. There are holy books and other documents; prophets; parables; geographical sites of special significance; buildings with recognizable architectural forms; logos; spiritual leaders; special clothing; public calls to worship that are transmitted by bells, amplified chants, and music; personal instruments and artifacts such as prayer beads, yarmulkes, prayer rugs; special food and drink; home decorations; jewelry; literature; radio stations, television programs, rock and rap groups; websites; and much more. Most importantly, religion offers people easy access to widely shared and simple discursive codes ("praise the Lord," "peace be upon the prophet," "Jesus loves you," "pray for me," "it's God's will," etc.) that comfort the faithful and inspire feelings of belongingness and hope for salvation. Religion facilitates opportunities for social contact and sexual interaction. For many, religion accounts for the origin of life, provides guidelines for living in the present, and promises a paradisiacal afterlife (as well as avoidance of the terrifying alternative). The total effect is hegemonic, enduring, and, in an important sense, natural.

Systems of thought and behavior such as religion congeal over time into primary units of cultural inheritance that, while not clearly genetic, are passed on with phenotypic power from one generation to the next as memes (Dawkins 1989, 2006). Like genes, memes emerge, function, and evolve in support of each other. In this sense, as Richard Dawkins suggests, "we could regard an organized church, with its architecture, rituals, laws, music, art, and written traditions, as a co-adapted stable set of mutually-assisting memes" (Dawkins 1989: 197). Religious rituals perform as "memory-enhancement processes" that co-evolve with religious documents and discourses, and are passed on to subsequent generations by means of cultural transmission (Dennett 2006: 142).

While religious individuals' and cultures' affiliations with a higher power are founded on largely subjective sentiments, the actual religious practices in which people engage are tangible, sensory, and available to everyone. By comparison, moral codes such as that which is represented in the Universal Declaration of Human Rights or in uncodified formulations such as "core moral ideas" or "universal ethics" enter people's consciousness as markedly abstract ideas. Even Appiah's transcultural "conversation" offers little in the way of mythology or iconography that can be employed to recruit adherents or foster loyalties. To combat this problem, as Smith and Szathmáry have proposed, "we need to create . . . myths that extend loyalty to the human species as a whole . . . and develop rituals that generate tolerance rather than hatred" (Smith and Szathmáry 1999: 148).

Notwithstanding daunting challenges like this and fully recognizing the immoderate passion with which fundamentalist ideologies tend to be asserted and defended, the principles of evolutionary biology and lessons from cultural history suggests that positive developments can eventually ensue. Although cultural values and practices persist from one generation to the next, even the most strongly held belief systems are subject to modification. Cultural adaptations – like biological mutations – develop in response to environmental challenges. Survival is a social project. Just as the individual gene needs a vehicle – a complex organism composed of many interdependent replicators – to survive, so too do individual human beings need the cooperation of each other. Collaborative "evolutionary interaction between roles" of biological beings is necessary for human development (Krebs 2006). And only the power of human communication can make that productive interaction happen.

Evolutionary processes enabled the progenitors of modern humans to become the dominant species on Earth more than 150,000 years ago and led to development of the myriad diverse cultures that exist today, replete with their various elaborate belief systems, traditions, and languages. But every culture exists in a perpetual state of becoming. Communication – the very means by which cultural groups form and sustain themselves – also has always been, and will always be, the primary agent of cultural change, beginning with the potential reduction of intergroup violence.

From the smallest interpersonal disagreements to the largest international and intercultural disputes, human communication often effectively reduces conflict. While people everywhere now are more aware than ever before of the violent struggles that are taking place around the world, for example, proportionately fewer wars, genocides, and human rights abuses are actually happening. The most notable reductions have taken place since 1990 (Center for Systemic Peace 2006; Human Security Centre 2006). Unprecedented levels of visibility, transparency, and accountability – global communication processes all – have led to the decline. Communication routinely deflates aggressive instincts in more common social contexts too. Human beings live in greater proximity with each other than any other species of mammal. We do so in relative harmony. Think of Shanghai, Mexico City, London, Cairo, Tokyo, and New York, for instance. Millions of people – often manifesting acute cultural differences – live in extremely close quarters that produce great stress but remarkably few acts of physical violence proportionate to the size of the population. The fundamental reason for this is the unique ability of humans to use oral and written codes to represent complex thoughts and feelings, to listen, discuss ideas, tolerate and negotiate differences, compromise, and ultimately, in many cases, even befriend the "other."

The prospects for long-term intercultural understanding stem directly from the spread of secular modernity and the positive force of human communication. That includes the fast-expanding, widespread circulation of information and cultural forms that broaden the life experience of people everywhere. Greater visibility and transparency brought about by mass media, the culture industries, the internet, and personal communications technology will heighten the level of accountability demanded of political and cultural systems. Global awareness and wisdom will spring from the torrents of discussion and dialogue that flow through constantly expanding communication channels.

More opportunities for human expression will also be vital to cultural development. Today's active, self-aware, increasingly sovereign subjects have much more room and many more resources with which to operate as culture creators. With advances in communication and cultural expression leading the way, we stand on the edge of a profound transformation of the global consciousness. The sweeping social interconnectedness and the organic nature of global communication today can bring about metacultural "emergence" – when a networked system of relatively simple elements self-organizes to form more intelligent, more adaptive, higher-level behavior (Johnson 2002).

In the Introduction to this book I referred to an inspiring vision articulated by Karl Popper in the classic volume *The Open Society and Its Enemies* (1945). Popper expressed what he considered to be the decisive role of an open and free exchange of ideas for reconstruction of the crisis world after World War II. The frame of mind necessary to accompany that massive project, Popper argued, is a dedicated belief in the idea that human beings have the ability to build "a better and freer world" (Popper 1945: xiii).

As Karl Popper prepared the second edition of his book five years after publication of the original, he contemplated changes he might make in the text. He considered adjustments not just in content but in the tone of the first edition. Upon initial reflection, Popper thought he might temper the optimism that was so fully present in the original. He worried that the enthusiasm that shone through so brightly might have come across as naïve and ultimately unproductive. Upon further consideration, however, Popper discarded the idea of a change in tone. He reclaimed his genuine spirit. In the preface to the second edition, Popper said he decided to "resist the temptation to subdue [the book's] tenor. For in spite of the present world situation, I feel as hopeful as I ever did" (Popper 1945: ix). The second and subsequent editions of *The Open Society and Its Enemies* were published with additions in material, but not with changes in voice.

Today we face challenges presented by a different crisis world. As we look to the uncertain future, we can continue to draw inspiration from not only Popper, but from the great naturalist, Charles Darwin. In the nineteenth century, Darwin described the dilemma we still face today. He noted that "so many absurd rules of conduct" and "so many absurd religious beliefs . . . in all quarters of the world" have become "deeply impressed on the mind of men," leading cultural groups ranging from indigenous tribes to "highly civilized nations" to divide up, sometimes violently, according to differences in appearance and habit (Darwin 1871/1998: 126). Despite this tendency, Darwin believed that

> as man advances in civilization, and small tribes are united into larger communities, the simplest reason would tell each individual he ought to extend his social instincts and sympathies to all the members of the same nation, though personally unknown to him. This point once being reached, there is only an artificial barrier to prevent his sympathies from extending to the men of all nations and races. (ibid.: 126–7)

Darwin believed that the greatest quality that separates humans from lower animals is the capacity to make moral decisions, the ultimate benefit accruing from man's superior cognitive development. "A moral being," Darwin wrote, "is one who is capable of reflecting on his past actions and their motives – of approving of some and disapproving of others" (Darwin 1871/1998: 633).

Moral reflection that is undertaken today occurs in a global environment bursting with information. Can that information help turn belief into knowledge, and knowledge into wisdom, so that the human race can continue to survive and prosper? The future will not be determined by humans as a species. In nature, species don't act. Individuals do, in concert with other individuals, each working to produce beneficial results. Only the most sophisticated social skill that humans have mastered in the millennia of their biological and social evolution – communication – has the potential to help the world's peoples do just that, hopefully, in the end, to the advantage of us all.

Notes

1. From *The Telling*, a culturally based science fiction novel by Ursula K. LeGuin. The line refers to deliverance from the influence of a fictional fundamentalist religious sect, the "Unists," which had forced its destructive belief system, "Unism," on the population.

2. A recent study by the United States Department of Education (2005) revealed that less than one-third of adult Americans, including a surprisingly low number of college graduates, were proficient at grasping and analyzing complex texts. The study concludes that having more information doesn't mean it will be understood and used well. The world has become more complex and much more information is available, but skills for interpretation lag behind.

3. Seventy percent of the cross-national variance in the factor analysis conducted on the quantitative survey data clustered into two polar dimensions: "traditional" v. "secular-rational" and "survival" v. "self-expression" values.

4. Economically flourishing societies develop greater existential security which gives further rise to individual autonomy, gender equality, social tolerance, political democracy, and freedom of expression. These cultural qualities then open up more space for creativity and innovation, which creates the conditions for generating additional economic capital (Inglehart and Welzel 2005).

References

ABC News (2003). Poll: "Most Americans Say They're Christian." http://abcnews.go.com/sections/us/DailyNews/beliefnet_poll_010718.html

Abdullah II, King of Jordan (2004a). Address to the World Affairs Council. San Francisco, April 16.

Abdullah II, King of Jordan (2004b). Amman message. Amman, Jordan, November 9. www.jordanembassyus.org/new/pr/pr11092004.shtml

Abdullah II, King of Jordan (2004c). Appearance on *Hardball*. MSNBC. December 10.

Agre, P. (2001). "Institutions and the Entrepreneurial Self." http://dlis.gseis.ucla.edu/pagre/

Almond, G. A., Appleby, R. S., and Sivan, E. (2003). *Strong Religion*. Chicago, IL: University of Chicago Press.

Appiah, K. A. (2006). *Cosmopolitanism: Ethics in a World of Strangers*. New York: W. W. Norton.

Arbanowski, S. (2003). "I-Centric Communications." Doctoral thesis. Technical University of Berlin, School of Electrical Engineering and Computer Sciences. http://edocs.tu-berlin.de/diss/2003/arbanowski_stefan.htm

Augé, M. (1995). *Non Places*. London: Verso.

Bachelet, M. (2006). www.presidencyofchile.cl/view/viewArticuloContraste.asp?idarticulo=5780&tipo=

Bagdikian, B. (2004). *The New Media Monopoly*. Boston, MA: Beacon Press.

Barber, B. (1995). *Jihad v. McWorld*. New York: Ballantine Books.

Barnett, T. P. M. (2005). *The Pentagon's New Map*. New York: Berkley Trade.

Bauman, Z. (2000). *Liquid Modernity*. Cambridge, UK: Polity Press.

Beck, U. (2000). "Living Your Own Life in a Runaway World." In W. Hutton and A. Giddens (eds.), *Global Capitalism*. New York: The New Press.

Beck, U. and Beck-Gernsheim, E. (2002). *Individualization*. London: Sage.

Benjamin, W. (1970). *Illuminations*. London: Jonathan Cape.

Bhagwati, J. (2004). *In Defense of Globalization*. New York: Oxford University Press.

Blombo Caves Project (2006). www.svf.uib.no/sfu/blombos/Press_Releases.html

Boulding, K. E. (1969). "The Interplay of Technology and Values." In K. Baier and N. Rescher (eds.), *Values and the Future*. New York: The Free Press.

Boulding, K. E. (1978). *Ecodynamics: A New Theory of Societal Evolution*. Newbury Park, CA: Sage.

Boulding, K. E. (1989). *Three Faces of Power*. Newbury Park, CA: Sage.

Bourdieu, P. (1998). *Acts of Resistance*. Cambridge, UK: Polity Press.

Brin, D. (1998). *The Transparent Society*. Reading, MA: Perseus Books.

British Broadcasting Corporation (2003). "What the World Thinks of America." www.bbc.com

Brooks, D. (2006). "Drafting Hitler," *The New York Time,* February 9, p. A27.

Canetti, E. (1984). *Crowds and Power*. New York: Farrar, Straus, & Giroux.

Castells, M. (1996). *The Rise of the Network Society*. Oxford: Blackwell.

Castells, M. (2000). "Information Technology and Global Capitalism." In W. Hutton and A. Giddens (eds.), *Global Capitalism*. New York: The New Press.

Castells, M. (2001). *The Internet Galaxy*. Oxford: Oxford University Press.

CBS News (2006). Poll: "Sinking Perceptions of Islam." www.cbsnews.com/stories/2006/04/12/national/main1494697.shtml

Center for Systemic Peace (2006). http://members.aol.com/cspmgm/conflict.htm

Chaney, D. (2002). *Cultural Change and Everyday Life*. Basingstoke: Palgrave Macmillan.

Chau, A. (2003). *World on Fire*. New York: Anchor Books.

Clark, A. (2003). *Natural-born Cyborgs*. New York: Oxford University Press.

Cole, J. (2003). *Surveying the Digital Future: The UCLA Internet Report*. www.ccp.ucla.edu

Coll, S. and Glasser, S. B. (2005). "Terrorists Turn to the Web as Base of Operations," *Washington Post*. www.washingtonpost.com/wp-dyn/content/article/2005/08/05/AR2005080501138.html

Commission on Global Governance (1995). *Our Global Neighbourhood*. Oxford: Oxford University Press.

Cook, M. (2000). *The Koran*. Oxford: Oxford University Press.

Cowen, T. (1998). *In Praise of Commercial Culture*. Cambridge, MA: Harvard University Press.

Cowen, T. (2002). *Creative Destruction*. Princeton, NJ: Princeton University Press.

Cramer, R. B. (2004). *How Israel Lost*. New York: Simon & Schuster.

Csikszentmihalyi, M. (1996). *Creativity*. New York: HarperCollins.

Cunningham, S. and Sinclair, J. (2000). *Floating Lives*. St. Lucia, Queensland, Australia: University of Queensland Press.

Darwin, C. (1859/1979). *The Origin of Species*. New York: Random House.

Darwin, C. (1871/1998). *The Descent of Man*. Amherst, NY: Prometheus.

Dawkins, R. (1989). *The Selfish Gene*. Oxford: Oxford University Press.

Dawkins, R. (2006). "Afterword." Address given at the London School of Economics and Political Science. London, England, March 16.

DeFleur, M. H. and DeFleur, M. L. (2002). "The Next Generation's Image of Americans." www.bu.edu/phpbin/news/releases/display.php?id=215

DeSoto, H. (2000). *The Mystery of Capital*. New York: Basic Books.

Dennett, D. (2006). *Breaking the Spell*. New York: Viking.

Diamond, J. (1999). *Guns, Germs, and Steel*. New York: W. W. Norton.

Dolhenty, J. (2005). "An Overview of Natural Law Theory." http://radicalacademy.com/philnaturallaw.htm

Dozier, R. W., Jr. (1998). *Fear Itself*. New York: St. Martin's Press.

Eagleton, T. (2000). *The Idea of Culture*. Oxford: Blackwell.

Ebadi, S. (2005). http://daily.stanford.edu/tempo?page=content&id=17363&repository=0001_article

Ebadi, S. (2006). *Iran Awakening*. New York: Random House.

Edgar, A. and Sedgwick, P. (1999). *Key Concepts in Cultural Theory*. London: Routledge.

Eickelman, D. F. and Anderson, J. W. (2003). *New Media in the Muslim World* (2nd edn.) Bloomington, IN: Indiana University Press.

El Fadl, K. A. (2002). *The Place of Tolerance in Islam*. Boston, MA: Beacon Press.

El Fadl, K. A. (2005). "The Great Theft: Wrestling Islam from the Extremists." Address given at the World Affairs Council, San Francisco, October 12.

El-Nawawy, M. and Iskandar, A. (2002). *Al-Jazeera*. Cambridge, MA: Westview.

Engelbart, D. (2005). "Bookstrap Institute." http://www.bootstrap.org

Evans, D. (2001). *Emotion*. Oxford: Oxford University Press.

Foucault, M. (1977). *Discipline and Punish*. Harmondsworth, UK: Penguin.

Friedman, T. (2000). *The Lexus and the Olive Tree*. New York: Farrar, Straus, & Giroux.

Friedman, T. (2002). *Longitudes and Attitudes*. New York: Farrar, Straus, & Giroux.

Friedman, T. (2003). "Searching for the Roots of 9/11." *Discovery Channel* DVD.

Friedman, T. (2005). *The World is Flat*. New York: Farrar, Straus, & Giroux.

Fukuyama, F. (1992). *The End of History*. New York: Harper.

Fukuyama, F. (2006). *America at the Crossroads*. New Haven, CT: Yale University Press.

Gans, H. (1974). *Popular Culture and High Culture*. New York: Basic Books.

García Canclini, N. (1995). *Consumidores y Ciudadanos*. Mexico City: Grijalbo.

García Canclini, N. (1999). *La Globalizacion Imaginada*. Mexico City: Paidos.

Giddens, A. (1984). *The Constitution of Society*. Cambridge, UK: Polity Press.

Giddens, A. (1994). "Living in a Post-Traditional Society." In U. Beck, A. Giddens, and S. Lash (eds.), *Reflexive Modernization*. Cambridge, UK: Polity Press.

Giddens, A. (1998). *The Third Way*. Cambridge, UK: Polity Press.

Giddens, A. (2000). *Runaway World*. London: Routledge.

Giddens, A. (2001). "The Great Globalization Debate." Address given at the University of California, Berkeley, October 25.

Giddens, A. (2002a). "The Future of Democracy." Address given at the London School of Economics and Political Science, January 30.

Giddens, A. (2002b). *What Now for New Labour?* Cambridge, UK: Polity Press.

Gillespie, M. (1995). *Television, Ethnicity, and Cultural Change*. London: Routledge.

Gillmor, D. (2004). *We the Media*. Sebastopol, CA: O'Reilly.

Gitlin, T. (1996). *The Twilight of Common Dreams*. New York: Owlet.

Gitlin, T. (2001). *Media Unlimited*. New York: Henry Holt.

González, J. (2001). "Cultural Fronts: Towards a Dialogical Understanding of Contemporary Cultures." In J. Lull (ed.), *Culture in the Communication Age*. London: Routledge.

Goodall, J. (2000). *In the Shadow of Man*. Boston, MA: Mariner Books.

Greenberg, Quinlan, Rosner Research (2004). www.gqrr.com/

Guardian (2004). "Muslims Poll, November." www.icmresearch.co.uk/reviews/2004/Guardian%20Muslims%20Poll%20Nov%2004/Guardian%20Muslims%20Nov04.asp

Guardian (2005). "Muslims Poll, July." www.icmresearch.co.uk/reviews/2005/Guardian%20-%20muslims%20july05/Guardian%20Muslims%20jul05.asp

Hannerz, U. (2001). "Thinking about Culture in a Global Ecumene." In J. Lull (ed.), *Culture in the Communication Age*. London: Routledge.

Hargreaves, A. (1997). "Satellite Television Viewing among Ethnic Minorities in France," *European Journal of Communication* 12: 4.

Harris, S. (2005). *The End of Faith*. New York: W. W. Norton.

Held, D. (2004). *Global Covenant*. Cambridge, UK: Polity Press.

Held, D., McGrew, A., Goldblatt, D., and Perraton, J. (1999). *Global Transformations*. Cambridge, UK: Polity Press.

Heller, A. (1984). *Everyday Life* (trans. G. L. Campbell). London: Routledge.

Hobsbawm, E. (2000). *On the Edge of the New Century*. New York: The New Press.

HomeNet (2003). www.HomeNet.hcii.cs.cmu.edu

Hotaling, E. (2003). *Islam without Illusions*. Syracuse, NY: Syracuse University Press.

Human Security Centre (2006). *Human Security Report 2005*. Oxford: Oxford University Press.

Huntington, S. P. (1996). *The Clash of Civilizations and the Remaking of World Order*. New York: Simon & Schuster.

Hutton, W. and Giddens, A. (eds.) (2000). *Global Capitalism*. New York: The Free Press.

Ignatieff, M. (1993). *Blood and Belonging*. London: BBC Books.

InfoWorld Media Group (2005). www.infoworld.com/article/06/04/11/77345_HNiceland_1.html

Inglehart, R. and Baker, W. (2000). "Modernization, Cultural Change and the Persistence of Traditional Values," *American Sociological Review* (February), 19–51.

Inglehart, R. and Norris, P. (2003). "The True Clash of Civilizations," *Foreign Policy* March/April: 63–70.

Inglehart, R. and Welzel, C. (2005). *Modernization, Cultural Change, and Democracy.* Cambridge: Cambridge University Press.

International Labour Organization (2006). World Economic Report 2004–5. Geneva: International Labour Organization.

International Telecommunications Union (2005). *World Summit on the Information Society.* http://www.itu.int/wsis/docs/geneva/official/dop.html

Internet World Stats (2006). www.internetworldstats.com/stats.htm

Ito, M. (2001). "Mobile Phones, Japanese Youth, and the Re-placement of Social Contact." www.itofisher.com/PEOPLE/mito/Ito.4S2001.mobile.pdf

Iwabuchi, K. (2002). *Recentering Globalization.* Durham, NC: Duke University Press.

Jayapal, P. (2000). *Pilgrimage to India.* Seattle, WA: Seal Press.

Johanson, D., Edgar, B., and Brill, D. (2006). *From Lucy to Language* (revised edn.). New York: Simon & Schuster.

Johnson, S. (2002). *Emergence.* New York: Charles Scribner's.

Johnson, S. (2005). *Everything Bad is Good for You.* New York: Riverhead.

Kelley, L. M. and Eberstadt, N. (2005). "The Muslim Face of AIDS," *Foreign Policy* July/August: 42–8.

Khuri, F. I. (2001). *The Body in Islamic Culture.* London: Saqi Books.

Kopomaa, T. (2000). *Birth of the Mobile Information Society.* Helsinki: Gaudeamus.

Krebs, J. (2006). "From Intellectual Plumbing to Arms Races." Address at the London School of Economics and Political Science. London, England, March 16.

Kunstradio (2005). www.kunstradio.at/PROJECTS/CURATED_BY/RR/mainframe.html

Kurtz, S. (2002). "Text and Context." In K. El Fadl (ed.), *The Place of Tolerance in Islam.* Boston, MA: Beacon Press.

Landes, D. S. (1999). *The Wealth and Poverty of Nations.* New York: W. W. Norton.

Leakey, R. E. and Lewin, R. (1993). *Origins Reconsidered: In Search of What Makes Us Human.* New York: Anchor Books.

Le Guin, U. (2000). *The Telling.* New York: Harcourt.

Lessig, L. (2004). *Free Culture.* New York: Penguin Press.

Levy, S. (2004). "Something in the Air," *Newsweek,* July 7.

Levy, S. and Stone, B. (2006). "The New Wisdom of the Web," *Newsweek,* April 3.

Lewis, B. (2002). *What Went Wrong?* London: Weidenfeld & Nicolson.

Lewis, B. (2003). *The Crisis of Islam.* New York: Random House.

Lull, J. (1991). *China Turned On.* London: Routledge.

Lull, J. (2000). *Media, Communication, Culture.* Cambridge, UK: Polity Press.

Lull, J. (ed.). (1988). *World Families Watch Television.* Newbury Park, CA: Sage.

Lull, J. (ed.) (2001). *Culture in the Communication Age.* London: Routledge.

Lull, J. and Wallis, R. (1992). "The Beat of West Vietnam." In J. Lull (ed.), *Popular Music and Communication* (2nd edn.). Newbury Park, CA: Sage.

Lyman, P. and Varian, H. (2003). "How Much Information 2003?" www2.sims.berkeley.edu/research/projects/how-much-info-2003/

Lynch, M. (2006a). *Voices of the New Arab Public.* New York: Columbia University Press.

Lynch, M. (2006b). "Q & A with Marc Lynch." www.columbia.edu/cu/cup/publicity/lynchqa.pdf

Maguire, K. and Lines, A. (2005). "Exclusive: Bush Plot to Bomb His Arab Ally." www.mirror.co.uk

Maher, B. (2002). *When You Ride Alone You Ride with bin Laden.* Beverly Hills, CA: New Millenium Press.

Manji, I. (2003). *The Trouble with Islam Today.* New York: St. Martin's Press.

Maslow, A. H. (1943). "A Theory of Human Motivation," *Psychological Review* 50: 370–96.

Mateo, D. (2004). "Una mirada supercultural a la labor de los ravers en Chile." Master's thesis. Universidad Diego Portales, Chile.

McCracken, G. (1990). *Culture and Consumption.* Bloomington, IN: Indiana University Press.

McDermott, T. (2005). *Perfect Soldiers.* New York: HarperCollins.

Mearsheimer, J. and Walt, S. M. (2006). "The Israel Lobby." *London Review of Books*: www.lrb.co.uk/v28/n06/mear01_.html

Menard, R. (2006). Quoted in www.nytimes.com/2006/02/02/international/europe/02danish.html?ex=1296536400&en=f0a294ee1fb65e8f&ei=5088&partner=rssnyt&emc=rss

Messaris, P. (1994). *Visual Literacy.* Boulder, CO: Westview.

Messaris, P. (1997). *Visual Persuasion.* Thousand Oaks, CA: Sage.

Middle East Media Research Institute (2006). www.memri.org/

Miles, H. (2005). *Al Jazeera: The Inside Story of the Arab News Channel That is Changing the West.* New York: Grove Press.

Mithen, S. (2006). *The Singing Neanderthals*. Cambridge, MA: Harvard University Press.

Morley, D. (2000). *Home Territories*. London: Routledge.

Naficy, H. (1993). *The Making of Exile Cultures*. Minneapolis: University of Minnesota Press.

Nasr, V. (2006). *The Shia Revival*. New York: W. W. Norton.

National Geographic Magazine (1999). Millennium Supplement: Culture. Vol. 196: 2 (August).

National Geographic News (2002). "Thousands of Women Killed for Family Honor." news.nationalgeographic.com/news/2002/02/0212_020212_honorkilling.html

NetAid (2006). www.NetAid.org

Newcomb, H. and Hirsch, P. (1987). "Television as a Cultural Forum." In H. Newcomb (ed.), *Television: The Critical View*. New York: Oxford University Press.

Newport, F. (2002). "Muslim Antipathy toward the US is Pervasive," *San José Mercury News*, March 3, pp. 1–3P.

Newsweek (2004). December 13, p. 51.

Newsweek (2006). June 12, p. 56.

Norberg, J. (2003). *In Defense of Capitalism*. Washington, DC: Cato Institute.

Notoji, M. (2000). "Cultural Transmission of John Philip Sousa and Disneyland in Japan." In R. Wagnleitner and E. T. May (eds.), *Here, There, and Everywhere*. Hanover, CT: University Press of New England.

Nye, J. (2004). *Soft Power*. New York: PublicAffairs.

Parker, J. (2004). "New Survey Reveals Evangelical America's Diversity." http://headlines.agapepress.org/printver.asp

Parsons, T. (1978). *Action Theory and the Human Condition*. New York: Free Press.

Pei, M. (2003). "The Paradoxes of American Nationalism," *Foreign Policy* (May/June): 31–7.

Peters, F. E. (2003). *The Monotheists*. Princeton, NJ: Princeton University Press.

Pew Forum on Religion and Public Life (2004–5). http://pewforum.org/

Pew Global Attitudes Project (2002–6). www.pewglobal.org

Pew Internet and American Life (2003–6). www.pewinternet.org

Pew Research Center for People and the Press (2005). http://people-press.org/

Phillips, K. (2006). *American Theocracy*. New York: Viking.

Plant, S. (2002a). *On the Mobile: The Effects of Mobile Telephones on Social and Individual Life*. www.motorola.com

Plant, S. (2002b). "How the Mobile Changed the World," *The Sunday Times of London*. May 5: section 4, p. 9.

Popper, K. (1945). *The Open Society and its Enemies* (2nd edn.). London: Routledge.

Project for the New American Century (2006). www.newamericancentury.org/index.html

Putnam, R. D. (2000). *Bowling Alone*. New York: Simon & Schuster.

Ramadan, T. (2004). *Western Muslims and the Future of Islam*. New York: Oxford University Press.

Rantanen, T. (2005). *The Media and Globalization*. London: Sage.

Rauf, F. A. (2004). *A New Vision for Muslims and the West*. San Francisco, CA: HarperSanFrancisco.

Real, M. (1989). *Super Media*. Newbury Park, CA: Sage.

Reeves, B. and Nass, C. (1996). *The Media Equation*. Cambridge: Cambridge University Press.

Rheingold, H. (2002). *Smart Mobs*. Cambridge, MA: Perseus.

Ritzer, G. (1993). *The McDonaldization of Society*. Thousand Oaks, CA: Pine Forge.

Roy, O. (2004). *Globalized Islam*. New York: Columbia University Press.

Rushdie, S. (2001). "Yes, this is about Islam," *The New York Times*, November 2. www.nytimes.com/2001/11/02/opinion/02RUSH.html?

Rushdie, S. (2005). *Shalimar the Clown*. New York: Random House.

Said, E. (1997). *Covering Islam*. New York: Vintage Books.

Schiller, H. (2000). *Living in the Number One Country*. New York: Seven Stories Press.

Sennett, R. (2000). "Street and Office: Two Sources of Identity." In W. Hutton and A. Giddens (eds.), *Global Capitalism*. New York: The New Press.

Silverstone, R. (2001). "Finding a Voice: Minorities, Media, and the Global Commons," *Emergences* 11: 13–27.

Silverstone, R. (2006). *Media and Morality*. Cambridge, UK: Polity Press.

Simon, E. (2004). "Digital Cameras Change Perception of War." www.msnbc.msn.com/id/4925611/

Sim, S. (2005). *Fundamentalist World*. London: Icon Books.

Smith, A. (1996). *Software for the Self*. Oxford: Oxford University Press.

Smith, C. (2005). *Soul Searching: The Religious and Spiritual Lives of American Teenagers*. New York: Oxford University Press.

Smith, J. M. and Szathmáry, E. (1999). *The Origins of Life*. Oxford: Oxford University Press.

Soros, G. (1998). *The Crisis of Global Capitalism*. Oxford: Public Affairs Ltd.

Soros, G. (2002). *George Soros on Globalization*. Oxford: Public Affairs Ltd.

Soros, G. (2004). "The Bubble of American Supremacy." Address at the University of California, Berkeley, March 3.

Sowell, T. (1994). *Race and Culture*. New York: Basic Books.

Sreberny, A. (2002). "Globalization and Me." In J. M. Chan and B. McIntyre (eds.), *In Search of Boundaries*. Westport, CT: Ablex.

Stewart, E. (2001). "Culture of the Mind: On the Origins of Meaning and Emotion." In J. Lull (ed.), *Culture in the Communication Age*. London: Routledge.

Stiglitz, J. E. (2002). *Globalization and Its Discontents*. New York: W. W. Norton.

Stiglitz, J. E. and Charlton, A. (2006). *Fair Trade for All*. New York: Oxford University Press.

Straubhaar, J. (1997). "Distinguishing the Global, Regional, and National Levels of World Television." In A. Sreberny-Mohammadi, D. Winseck, J. McKenna, and O. Boyd-Barrett (eds.), *Media in Global Context*. London: Edward Arnold.

Takahashi, T. (2003). "Japanese Engagement with Media in Everyday Life." Doctoral dissertation. London School of Economics and Political Science.

Telhami, S. (2006). "Overshadowed," *San Jose Mercury News*, July 30. www.mercurynews.com/mld/mercurynews/news/editorial/15157817.htm

The Davos Report (2004). Geneva/Washington, DC: World Economic Forum/*Foreign Policy*/Carnegie Comission for International Peace.

The Economist (2006). www.economist.com/opinion/displaystory.cfm?story_id=5494602

The New York Times (2006). "As barrier comes down, a Muslim split remains," p. 13.

Thompson, C. (2006). "Google's China Problem (and China's Google Problem)," *The New York Times Magazine*, April 23, pp. 64–71, 86, 154–6.

Thompson, J. B. (1995). *The Media and Modernity*. Cambridge, UK: Polity Press.

Tibi, B. (2002). *The Challenge of Fundamentalism* (2nd edn.). Berkeley, CA: University of California Press.

Tomlinson, J. (1991). *Cultural Imperialism.* Baltimore, MD: Johns Hopkins University Press.

Tomlinson, J. (1999). *Globalization and Culture.* Cambridge, UK: Polity Press.

Transparency International (2004). www.transparency.org

Turner, J. H. (2000). *On the Origins of Human Emotions.* Stanford, CA: Stanford University Press.

United Nations (1999). *United Nations.* New York: Department of Public Information.

United Nations (2006). *Declaration of Human Rights.* www.un.org

United Nations Development Programme (2002a). *Human Development Report: Deepening Democracy in a Fragmented World.* New York: Oxford University Press.

United Nations Development Programme (2002b). *Arab Human Development Report: Creating Opportunities for Future Generations.* New York: UNDP.

United Nations Development Programme (2003a). *Human Development Report: Millennium Development Goals.* New York: Oxford University Press.

United Nations Development Programme (2003b). *Arab Human Development Report: Building a Knowledge Society.* New York: UNDP.

United Nations Development Programme (2004). *Human Development Report: Cultural Liberty in Today's Diverse World.* New York: Oxford University Press.

United Nations Development Programme (2005). *Human Development Report: International Cooperation at a Crossroads.* New York: Oxford University Press.

United Nations Educational, Scientific and Cultural Organization (2005). General Conference, 33rd session. Paris, October 3–21.

United Nations Information and Communications Technology Task Force (2005). www.unicttaskforce.org

United States Department of Education (2005). "National Assessment of Adult Literacy." http://nces.ed.gov/naal/

Uribe, A. (2003). "Re-imaginando Mexico con la Telenovela." Doctoral dissertation. El Colelgio de la Frontera Norte, Tijuana, Mexico.

Wallerstein, I. (2003). *The Decline of American Power.* New York: The New Press.

Weber, S. (2004). *The Success of Open Source.* Cambridge, MA: Harvard University Press.

Webster, J. and Phalen, P. (1997). *The Mass Audience.* Mahwah, NJ: Lawrence Erlbaum.

Wellman, B. (2002). "Little Boxes, Glocalization, and Networked Individualism." In M. Tanabe, P. van den Besselaar, and T. Ishida (eds.), *Digital Cities II: Computational and Sociological Approaches.* Berlin: Springer-Verlag.

Willis, P. (1977). *Learning to Labour.* Farnborough: Saxon House.

Willis, P. (1990). *Common Culture.* Boulder, CO: Westview.

Willis, P. (2000). *The Ethnographic Imagination.* Cambridge, UK: Polity Press.

Wilson, B. (1966). *Religion in a Secular Society.* London: Watts.

Wilson, E. O. (2006). *From So Simple a Beginning.* New York: W. W. Norton.

WITNESS (2005). www.witness.org

Woodward, B. (2004). *Plan of Attack.* New York: Simon & Schuster.

World Bank (2003). *World Development Report: Sustainable Development in a Dynamic World.* New York: Oxford University Press.

World Economic Forum (2005). *Women's Empowerment: Measuring the Global Gender Gap.* Geneva: World Economic Forum.

World Values Survey (2005–6). www.worldvaluessurvey.org

Wright, L. (2006). *The Looming Tower.* New York: Alfred A. Knopf.

Yamani, M. (2000). *Changed Identities.* London: Royal Institute of International Affairs.

Zachary, G. P. (2000). *The Global Me.* New York: Public Affairs.

Zakaria, F. (2003). *The Future of Freedom.* New York: W. W. Norton.

Zakaria, F. (2004a). "The good, the bad, the ugly," *Newsweek,* May 31: 33.

Zakaria, F. (2004b). *Newsweek,* September 27, p. 39.

Zizek, S. (2006). "Defenders of the Faith," *New York Times,* March 12: 12.

Index